The Community Press in an Urban Setting

The Community Press in an Urban Setting

The Social Elements of Urbanism
Second Edition

By Morris Janowitz

with a Postscript by Scott Greer

THE UNIVERSITY OF CHICAGO PRESS
CHICAGO AND LONDON

Library of Congress Catalog Card Number: 67-21391

THE UNIVERSITY OF CHICAGO PRESS, CHICAGO &
  LONDON
The University of Toronto Press, Toronto 5, Canada

To Bruno Bettelheim

Preface
to Second Edition

If the term "urban community" has any distinctive meaning, it is because it connotes more than the dense aggregate of human settlement. It must imply the special consequences of locality on social organization and cultural values. Therefore, the sociological study of urbanism is more than the quantitative analysis of population, residence, transportation, and location of social institutions.

The urban community, like any social system, encompasses a process of communications and a system of values. It implies sentiments and attachments to a geographical area, no matter how transitory or complex. The boundaries of human communities in our industrialized society are not only diffuse but are multiple. They stubbornly defy simple cartographic representations, but they create the life space in which men and their families pursue the search for status and self-respect. In its totality the urban community, despite its growth and proliferation, is a social form distinct from the modern nation-state. Even the largest metropolis has some internal unity because it is a network of social relations generated by the daily journey to work and by the daily transactions which are required to meet sustenance needs.

The study of the urban community includes the search for social indicators of the symbolism and collective representations of the city and its suburbs. Indicators of these collective representations must both reflect underlying values and aspirations and at the same time be sensitive enough to reflect rapidly social change. The community press—its institutional structure, its content which can be examined in historical perspective, and its audience—is one such social indicator precisely because of its diffuse and transitory character.

The Community Press in an Urban Setting, completed in 1952, was an exercise in the Chicago school of sociology with an attempt to incorporate more systematic research procedures. Since its publication, through the efforts of various social researchers (especially Scott Greer), the study of urban journalism has become an element of "urban sociology" and the study of the metropolitan community.[1] A variety of replications and alternative lines of inquiry have been undertaken which make use of the newspaper to probe interpersonal and social relations

---

1. Otto N. Larsen and Alex S. Edelstein, "Communication, Consensus and the Community Involvement of Urban Husbands and Wives," *Acta Sociologica* (1960): 15-30; Scott Greer, *The Emerging City: Myth and Reality* (New York: Free Press of Glencoe, 1962); Scott Greer and Ella Kube, "Urbanism and Social Structure: A Los Angeles Study," in *Community Structure and Analysis*, edited by Marvin B. Sussman (New York: Thomas Y. Crowell Company, 1959); Scott Greer, "The Mass Society and the Parapolitical Structure," *American Sociological Review* 27 (October, 1962): 634-46; Scott Greer, *Metropolitics: A Study of Political Culture* (New York: John Wiley and Sons, 1963), see especially Chapter 5, "Who Was Listening?"

in the American metropolis.[2] As a result, in this second edition of *The Community Press in an Urban Setting*, we are able to present a postscript in the form of a report of a research continuity by Scott Greer which contrasts the original findings with those he gathered in Los Angeles, St. Louis, and elsewhere in the United States. His materials have particular relevance since he is able to link community journalism more explicitly to patterns of political behavior. The convergence of our sociological perspectives does not obscure our differences in values and aspiration. Scott Greer is the southern Californian transplanted to the Evanston suburbs who anticipates and heralds the end of the central city and the rise of a new decentralized urban complex, whereas I still remain the offspring of industrial Paterson, New Jersey, transplanted to Hyde Park, Chicago, who is committed to a central city with a center.

Since the period of the original study, two trends are worthy of comment. One deals with the growth in the number of papers and readership of the community press as well as the strengthening of its economic base. The second is the greater articulation of the community press with downtown institutions, reflecting the increased interdependence between the local community and organs of government and politics. If only because of the new and emerging federal programs of the past ten years, the local community has greater relevance as a unit of political decision making.

From 1945 the community press, both in the suburbs and in the central city, has had a vigorous growth. The growth in the suburban areas has been much more marked than that in the central city. However, given the predictions of the sociologists of a decline of the vitality of the inner city, even this more

---

2. Studies in comparative community journalism have been undertaken in Great Britain by Mark Abrams, Research Services, Ltd., and by Rene Koenig, University of Cologne, West Germany.

modest expansion in the city requires explanation. In 1950, when the field work for *The Community Press in an Urban Setting* was undertaken, there were eighty-two newspapers within the political boundaries of the city of Chicago. They had a total circulation in excess of 983,000. These were English-language weeklies addressing themselves to a specific geographical sector of the city and did not include either the foreign-language or the Negro press, which at that time sought to cover the entire Negro population. The 1950 number represented a growth from thirty-one community newspapers in 1910—a growth which had been steady except for an extensive contraction during the depression.

In 1966 the number of community newspapers in the central city had grown to ninety-four, with a combined circulation of over 1,200,000. These figures should not obscure the constant adjustments that the Chicago community press had to make to survive and to grow. Deaths of publishers, the changing social composition of neighborhoods, radical shifts in transportation and shopping patterns, and rising production costs—all have had their impact. The changing boundaries of the community press reflect this constant state of flux. Twenty-seven of the newspapers operating in 1950 (or almost one-third of the total) were no longer being published fifteen years later, either because they had become defunct or because they had been consolidated with other newspapers. In turn, thirty-seven new papers have been started, so that there has been an over-all increase of 14 per cent in the number being published.

The growth in number of papers and in circulation reflects both increased economic resources and higher levels of literacy. Average family income in Chicago has risen, so that there is more disposable income for leisure-time activities and for the purchase of reading materials, including community newspapers. The percentage of paid circulation has grown. While adequate data are not available on the profitability of the community press, the economic position of the average operator is clearly superior to that of fifteen years ago. Marginal newspapers continue to be in a precarious position since they are unable to modernize their equipment, and the most profitable ones are those with their own printing equipment. As a result, there has been a limited consolidation trend.

The economic position of the community press has been strengthened mainly by more adequate advertising revenue. The growth of the supermarkets has resulted in more advertising than small individual stores could produce. In addition, there are new and important sources of revenue from city-wide organizations such as public utilities which have come to support the community press, plus an expansion of classified advertisements, particularly for the recruitment of labor. In turn, the daily newspapers seek to be more competitive by publishing more local news. One metropolitan daily has even introduced a special Thursday community edition which offers neighborhood news and advertising coverage zoned for specific sectors of the city at reduced rates. Essentially, the success of the community press is a result of continued economic prosperity and the economies of scale. The community press serves both audiences and market areas which are uneconomic for the larger daily press.

The community press finds itself in a changing division of labor among the mass media. The rise of television has not undermined the other media. To the contrary, exposure to the mass media is not competitive in the sense that exposure to one media prevents exposure to another. Moreover, television has become the main source of entertainment and features, while the printed media focus on the immediate environment. Along with the growth of the local community press has been the development of the local religious press, particularly the

Catholic diocesan press, reflecting a new basis of community organization.

The social ecology of the community press continues to change gradually. Each section of the entire city, except for some of the most economically depressed areas, is covered by at least one newspaper. The increased number of community papers has meant that more areas of the city are covered by two newspapers, which means some journalistic competition. Although the increase is the result of more available resources, new papers are also the expression of competing socio-political interests which come to feel the need for an outlet for their point of view. At election time new papers spring up, some merely a temporary expression of the local political organization, others the result of broader interests.

In 1950 the social ecology of the community newspapers reflected the great divide of race relations. Community newspapers were to be found in white areas at all social economic levels, while in the Negro areas the Negro press sought to appeal to the Negro community as a whole. By 1965, important changes had taken place. Within the Negro residential areas community newspapers were beginning to show vitality. Some community newspapers survived the transition in racial composition, while in middle-class neighborhoods new papers were being established. This reflects the breakup of the Negro metropolis into more distinctive local communities paralleling the pattern of the white society.

Likewise, the stance of the community press toward the race issue has been transformed since 1950, when the issue was dealt with mainly by denial, fierce maintainence of the status quo, or covert opposition to change. By 1965 there was more extensive coverage of the basic social trends and problems in the city. At the overt level, race labeling in advertisements had been given up as a result of the efforts of the Mayor's Commission on Human Relations. In many transitional areas, shifting from white to all Negro, the community press and its publisher were involved in efforts to maintain law and order and to assist in stabilizing the community patterns, although in the absence of effective school policies (especially in low income areas) these efforts were at best temporary and without marked success. In the two major middle-class local communities which had achieved stable integration, the community press was overtly integrated in its editorial stance and its contents.

In other cities the growth of the community press has been visible in varying degree. One of the most conspicuous cases is in the Los Angeles area. A striking index of the vitality of community journalism is to be seen in New York. In 1950, community publishers pointed to the low concentration of newspapers in New York, particularly in Manhattan, although the community press was somewhat stronger in the other boroughs and especially so in Brooklyn and Queens. New York was thought to be the epitome of mass urbanism and communications. In retrospect, its social ecology was resistant to community journalism. The stronger survival of the ethnic and foreign-language press served for a time as a partial substitute until the economies of scale began to operate so that a community press could develop when the major newspapers could not serve more localized needs. By 1963 the number of weekly community newspapers in New York had risen to sixty-three, including an expansion in Manhattan.[3] By now there are new limits of scale and geographical coverage. In the struggle to maintain a sense of locality and even provincialism, community newspapers have become too large to sense specific needs. Individual housing projects have developed their own house organs, reflective of the gossip sheets of the coffee shops of

---

3. *New York Times*, Nov. 26, 1963, p. 39.

eighteenth-century London. The vital news of a single large apartment house is even circulated by means of a mimeographed sheet edited by a resident editor who gives modulated expression to the negativeness toward the landlord and who looks upon each tenant as a potential correspondent.

The community press is more closely articulated with the central downtown institutions of the government, education, and social welfare, which represent a high degree of centralized authority. But in turn, the local community has emerged as a more important locus of political decision making and social action. This is due to the new programs and services of government in education, health, employment, and urban renewal, which, although they are extensions of federal government activity, require various forms of community participation by local leaders and voluntary associations.

The closer articulation of the community press with the larger metropolis can be seen in every phase of its operations. The content of the community press is no less concerned with the endless details of family and neighborhood life, but the broader context of city-wide affairs is perceptibly stronger than in the past. The amount of external news has grown. In addition to the greater amount of advertising support from outside the community, the community press receives a much greater flow of news and materials from city-wide agencies seeking local support. The community newspaper list is now a standard tool of the downtown public relations officers, particularly of governmental and social service agencies, as well as of the Community Chest and related funds drives. These lists are constantly kept up to date with notations of the practices and policies of the smallest newspapers, for the importance of community journalism and local support has become a new slogan and belief system.

Perhaps the most realistic and shrewd evaluation of the

influence of the community press is to be found in the attitudes and behavior of the professional political leaders. These men pay full respect to the community press, seeking to cultivate their personal connections and supplying a stream of releases. If they have any doubts about the positive effectiveness of the community press as a medium of help and support, they are generally convinced that each publisher has the potential of hurting their cause or at least making trouble. They fully understand that community papers approach controversy with caution, so that when a community newspaper does oppose an elected political leader such a stand commands considerable attention.

Political leaders make it a practice to call on community publishers and editors as part of the protocol of an election campaign. Interest in the community press extends to the very top of the ticket, and local staffs are proud of the interest that congressmen and even senators show. It is an open secret that such candidates frequently organize campaigns to have letters written to the editors, for these letters form one of the most heavily read portions of the paper. The community press is still a vehicle of local gossip, and the political leaders are fully aware that politics thrives on favorable gossip.

The politicians' interest in the community press has come to extend well beyond the publicity and news generated around election time. In the past fifteen years the political campaign has become a year-round activity, so news and material are created to meet the needs of each season. The ward organization must respond to the pressure of the office of the mayor and produce support for crucial programs which the Democratic party has defined as essential. At the top of the list are bond issues and urban renewal. Both these issues have in the past had powerful sources of local community opposition, and the political leaders have carefully sought to mobilize the community press in support of them. In 1962 the community press was passive as the city-wide bond issues were defeated, but in 1966 the publishers were effectively involved and assisted in the ultimate victory. The community press has come to accept the concept of urban renewal. Negro papers have generally abandoned the idea that "urban renewal is Negro renewal." The details of specific renewal and conservation program continue to fill the news columns and supply the basis for editorial debate.

If there is a great deal of stability in format and content of the community press, its columns now report selectively on the new health, educational, and social welfare programs of the federal government. These programs, although in many instances designed to serve the lowest income groups, offer important benefits to social groups throughout the entire central city, with the health and college-oriented programs being the most widely reported. The information presented by the community on these programs is usually supplied by the operating agencies and cooperating voluntary associations.

Elected officials have only slowly sought to become identified with these programs, but the columns of the community press reflect the ever extending involvement of aldermen and congressmen in these activities. The broadening and transformation of the welfare state create new roles for the elected official as a source of information, broker, *ombudsmann,* and a symbolic leader. The columns of the community press reveal that it is premature to assume that the welfare state deprives the local alderman of political visibility and local function.

An additional observation can be made which is only partially a discernible trend and partially a reinterpretation of the standpoint of the original research. The community press has been assumed to be both a reflection of underlying social organization and at the same time an active ingredient in social change. All systems of mass communications partake of this double aspect. It is of course much more feasible to see the community press as a reflector of social structure than as an independent variable. In particular, the contents of the community press and its readership supplied a subtle and rich indicator of community participation. It turned our attention away from the simple dichotomy of participation versus non-participation to a fuller observation of the complexity, range, and particularly the variation in intensity of community involvement and attachments. While there were differences in levels of involvement from community to community, the important variation was that encountered within a community as human beings distributed themselves according to the "normal" pattern—the majority clustered at some typical average while one minority was heavily committed and the other minority totally removed. In the end there emerged a better understanding of the nature of the human bond in the local community, with both its intensity and its fragility, which we labeled the community of limited liability to distinguish it sharply from the human bond of so-called traditional settlements.

What about the community press as an agent of social stability and social change? No doubt we are able to identify the social role of this particular institution as one aspect of the normative system of the urban community. In another sense our definitions and our assumptions in retrospect were too limited. There was an excessive concern with the strategy of communications research which focuses on specific responses, and not enough on the natural history of a social institution and the collective representations it created. The environment—ecological, economic, and even political—was taken for granted, and the research probed the social and psychological response. We recognized that men create transportation systems, locate factories, and build homes with purposive intent. Naïvely we were almost reassured when we found the existence of an expressive symbolic content which gives some communal meaning to these accomplishments. It was as if we were blind to the notion that men also seek to create collective representations and a symbolic order to give to these accomplishments meaning and a sense of community.

The community press is a minor element in this human enterprise, but one which has its special role because it is concerned with locality and therefore with status and self-respect. We were following up on the leads of Robert Park and Ernest Burgess when we probed the social space and the social definitions of the neighborhoods and the communities in which the members of our sample resided. In retrospect we were primitive in the research techniques we used to record the concepts they held of their life space. For example, men and women are much better equipped to locate social space by means of a self-drawn map than by verbal descriptions. But even our crude techniques forced us to remember that self-respect and status—identity, if you will—include an expression of the conception of one's geographical locality, and that for many the very name of their locality, as they defined it, held a very special meaning.

In the earlier efforts of Park and Burgess to describe the local areas of Chicago, there was an excessive concern with identifying physical boundaries and identifying generic names.[4] In

---

4. Ernest W. Burgess and Charles Newcomb, editors, *Census Data of the City of Chicago, 1920* (Chicago: University of Chicago Press, 1931); Louis Wirth and Margaret Furez, *Local Community Fact Book* (Chicago: Chicago Recreation Commission, 1938); Louis Wirth and Eleanor H. Bernet, *Local Community Fact Book of Chicago* (Chicago: Chicago Community Inventory, 1949); Philip M. Hauser and Evelyn M. Kitagawa, editors, *Local Community Fact Book for Chicago, 1950* (Chicago: Chicago Community Inventory, 1953); Evelyn M. Kitagawa and Karl E. Taeuber, *Local Community Fact Book, Chicago Metropolitan Area, 1960* (Chicago: Chicago Community Inventory, 1963).

retrospect their results seem a bit too neat and too precise, although this is not to underestimate the empirical relevance of their efforts to record in the 1920's local community history and boundaries. In part they were describing social reality, and in part they were trying to create collective representations. The seventy-five communities that emerged contributed to the social integration of Chicago. These units became the basis of social planning, social action, and even a popular concept. Cities which created more artificial units were no better—and probably worse—off.

The community newspapers, organized along geographical boundaries, were the mass equivalents of the Burgess community areas. Community publishers, pursuing economic enterprise goals with an admixture of sentimentality, made a positive contribution to the collective representations of urban life. In one sense their boundaries of the community were more meaningful, since theirs were continuously in flux while the constructs of the social scientists have been fixed and have become out of date.

In the past fifteen years the effort to create local communities in the inner city has intensified rather than declined. Perhaps one of the most dramatic changes in the social institutions of the inner city since the publication of the original research findings has been the rise to public prominence—if not necessarily to influence—of the community organizer, the professionally trained specialist, the ideologically inspired and externally financed agent, and the self-appointed local spokesman. For all of them the notion of a local community is not artifact but an essential social requirement. If one does not exist, he is prepared and committed to create one. There is no decline of utopia in the United States, for these men are convinced that all men have the right to local community attachments. Businessmen are consciously and perhaps more realistically involved through their efforts to build shopping centers and make use of urban renewal funds.

A new generation of University of Chicago graduate students is engaged in the direct observation of local communities. It is striking to read in their reports the rapidity with which geographical referents can be implanted in the minds of men to create the hope if not the reality of a sense of community. Such a sense of community may be no more than a negative one. The result of community agitation on recent migrants who have lived in Uptown for six months can be a profound desire to leave Uptown. The images of community are fashioned not only by the local press but by the metropolitan dailies which have increased their coverage of the "sociology" of urban life.

The process of community mobilization has striking similarities to the search for nationalism in an emerging nation, where the emphasis on expressive content and symbols of identification can outrun actual institution building and social change. If what men define to be real is real, in the words of W. I. Thomas, there is a striking amount of effort to fashion directly the contents of men's definitions by the contents of the mass media and the work of voluntary associations. Of *The Community Press in an Urban Setting* and contemporary sociological research, the question must still be asked whether symbolic and cultural content is being adequately considered as a system of "action" and influence.

Preface
to First Edition

While the daily press addresses itself to the whole of the metropolitan center, the unique character of the community press arises from the fact that it has as its audience the residents of a specific sector of the urban metropolis. Its local community audience conditions its content, determines its appeal, and facilitates its impact. As such, social science research into the operations and impact of the community press ought to be relevant to the student of the metropolitan community. But the practicalities of this specialized medium make research into the community newspaper a matter of concern for communications specialists, advertising personnel, community relations experts and the responsible citizen. . . .

The decision to undertake this research was the result of deliberations of the Committee on Communication of the University of Chicago. However, the collection of data was made possible only by extensive, time-consuming and unreserved cooperation from community newspaper publishers and their staffs. While it is impossible to mention separately the dozens of individuals who gave freely of their time and effort, I wish to thank them all. Mr. Jack Feldman, Mr. Leo Lerner and Mr. John L. Showel as well as the national officers and trustees of Controlled Circulation Newspapers of America, Inc., were especially helpful. In the course of the research, the records and files of community newspapers were thrown open to me. Statistics on operations, as well as the opportunity for independent audit were never denied. All that I guaranteed was anonymity in the final report as far as identifying individual newspapers and communities was concerned.

This guarantee was designed to insure objectivity by decreasing the possibilities of misrepresentation, favorable or unfavorable. The object was to remove the study completely from the context of commercial advantage or disadvantage that the results might have for individual papers. Although the community newspaper publishers frequently had no objection to the identification of their newspaper it did not seem appropriate to reverse the original guarantee of anonymity. In any case, the names of the newspapers and all the details of the research are available in my files and are open to inspection and re-analysis by qualified social scientists and communications researchers.

The study itself was sponsored by a joint grant from the Social Science Research Committee and the Chicago Community Inventory of the University of Chicago. The author wishes to express his gratitude to Dean Ralph W. Tyler, chairman of the Committee, and Professor Philip Hauser, director of the Inventory, for their valuable suggestions and active support of the research.

In the course of the study, a wide variety of data was accumulated by the Committee on Communication, only a portion of which is presented in this volume. In particular, Mr. Fred Davis was responsible for the execution of the content analysis phases of the study and, together with Mr. George Nollet, assumed the task of interviewing the publishers and editors of the Chicago community newspapers. Their field work made possible the collection of historical background data, as well as information on the organization of the industry and basic statistics of circulation and finance. Mr. Louis Kriesberg was responsible for supervising the staff of interviewers during the survey aspects of the study.

The author was fortunate in being able to have the continuing criticism and advice of the members of the Committee on Communication. In particular, I am indebted to Dr. Bernard Berelson for his very valuable assistance on the construction of the content analysis categories, the designing of the interview schedule and for his careful reading of the final manuscript. In addition, Professors Albert J. Reiss, Jr., David Ricsman and Louis Wirth were most generous in offering help and advice.

Contents

I

Communications and the Urban Metropolis

Social Elements of Urbanism

In 1950, eighty-two community newspapers were being published within the city limits of Chicago with a total weekly circulation in excess of 983,000. For the Chicago metropolitan district as a whole, the total number reached 181. A similar pattern repeated itself with local modifications in every metropolitan district of over 1,000,000 in the United States,[1] for it is at this population level that the urban community press begins to take hold. Measured by dollar volume, the last thirty years have witnessed the development of the community newspaper "industry" into a profitable business despite

1. New York City constitutes an exception. See page 45.

the drastic competition of the "big" mass media. Measured by circulation, the community press offers national advertisers facilities for delivering any advertisement into the homes of the vast majority of the urban families of these metropolitan centers.

The world at the level of the community press appears as a mass of details of parochial concern and the contents of the community press can only take on meaning with some degree of personal acquaintance with the area. For the sophisticated detached observer who cannot react to the specific details but who perceives the press content with its personalistic overtones, the invariable reaction is: Are the contents of the community newspaper appealing to something real and meaningful? Or are the readers being manipulated for the benefit of local commercial interests?

In fact, the urban community newspaper, according to some, should have ceased to exist. That variety of sociological theory which is oriented towards viewing our modern mass society as movement from the simple to the complex, from the small scale to the large scale, has difficulty in accommodating itself to the persistence of old forms or to the development of counter-trends. From such a point of view, counter-trends, such as the growth of the urban community press, are viewed as mere survivals destined to be eliminated in the so-called "long run." But even the most superficial examination of the contents of a single community newspaper presents the social scientist with a revealing reflection of the complexities, ambiguities and viability of the local community. A systematic analysis of the urban community press such as that attempted in this research study becomes a relevant method of analyzing social organization and social control at the local community level.

The community press exists, grows and has an impact because, for most urban families, the place of work of the principal wage earner and place of family residence are physically separated. Integration into the urban social structure involves interests and conflicts generated by the factory system, a problem which has been among the main concerns of social scientists. It also involves the interests and conflicts centering in the residential community. The vitality and impact of the community press hinge on the forms of social participation which these interests and conflicts generate.

Politics and the governmental process is a case in point. The growth and shifts in population in our metropolitan centers present the political parties which are linked to older units of population concentration with profound tasks of mediation in order to maintain a democratic consensus. For example, there has been a marked trend for middle class residents to move to localities far removed from the place of their employment and these changes have frequently taken place without appropriate changes in political jurisdiction. Thus, the "class struggle" is joined by the "geographical struggle," as the new outlying portions of the city pose themselves against the older districts, the city against the suburbs, and the metropolitan district against the hinterlands.

Within the confines of the metropolitan district, traditional economic power blocs, and social prestige groups have sought to extend their influence to those areas of residence where the balance of political power lies. More recently, there have been efforts by the trade union movement to extend its power from the factory system into the residential community through political action organizations.[2] In the

---

2. Even the revolutionaries must address themselves to this context. The Communist Party of America before World War II debated endlessly whether it would organize and appeal to the workers factory by factory or whether the banners would be raised community by community. In periods of revolutionary

past, the professional politician has been of crucial importance in effecting a "compromise" between competing geographical interests.

Until recently, extraordinary viability has been demonstrated by the political organization in effecting political compromise between competing community areas. No group is more sensitized to these trends, and the difficulties involved in effecting compromise, than the community newspaper publishers whose very existence is tied to population shifts and to the implications of these shifts for the social relations and politics of the local community.

In the process of urban growth in America, the maintenance of consensus has also been closely associated with the development of the mass media of communications. Mass media contributed to the growth of urban centers by providing the channels of information and symbolism required for the integration and social solidarity of vast aggregates of population. In turn, urbanism has promoted the development of the mass media by providing geographically a concentrated audience and a concentrated market for their support.

The mass media are generally viewed as reaching the widest possible audience within the urban centers, and hence as minimizing differences and promoting the most general identifications. However, just as the development of urbanism allows for and stimulates the organization of various local and specialized institutions in the community, so the growth of the mass media is accompanied by the development of specialized and local channels of communication. A vast proliferation of special publications addressed to members of specific class, skill and special interest groups has taken place.

---

fervor the factory has been the center of agitation, but in popular front periods political action involving alliance shifted to the residential community.

The growth of the urban community press within the major metropolitan areas represents another phase of "specialization within generalization," one in which this geographical distinction between work and residence is fundamental. Social scientific theorizing on the problems of urbanism has been considerable although hardly unified. However, research on the process of urbanization has been molded to a considerable extent by those theories which stress the one-way modifications from small-scale to large-scale organization with attendant shifts in human values, forms of social control, and centers and techniques of dominance.[3] Within this formula, some social scientists have assembled data which have led to an outlook that stresses the impersonality and disorganization of urban life. According to this view, the moral order is conditioned by the individual's functional and economic interests rather than by any social order in the local community or in the local neighborhood. In fact, this view envisages hardly enough social contact or organization on the local level to condition individual behavior.

Such a perspective fails to describe accurately urban social organization. The "obvious fact" of a decline in the importance of the local community—as compared with its importance in an idealized blood kinship society—precludes understanding how some measure of consensus persists at the lowest community levels, or, in short, how it is that urban society persists at all. If society were as impersonal, as self-centered and barren as described by some who are preoccupied with the one-way trend from "gemeinschaft" to "gesellschaft" seem to believe, the levels of criminality, social disorganization and psychopathology which social science

---

3. This point of view finds classic expression in the work of Ferdinand Toennies' *Gemeinschaft und Gesellschaft.*

seeks to account for would have to be viewed as very low rather than as alarmingly high.[4]

However, not all theory and research on urban communities has been dominated by such an outlook. The fact that a mass society has emerged need not prevent interest in the complex processes by which social adaptation to the growth of the metropolis takes place.[5] Some concrete studies can be pointed to which give a more accurate description of the local community and its facilities, and social organization.[6] Although

4. It may be an incomplete statement, but an analysis of the value position of many of these earlier sociologists who discovered such trends and raised them to universals points to a peculiar conclusion. These men were marginal to society—as are all intellectuals and all critics. They stood in a highly impersonal relation to society, and their marginality, remaining largely unknown to themselves, manifested itself in exaggerating the rootlessness of urban existence and the inevitability of these trends.

5. Georg Simmel, for example, delineated social forms which he believed helped to account for the persistence of society. Robert Park sought for an analysis of the communications processes and loyalties which developed as means of integrating the individual into the spatially rooted social arrangements of the metropolis. These men and others had the merit of focusing attention on a wide range of social forms that have to be considered as dimensions in analyzing the local urban community.

6. The following are some selected examples: Roderick D. McKenzie, *The Neighborhood: A Study of Local Life in the City of Columbus, Ohio, 1923* (Chicago: University of Chicago, 1923) one of the earliest studies of a so-called disorganized neighborhood, analyzed the intricacies of social organization at the local level. Bessie Clenahan's *The Changing Neighborhood* (University of Southern California Studies, Los Angeles, 1929), not only points to the "decline of the neighborhood," but also traces to what degree and in what manner "participation and the degree of intimate social contact is conditioned by locus." Frank Sweetzer, *Neighborhood Acquaintance and Association: A Study of Personal Neighborhoods* (New York, 1941), found that interaction could be best described on a person-to-person level rather than on a family-to-family level, as the basis for isolating in a more refined fashion the levels of community involvement. William F. Whyte, *Street Corner Society* (Chicago: University of Chicago Press, 1942), combined an analysis of social interaction among primary groups in a slum community and their interaction with the larger mechanisms of social control and as a result helped dispel the belief that the slum is a community without clearcut social organization. In "The Use of Local Facilities in a Metropolis," *American Journal of Sociology*, LVI (November 1950), 238-46, by Donald L. Foley, it was ascertained that between one-third and one-half of the reported facility use was local, and that,

wide differences exist in the definition of the local community in these and other studies, the general conclusion emerges that in our large cities impressive degrees and patterns of local community life exist within their metropolitan limits. The large city involves an intricate balance between the relative use of local and non-local facilities, and a complex of social institutions for integrating the individual into his "residential" community as well as his "employment" community. Within such a social context the community press operates, and requires analysis in these terms. In turn, the analysis of the community press might help clarify the character of the "residential" community, and in particular, help answer the question actually how rootless is the resident of the metropolis.

Research Dimensions and Hypotheses

The urban community newspaper is defined as a weekly English-language publication addressed to the residents of a specific area of the urban metropolis.[7] The mode of production and distribution may vary considerably, as may their financial base. Nevertheless, urban community newspapers—both city

---

contrary to expectation, older more densely built up sections with greater tenancy showed somewhat more extensive use of local facilities than the sparse, single-family sections where home ownership rates were high. Other studies have shown that residential mobility is not a progressive function of urbanism, as found in Theodore Caplow, "Incidence and Direction of Residential Mobility in a Minneapolis Sample," *Social Forces*, 27 (May 1949).

7. The requirement of weekly publication—and, in a few cases, semi-weekly publication—is necessary in order to eliminate those occasional daily English-language papers found in the urban metropolis that address themselves not to specific communities but to wide sections of the metropolitan district. These newspapers are associated with older municipalities and political units that were in existence before the growth of the metropolitan district. They are invariably published outside the central business district.

and suburban—may be considered as constituting a homogeneous class inasmuch as they are directed to a geographically and ecologically delimited audience within the metropolitan district.

The definitions of the U. S. Census Bureau, as of 1940, supply the basis for delimiting the urban metropolis in this study. These boundaries are well suited for analyzing certain aspects of the community press. However, the traditional political limits of the city supply a convenient boundary if one is interested in community newspapers operating in more urbanized areas.

The specific areas in the metropolis to which the community press addresses itself can be thought of as "community areas." Even to the superficial observer the modern metropolis is a collection of little worlds and local communities. Chicago, in particular, is known as a city of seventy-five community areas. These seventy-five communities are based on the analysis of a wide range of data produced by a generation of research at the University of Chicago.[8] Nevertheless, these community areas are not mere statistical devices. Their dimensions are readily discernible. "It has been found useful to view the city as made up of seventy-five component local communities each of which has a history of its own, and is marked off from the others by distinctive physical and social characteristics and by natural boundaries. The names of these seventy-five communities have acquired considerable currency and renown and evoke among the inhabitants a sense of identification if not loyalty. In the face of the movements of population, of industry and the rise and decline of specific areas within the city, these communities nevertheless retain a certain constancy."[9] The growth of the community press, the

8. Wirth and Bernert, *Local Community Fact Book of Chicago*, 1949.
9. Wirth and Bernert, *op. cit.*, p. vii.

boundaries of its audience and its present character are intimately linked to the community area concept. For example, a preponderant number of community newspapers in Chicago bear on their mastheads the names of particular local community areas, although their circulation areas may vary somewhat from these community area boundaries.

The community press, like any other form of mass communication, can be seen as an operating system. To consider the community press as a system involves linking the characteristics of the producers of community newspapers to their content and linking the content to the impact of the media on the readership (and to the lack of impact on non-readers). But it means more. It requires investigation of the range of communications—direct and indirect—by which the readers contact and influence the controllers and producers of the community press. The publisher creates a communication which is intended for an audience which not only reacts to the communication but which, in one form or another, itself initiates communications back to the original communicator. The classic formula of Lasswell, "who says what, to whom, with what effect," implies, in turn, how does "whom" affect "who" so that the "what" can be modified to changing needs. The community press presented a rather unique opportunity for studying a communication system in a comprehensive and integrated fashion. Though complex, the investigation could be reduced to a manageable research task involving all elements of a communication system. Moreover, it seemed possible to relate the communication system to the specific social organization of the audience, a research requirement for communication research which is all too seldom fulfilled.

Thus, the basic orientation of this research views the urban community press as one of the social mechanisms through which the individual is integrated into the urban social structure. All mass media of communication need not invariably be conceived as disintegrating factors in modern society. In fact, the underlying question is whether the community press helps to maintain local community activities and identifications and to interrelate them to non-local activities and identifications. Concretely, the following series of hypotheses were employed as a departure for analyzing the various aspects of the community press:

1. *The community newspaper arose out of predominantly commercial requirements connected with the decentralization of the central business district but which in turn have led the community newspaper to serve a wider range of unanticipated social, political, and affectual needs.* In the long run, the community newspaper, like other forms of organized communication, develops through its struggle to survive, functions and services it was never intended to perform.

The community newspaper arose out of the development of the satellite business center in the metropolitan district, which made possible a base of advertising revenue. In fact, it soon emerged that only a small minority of urban community newspapers represent the outgrowth of village-type newspapers in communities which were incorporated into the metropolitan district. The majority arose in areas where no village or small town antecedents could be found. The development of the satellite business district reflected changes in population distributions along community lines and created an audience which could be addressed in terms of local geographical identifications.

The community press constitutes an interesting case of modern entrepreneurship. It required examination as a form which developed in contradistinction to large-scale tendencies. The large-scale daily newspaper left unfulfilled certain local functions of communication. This does not deny that the community press itself might display tendencies of consolidation at a certain point in its development.

2. *The community press acts as a mechanism which seeks to maintain local consensus through the emphasis on common values rather than on the solution of conflicting values.* If true, such a mode of discourse could be a function of the economic origin of the community newspaper, the characteristics of the publisher, his relationship to his advertisers, the close social distance to other community leaders and to his audience, all of which seemed in advance to limit his ability to be openly controversial in news and editorials.

Despite its economic origin and its economic struggle for existence, the content of the community newspaper appeared less commercialized than that of the daily newspapers. Is the publisher less able to take an impersonal view of his operations and less able to give unbridled expression to the desire for profit? The same factors which limit controversy might also limit commercialism. As a result of his closer contact with his readers and the general community pressure on the community press, the content of the community press, it is contended, reflects a wide range of attitudes and aspirations of the local community more closely than does the daily press. Decentralized ownership of the community press further serves to reinforce such sensitivity and thereby to enhance the significance of the local community press as an indicator of community values.

It has been traditional for market researchers to claim low readership or readership indifference to community newspapers and to label them contemptuously as "little sheets" and the like. As shall be shown later, this claim represents a complex of commercial attitudes and advertising ideology which is not in the slightest degree based upon research for such research did not exist prior to this study. To the contrary, early in the course of this research it became clear that high exposure among readers to community newspapers is in part a function of the relatively smaller number of pages contained in each issue than in the daily press. Compared with the bulky editions of such papers as the *Chicago Tribune*, each portion of the community newspaper is in less competition for attention, and thereby more likely to penetrate the consciousness of the reader. (Testing of this hypothesis in its full scope lies beyond the limits of this study.)

3. In the "neighborhood" community, not only the socialization of the next generation takes place, and certain primary group relations are manifested, but also patterns of consumption are expressed and important mechanisms of politics are extant. If it is true that the community newspaper is related to the process of integrating the individual into the local urban community, then the attributes of readers should reflect both this process and the local social structure which makes possible this process.

First, the local community resident can be viewed as a member of a family and status group; *as such, indices of greater family and social cohesion should be related to local community readership, for such cohesion is a requisite to community orientation.* Second, the local community resident in varying degrees participates in and identifies with the facilities and institutions of the local community; *as such, indices of greater community integration should be related to more community newspaper readership.*

The association of community press readership with community integration might well be merely on the "ideological" level; at least a portion of the population might have their community participation limited to a strong positive belief which is seldom practiced. Community integration had to be defined so that actual community behavior was of crucial importance, in order to isolate pseudo-community identification or the desire for community orientation from actual community integration.

4. *As a communications system, at every point in its operation, the mass communications aspects of the local community press are inextricably interrelated with the personal communications which link together the community newspaper personnel, the community leaders, and the readership clientele.* Thus, in a sense, the community press is seen as operating "midway" between the mass media (the daily press) and informal communication (word of mouth).

In a division of labor between these modes of communication, the community press assumes functions that cannot be performed by either the mass media or word of mouth. It becomes relevant to investigate the specific types of content the daily press is unable to carry but which the community press publishes in order to meet the information requirements of local residents, and thus maintain various levels of local identification. On the other hand, in the local community the network of relationships between individuals, especially between community leaders, is too complicated to be carried by word of mouth.

The impact of the community newspaper was studied in terms of the continuity of personal communications and the mass communications content of the press. This continuity involves not only the contact of readers with other readers, but the contact of readers, especially those in community leadership positions, with the publisher and other personnel who control and produce community newspapers. Because of these patterns of interaction, the social role of the men who operate the community press seems to offer a key for analyzing how the various elements of this communications system are interrelated. Moreover, the role of the publisher becomes an index to understanding how conflicting group interests are resolved at the local level.

All of the above hypotheses, if correct, indicate that the community press need not be viewed as a survival, rural or otherwise. Instead, it is assumed that the contents of the community press and the function it performs for its readers are linked to the social requirements of the urban community which are ever changing and not merely survivals of "village-type existence." In a fundamental sense, the ethics and the values of the community press need not be traced to historical analogues but have their own validity in the requirements of the local urban community and of urban personality.

The analysis of the community press as a specialized form of communication raises a number of complex value judgments concerning democratic ideology. Nevertheless, the following simple hypothesis is offered; namely, that individuals who display strong local community identifications are people who display a higher sense of political competence required for democratic consensus than those who have low or no local community identifications. Of course, a minority of individuals may have their sense of political competence rooted in strictly ideological considerations. Yet it may well be that this hypothesis is an over-simplification; it is certainly designed to modify the oft-repeated contention that the individual who is not provincial is truly the individual of democratic political motivation. But community orientation and provincialism are not the same thing, for the latter excludes or at least hinders wider orientations, while the former need not operate to such an end.

In constructing a research design to test these hypotheses, two important methodological problems were central. First, community-oriented research into urbanism has been characterized by the energetic development of efforts to chart the class stratification and interaction patterns of small communities. Small communities are presumed to be more amenable to systematic research and from the analysis of such small-scale communities, it is assumed, projections can be made to assist the understanding of our mass society. As yet such projections remain to be accomplished. This research attempts an alternative, by analyzing community communications as a dimension in the direct observation of metropolitan social organization.

Second, a considerable body of data on attitudes and identifications has been collected by survey methods which should throw light on the processes of coordination and indirect control in urban communities. Since, in the urban community, integration is conditioned by systems of identifications and images, attitude data should be of crucial importance in understanding large-scale social organization which involves indirect social contacts. But the survey research technique as a method for studying urban "collective representations" has not been highly relevant for community-oriented research.[10] The use of the survey technique for such problems requires a research design that takes into account both the ecological and community realities of the metropolitan district instead of selecting respondents merely on the basis of national sampling characteristics (e.g., age, sex, income, etc.).

Therefore, in this study, the research design was limited to metropolitan Chicago and included (a) historical and ecological analysis of growth and organization of the community press, (b) interviews with the personnel involved in the community press, (c) content analysis of the community press

---

10. By "collective representations" is meant those symbols and attitudes which are of crucial importance for guiding social action in that they reflect significant patterns of shared values and group goals.

and (d) a survey of readers and non-readers of the community press in three selected communities. In studying both the personnel and the readers, special emphasis was placed on the range of communications and social devices by which the audience made known their reactions to the contents. Finally a special sample of community leaders was required to test many hypotheses which required comparative data.

II

The Growth
and Organization
of the Community
Press

The Decline of the Immigrant Press

The growth of American cities began in earnest after the Civil War. Population increases due to the birth rate and internal migration were augmented by the tremendous influx of immigrants. Adjustment to urban life modified old institutions and brought new ones into existence, one of which was the expanding immigrant press. These foreign language newspapers, flourishing in a period before the urban community newspaper developed, sought to mediate the impersonalized aspects of urban life for a wide portion of the population.

The waves of immigrants who fed the growth of America's centers of commerce and industry contributed to a particular ecological pattern. Foreign-language immigrants found the big cities segregated into cultural and ethnic enclosures. Their arrival contributed to the strengthening and expansion of these ghettoes within the metropolis. Before the "closing of the gates," the foreign language publisher found his audience not only ethnically united but, in all likelihood, living in some sort of geographical community.

The popularity of the immigrant press was immense. Neither skillful journalism nor the technical production which characterizes the contemporary newspaper was its basis. Certain of the immigrant newspapers were striving in this direction, but most showed an almost studied disregard of such "standards." Park, in his study, *The Immigrant Press and Its Control*, traces the origins of its powerful pull.[1] His elaborate analysis of emerging European nationalism and aspirations for ethnic liberation in the 19th and early 20th centuries as the background for the immigrant press dispelled the belief that the immigrant press was some sort of survival, or appendage of the European press. To the contrary, the immigrant press in this country and its transitory success served as an expression of emancipation, in the same sense as was immigration to this country.

"The popularity of the foreign language press is due to various causes. One reason why immigrants are eager to read their own language in this country is that they have not been permitted to do so in their own. Sometimes they have not learned to read before they come here; they have not been permitted to do so. Sometimes the journals they might read (in Europe) were not interesting or not intelligible. Frequently the 'oppressed and dependent' peoples of Europe were not allowed to publish journals in their own language. Immigrants who have struggled for the right to print and read their native languages

---

1. Park, R. E., *The Immigrant Press and Its Control* (New York: Harper & Bros., 1929).

at home are bound to have sentimental views in regards to the press which prints their language in America." [2]

Liberation here meant social and intellectual liberation even more than political. The spoken vernacular of the European peasant, even if his ethnic group was in political power, was not found in the columns of the European press of this period. The press was usually addressed to the educated classes. In Poland, at least, there was an interesting exception, for here there came into being a press published for and addressed to the interests and understanding of the ordinary peasant.[3]

The "survival" interpretation is further weakened by a consideration of the motives of the readers:

"One reason why immigrant peoples read more in America than they do at home is because there is more going on that they need to know. There is more novelty and more news.

"News is a kind of urgent information that men use in making adjustments to a new environment, in changing old habits and in forming new opinions." [4]

Since assimilation was an ultimate goal, the success of the immigrant press could in some part be measured by its ability to destroy itself. For if the ghettoes had not declined as rapidly as they did, the immigrant press might have had a prolonged importance.

The economic origin of the immigrant press hardly foreshadowed the role it was to play in the United States. Its economic basis, moreover, was least stable and respectable in the years when its role was most crucial. Many foreign language newspapers had their origin in an advertising sheet sent out by steamship ticket agents. These agents, looking for steam-

---

2. Park, *Ibid.*, p. 9.
3. Thomas, W. I., and Znaniecki, F., *The Polish Peasant* (Chicago: University of Chicago Press, 1918). Vol. IV, pp. 241-70.
4. Park, *op. cit.*, p. 9.

ship business, circularized recent arrivals who were concerned with bringing to America the rest of their families and their relatives. Eventually, the proprietor hired an "intellectual" who edited the advertising sheet, wrote news and editorials, and thus converted it into a regularly established newspaper.

Park pointed out that, "if the editor made a success of the paper he might, in course of time, become the proprietor. Frequently, it was the other way. Some impecunious intellectual started a paper, but was unable to make it go, and the steamship agent and banker took it off his hands." [5]

For long periods, the foreign-language papers had many problems in obtaining suitable advertising revenue. A good many foreign language papers could not have continued to exist if they were deprived of medical and patent medicine advertisements unless they became the organ of some society, party or faction. Just before World War I national advertising, including political advertising on a national basis, was made available to the foreign-language press through the activities of Louis N. Hammerling and his American Association of Foreign Language Newspapers. Hammerling, who had a genius for personal intrigue and negotiation, operated as a middleman between two groups who had mutual interests, the foreign language press and large American business organizations. He made the first serious attempt to put advertising in the foreign language papers on a sound business basis. He lost his monopolistic control of foreign language advertising because he was exposed for dealing with German propagandists and because he made too extensive use of the opportunities for honest graft. Nevertheless, the precedent had been established and national advertising in the immigrant press became more of an accepted practice. Soon the

5. Park, *Ibid.*, p. 339.

cessation of immigration was to bring about a decline in the importance of this medium to national mass-production-minded advertisers.

The foreign-language publisher was probably always engaged in an intense struggle for survival, although some of the largest immigrant papers became profitable ventures. However, Park makes a remarkable observation on the attitude of the publisher toward his paper, an observation which suggests application to the community press.

"Very few publishers of the foreign-language press have learned to take the detached and impersonal attitude of the American newspaper man toward the contents of the paper they print. They do not quite accept the philosophy of the editor who said he was 'willing to print anything that God would let happen.' The foreign language newspapers are never indifferent to quite the extent that this is true of an American business institution." [6]

The publishers' ties with the foreign-language community, and their close involvement with ethnic values acted as a barrier to the development of a completely commercial and instrumental outlook. Likewise, the community newspaper, although a creature of commercial interest, and engaged in a fierce struggle for survival, might well behave in a similar mode because of the publishers' close connections with the local community and its values.

Statistical data on the foreign-language press reveal the obvious connection between the waves of immigration and the changing composition and size of the immigrant press. During the years of World War I it reached its highest figure, because there was a heightened interest in news about the belligerent countries among those who could not read English. In 1910, it was estimated from N. W. Ayer's sources that there were 1,198 foreign language newspapers of all varieties.

6. Park, *Ibid.*, p. 114.

By 1917, the number had risen to 1,323. When the decade ended in 1920, the number had receded to 1,052. Since that time the decline of the foreign language newspapers has been steady but the attrition proceeded at a slower pace than once predicted. In 1950, the Common Council of American Unity estimated that there were over 900 foreign language publications; however this figure fails to reflect the decline in circulation and the less frequent periodicity of many papers in 1950 as compared with 1920. The present immigration policies may well temporarily halt the decline, but the long term prospects remain unaltered.

The decline in the numbers of the foreign-born together with significant shifts in their residence have resulted in a fundamental ecological shift in audiences for the foreign-language press. The decline of rigid ethnic segregation is perhaps just as important as the decline in numbers, for the foreign-language newspaper has lost most of its community orientation. At a specific point in the decline of its circulation, and in the face of the patterns of dispersal of residence of its readers, the immigrant press no longer addresses an audience predominantly located in a specific community of the urban metropolis. From ethnic minority to ethnic minority and from city to city this process takes place with varying speed. The foreign-language paper becomes oriented to all the members of the ethnic minority who reside in the metropolis and eventually it assumes the character of a regional and a national ethnic paper. As its ecological base is altered, its content seems to shift from local news and gossip to national ethnic politics.

The link between the decline of the foreign language press and the rise of the urban community press is not a direct one. An occasional foreign-language publisher appears in the ranks of the community publishers, but this is indeed rare.

The link is one of ecological, ethnic and economic development. As the ecological basis of the city changed, as new economic institutions arose and as the foreign-born and their children developed new perspectives, the trend lines of decline and growth overlapped.

The foreign language press, because of its position midway between large-scale mass communications and personal communications and because of its social and psychological implications supplies an analogy for comparison with what Park would call the "natural history" of the urban community press.

The Satellite Business District and the Rise of the Community Newspaper

The growth and present form of the community press is directly linked to the decentralization of the central business district and the development of secondary retail shopping areas in various sectors of the city and suburbs. For Chicago, at least, within the city limits the establishment of satellite shopping centers led to the creation of the majority of community weeklies in localities where such newspapers had never before existed. A minority of community newspapers grew out of the village-type weekly which existed before these villages were annexed in the expansion of the city and converted into satellite shopping centers. (Less than 10 percent of the papers published in 1950 could trace their beginnings either directly or indirectly to such an origin.)

By contrast, the origin of the suburban community newspaper is closer to the country newspaper. Such papers frequently developed out of printing establishments which sought to supply an outlying community with a newspaper. These beginnings still condition the operations of community newspapers, although changes in management and altered economic conditions have had drastic effects.

Although there have been marked fluctuations in response to business conditions, community newspapers in the Chicago metropolitan district have increased in number and circulation during the period 1910–50. From a total of 82 papers in 1910, the number of papers now stands at 181 (Table No. 1 (II)).[7] Contrary to expectation, the percentage of increase in the number of community newspapers during this period has been greater within the city limits than in the suburbs.

TABLE NO. 1 (II)—*Growth of Community Press in Chicago Metropolitan District, 1910–1950*

| | NUMBER OF PAPERS | | |
	City	Suburbs *	Total
1910	31	51	82
1915	30	58	88
1920	29	47	76
1925	30	58	88
1930	75	93	168
1935	15	71	86
1940	51	102	153
1945	61	95	156
1950	82	99	181

* According to 1940 census boundaries of the Metropolitan District.

In the city proper, the growth from 31 papers in 1910 to 82 · papers in 1949 constitutes an increase of 165 percent. In the suburban areas the increase was 94 percent, from 51 to 99 papers.

7. The data on the growth of community newspapers and circulation are based on N. W. Ayer's *Directory of Newspapers and Periodicals*, unpublished research reports, historical accounts, interviews, and other sources of estimates.

World War I and its economic dislocations brought the first interruption in the growth curve of the community press. Only by 1924 did business revive to the level necessary for further expansion. Nevertheless, since the first major steps in the decentralization of the central business district occurred in Chicago in the 1920's, the growth curve of community newspapers within the city limits was most marked by 1930 (75). The counter swing of the Great Depression wrought havoc with the majority of the city community newspapers. In fact only a minority (15) with real financial stability were able to survive. Recovery from the Depression was slow; by 1940 the number of papers (61) had not reached the 1930 level although circulation surpassed the 1930 level. (Table No. 2 (II).) World War II, in contrast to World War I, was not a period of decline. In fact almost ten new papers were established before the hostilities ended, and with the period of continued high level of business activity after the war, the growth curve had another sharp rise from 61 to 82 papers. During this entire period the suburban papers were much less sensitive to shifts in the business cycle, thus indicating a greater financial stability. However, during the last decade, there has been almost no increase in their number. This represents more the effects of a consolidation movement than a decline in circulation.[8]

---

8. In Chicago, as in many other metropolitan areas, the growth of community newspapers took place while efforts were undertaken to develop advertising newspapers. Advertising newspapers, usually referred to as "shoppers" or "shopping newspapers" are devoted almost exclusively to advertisements and are usually owned by groups of large department stores located in the central business district. In Chicago, because of the strong competition from the local community press, and the marked decentralization of the central business district "shoppers" have declined and are now nonexistent. In some other cities "shoppers" operate and naturally divert advertising revenue from the community press. See pp. 31-34, "National Trends in the Community Press" for details.

The increase in the number of community newspapers within the city of Chicago was accompanied by a tremendous expansion in weekly circulation (Table No. 2 (II)). In 1910, 31 publications circulated each week an approximate total of 113,000 copies; by 1950, 82 papers reached a weekly circulation of approximately 983,000 copies. This increase in circulation of 770 percent is probably a more significant indicator of growth of the community press than is the number of papers. In 1950, the total combined weekday circulation of daily papers within the city limits of Chicago was over 1,700,000.

TABLE NO. 2 (II)—*Weekly Circulation of Chicago Community Press*

YEAR	NUMBER OF PAPERS	TOTAL WEEKLY CIRCULATION	MEAN WEEKLY CIRCULATION
1910	31	113,000	3,645
1920	29	95,000	3,275
1930	75	756,000	10,080
1940	51	848,000	16,630
1950	82	983,000	11,990

A complex of ecological and economic factors affecting both the daily and community press throws light on the function of the newspaper as a marketing device. These interrelated factors assist in the explanation of the growth of the community press, since they condition the limits of the usefulness of the advertising medium and establish the effective "advertising area." [9] They consist of:

1. Accessibility of reaching the advertiser's place of business. The physical difficulty involved in reaching the advertiser's place of business, the arduousness, discomfort and time

9. Malone, John, unpublished manuscript, University of Kansas, 1950.

for travel by public conveyance or auto supplies a basic limitation on the "advertising area" which can be covered by any newspaper. (Phone and mail purchasing alter these limits.)

2. The size and number of firms or stores able to supply advertising revenue. The development of an "advertising area" requires not only a minimum of advertising revenue but also a reasonable expectation of long term continuation of advertising revenue.

3. Sheer physical size of the newspaper in pages. The size determines the cost and quantity of advertising competing for attention during the fixed time period between issues.

4. Attitude of the readers toward the news and advertising of the paper.

Of these factors, we are here concerned with the first and the second. (Physical size as a limiting factor is of little importance for most community newspapers; attitudes toward the paper are analyzed in Chapter IV and V). We are concerned with the ecological changes and economic developments necessary to support newspapers addressed to the residents of a particular area within the larger metropolis.

Theoretically, communities representing various levels of retail enterprise are able to support various communications networks. Five levels of economic integration can be identified which throw some light on the relation between community organizations and communications.

a. Hamlet—pop. 25-250—crossroad settlement, the metropolitan counterpart of which is the corner grocer, drugstore, filling station group. Communications media indigenous to this community are completely absent.

b. Market town—pop. 250-2,500—this center has its counterpart in the organized neighborhood within a metropolitan or suburban center at the edge of a regional city. Mass communications media appear for the first time, usually in the form of a weekly newspaper.

    c. County seat town—pop. 2,500-25,000—such communities represent the growth of a market town and serve as the hub of a number of hamlets and market towns. Mass communications indigenous to the community usually consist of a daily newspaper plus perhaps a weekly paper, in addition to an AM radio station.

    d. Regional city—25,000-250,000—a river confluence, a railroad center, a state capitol, or commercial and industrial development lead to the growth of the regional city. Such cities are characterized not only by central business districts but also by a number of community centers on the periphery of the larger city. In terms of communication, the central city is served by at least one daily newspaper while the smaller communities in the orbit of the central regional city have their own weekly newspapers. One or more radio stations will be present with national network hookups.

    e. Metropolitan area—pop. 250,000 and up—the metropolitan area is an urban center with dominating financial, administrative, manufacturing and distribution functions. In a population aggregate of this size, a morning and evening daily newspaper are likely to be found; available radio outlets include combinations of AM, FM, and television.[10] In population aggregates of this level the urban community newspaper begins to appear; as can be seen from the data presented on p. 46, it is only in centers of over one million that the community press develops effectively. The ever-growing strains on the internal transportation systems of the large metropolis are associated with the development of commer-

---

10. At each population center "local correspondents" supply news about the smaller population centers which are close by and thus extend the area of news coverage.

cial centers outside the central business district. In addition, certain smaller population centers are absorbed in the growth of the metropolitan district, which contain their own commercial centers.

In the case of Chicago the development of satellite business districts was a function of both population growth and population movement away from the central business district. By 1890 the basis for the metropolitan character of Chicago had been established. Subsequent changes in the legal limits of the city were negligible. In the decade 1910–1920, the population increased 24 percent, from approximately 2,200,000 to 2,700,000. During this period there was no comparable growth in the number or circulation of community newspapers. In the period of 1920–30, population growth was approximately 25 percent, from 2,700,000 to 3,400,000. This was the period of greatest expansion of the community press. In subsequent decades, although the population increased at lesser rates, the growth of the community press continued subject to fluctuations.

In a demographic sense, the growth of the community newspaper was as dependent on the dispersion of the population from the center of the city to outlying areas as it was on increases in total population. Between 1920 and 1934, the population of an "irregular" area extending four to five miles from the business center declined from 1,060,716 to 848,802, a drop of 20 percent, while the population of the rest of the city outside the area increased from 1,641,000 to 2,411,200, a gain of 74 percent.

At the same time, the dollar volume of business transacted in the outlying centers considerably increased. The volume of business outside the central business district as late as 1910 was relatively insignificant. By 1935 the total retail sales volume in the central business district was $275,766,000 as com-

pared with $785,487,000 in the remainder of the city; [11] and
it is from this economic basis that the community press draws
its advertising revenue.

Hoyt describes the consequences of these population movements in the following terms:

"The rapid growth of population in the outlying areas from 1921
to 1927, however, caused the upward course of values to be resumed
until the sales prices of the major corners tripled on the average between 1921 and 1928. Not only did an increase of population of one
million in these newly developed territories, combined with employment at high wages, furnish added consumer purchasing power for
local stores, but a number of factors tended to divert much of this
shopping away from the Loop to these community centers. The rapid
growth of outlying banks furnished depositories for local funds and
collected neighborhood savings for re-investment in local building
projects. The new palatial motion-picture houses furnished the same
entertainment that was afforded in the Loop. The Walgreen Drug
Store, the Woolworth or Kresge Store, or the Goldblatt or Wieboldt
Department Store offered a wide choice of merchandise. Hence the
residents of these new areas, finding it increasingly difficult to park
their automobiles in the downtown areas, came to prefer to do their
banking, shopping, and to seek their entertainment close to home." [12]

A comparison of the trends in the location of the satellite
business districts in Chicago and the trends in the location
of the community press presents a striking index of the close
connection between these two developments. In fact, the
growth of community newspapers and the boundaries of their
circulation area follow more closely upon the growth of these
satellite business districts than any other ecological factor.
This pattern of expansion which involved the majority of the
papers can hardly be called a rural survival.

---

11. Harold M. Mayer, "Patterns and Recent Trends of Chicago's Outlying
Business Centers," *Journal of Land and Public Utility Economics*, XVIII,
Feb. 1944, p. 4.

12. Hoyt, Homer, *One Hundred Years of Land Values in Chicago* (Chicago: University of Chicago, 1933) p. 36.

National Trends in the Community Press

The patterns of urban development, the decentralization of the business district and the resultant growth of the community newspaper which took place in Chicago were duplicated in other major metropolitan areas subject to variations in local conditions. Aside from deviations which can be traced to modification in the patterns of urbanism, in certain cities, particularly in Detroit and Cleveland, the owners of large department stores retarded the development somewhat by publishing their own advertising newspapers which diverted revenue from the community press.

Precise statistics on the number and circulation trends of the community press are not available for the country as a whole. In 1949, Controlled Circulation Newspapers of America, Inc., the trade association of the community press, listed as members over 130 community newspapers with a circulation of over 1,800,000. This represents only a portion of the industry.

Ayer's Directory gives a considerably fuller picture but a large number of community newspapers, especially those in the highly built up portion of metropolitan districts, are not listed due to indifference on the part of the publishers. A tabulation was made of weekly English-language newspapers in the 1949 edition of Ayer's which were not organs of special interest groups or which did not appeal explicitly to special interest groups but instead appeared to be oriented toward general audiences within geographical subdivisions of the metropolitan district. The tabulation was limited to metropolitan districts with over a quarter of a million population.

A total of 1019 newspapers were found with 749 in metropolitan districts of over a million population.

Papers printed for the population residing within the legal limits of the central city area are less in number than those printed for populations in suburban areas, although in terms of total circulation there is reason to believe that a closer balance between city and suburb is present.[13] If the mean circulation for Chicago community papers is projected to all metropolitan districts of over one million, a total circulation of about 10 million copies weekly is estimated.

Variation in the development of the community press has led to the belief that certain metropolitan areas constitute community newspaper centers and they are recognized as such in the lore of the industry. Chicago and Los Angeles are most frequently mentioned as ideal cities for community newspapers. The scope of community newspapers in Los Angeles can be seen in the ill-fated efforts of James Parton, associate of Henry Luce, to consolidate community newspaper publishing in that area. He purchased the *Down Town Shopping News* for half a million dollars, raised its circulation to 600,-000, changed its name to the *Los Angeles Independent*, hired 50 news men and 150 advertising salesmen, organized 15 sub-editions and went out of business in less than a year because of the strong competition of the existing community newspapers.

Examination of the distribution of the community press seems to indicate that with some exceptions the number of community newspapers correlates roughly with the total population of the metropolitan district. The major exception is

13. The distinction between city and suburban papers is not significant for delimiting types of local community newspapers in most metropolitan districts; the distinction involving types of payment for circulation is more crucial. (See page 41.)

New York City. "New York City is another kind of a world," in the language of the community press trade. Manhattan Island has a unique ecology; namely, a tremendous daytime population concentration, a transportation system which deemphasizes satellite business districts, and shifts in land utilization which alter local residential communities with great rapidity. The result seems to be that only in a few areas can community newspapers survive. Among those better known are *The East Side News*, a prosperous and politically influential weekly on the lower East Side; and *The Villager*, which circulates in Greenwich Village, an area where artists once lived, which has now become a fashionable residential district. At the same time, ethnic ghettoes still persist and new ones have been created by recent immigration with the result that the foreign language press in New York City still persists with some community overtones.

Off Manhattan Island, in some of the boroughs where satellite business districts flourish, the prevailing patterns of community newspapers are present. In Brooklyn alone, 20 community papers have been reported.

A tabulation of weekly metropolitan papers for metropolitan districts of over one million population based on Ayer's, is presented in Table No. 3 (II). The extent of under-enumeration is extreme in the case of Los Angeles where Ayer's lists only 108 while one recent survey covered over 230. From this table it can be inferred generally that the number of papers roughly parallels population concentration. Proportionately the small metropolitan districts seem to have a lower concentration of papers than the largest ones. This leads to the impression that the community press has had its greatest development in the largest metropolitan communities, with the exception of New York.

TABLE NO. 3 (II)—*Distribution of Community Press in Metropolitan Districts of Over One Million Population**

Metropolitan District	City Limits	NUMBER OF PAPERS Suburban Areas	Total
New York	25	70	95
Chicago	82	99	181
Los Angeles	57	51	108
Philadelphia	48	59	107
Boston	22	75	97
Detroit	22	29	51
Pittsburgh	10	43	53
San Francisco †	4	28	32
Cleveland	11	6	17
Baltimore	5	3	8
	286	463	749

* According to 1940 Bureau of the Census definition and data.
† Ayer's does not list one of the major chains in San Francisco.

Economic Organization and Operation

The development of a satellite shopping center and the competitive position it occupies within the larger metropolitan economy not only delineates the economic base for community newspapers but conditions a wide range of practices and attitudes which are common among community newspaper publishers. These, of course, fashion indirectly the contents of the paper and ultimately determine readership response.

The small merchant's desire for a greater slice of the consumer's dollar may be regarded as a constant. The local shopping area's struggle against intense competition with the giant department store of the central business district is a powerful incentive to overcome a completely individualistic approach to the problem. Most goods and services available in the downtown shopping area are also available in the local shopping area. But just as transportation and ecological factors limit movement to and from the Loop, these factors to a greater extent delimit the universe of shoppers on which the local center can draw.

The 1920's, the period of the greatest growth of community newspapers, also constituted a period of expansion of neighborhood businessmen's associations. These associations basically were formed to promote local business. They attempted all sorts of promotional devices from handbills to banners strung across the shopping center's main thoroughfare. But it soon became evident that the community newspaper was the one vehicle that guaranteed a regular, continuing and economical medium for presenting commercial messages. The prospective community newspaper publisher had an advantage over the daily newspaper because he could tailor his circulation area to the limits of the shopping area.

A neighborhood businessman's association or local chamber of commerce seldom had the time, outlook, or energy to create a community newspaper. Only one case was found in which a local association actually established a community newspaper. The pattern was to "invite" or "sponsor" the founding of a local newspaper. It is abundantly clear that such an invitation or sponsorship usually involved a great deal of promotion by prospective publishers. Since little investment was needed to establish a community newspaper, many were willing to venture the risk. Although the local businessmen were anxious to compete with those in the central business district, great persuasion was required to sell the idea to reluctant and conservative members of the local businessmen's fraternity. Thus even in their very inception many of the community newspapers had a promotional flavor.

Even the minority of community newspapers of older origin—those which had developed out of village newspapers —had to alter their operations along the lines of the newer papers. As the city expanded and as these villages became secondary shopping districts, these older papers were forced to undergo changes in outlook and to become instruments of the local merchants and their associations. Thus today as an outgrowth of its origin and because of its main sources of revenue, the community newspaper's interest and the interests of the secondary shopping center are usually identical. A sample of publishers and editors was intensively interviewed as part of the effort to study the community press as an over-all communication system. Of the 42 publishers and editor-publishers interviewed in the Chicago metropolitan area, only four do not belong to any local businessmen's association, while more than half belong to two or more such organizations. Membership in these organizations is far from nominal. Holding office is more typical than exceptional and publishers have been presidents of such groups. Almost 40 percent of the sample of community newspaper executives rated a businessmen's association as the group in which they were most active.

A few publishers spoke of meeting regularly with local businessmen's associations; others reported intermittent contacts when special campaigns were being arranged. However, throughout the entire study no evidence was found in which even partial financial interest in a community newspaper was held by a businessmen's association.

To make the community newspaper viable and to overcome the resistance to innovation, the community newspaper executive had to exercise effective entrepreneurship. Promotional skill was not enough; the industry had to devise operating procedures for the special problems of community journalism. Since the community newspaper industry was looked upon as a marginal enterprise at best, large amounts of capital were not forthcoming. In fact, the opposite was true. The possibility of lucrative profits with low capital investment made it attractive to the adventuresome. (It appeared so attractive that in Chicago a few doubtful promoters started newspapers and were for a number of years disturbing factors to the legitimate enterprises.) Low capital investments were required because the basic factors of production could be contracted for, rather than purchased or established. Thus many more were attracted than could succeed, and those who actually built a community newspaper developed a strong sense of pride in their business success.

The very location and physical appearance of the community newspaper reflects its economic position in the satellite business district and represents a compromise between two competing requirements. On the one hand, the publisher would like to be located as close as possible to the main intersection of the satellite business center in order to increase his accessibility to local merchants and residents who produce the advertising revenue of display and want ads. On the other hand, his financial position leads him to want to select a low-cost location. The result is an almost uniform location of community newspaper offices on street level store front premises "just around the corner" from the main thoroughfare of the satellite business district. Where community newspapers are operated in chains, publishers seek to decentralize their editorial, or if not their editorial, at least their business offices, so that the organization is represented in each of the communities they serve. As one chain publisher said, "We are merchants of decentralization, therefore we ourselves must practice decentralization. I have thirteen separate offices where my staff can meet the public, and I want more. The smart-alec management experts recommend that I centralize. They would put me out of business."

The economics and technical efficiency of the large rotary press was an important factor in enabling the community newspaper publisher to develop his enterprise. The large rotary press requires a heavy capital investment but makes possible cheap and high speed production required for a weekly publication. The urban community press would hardly have taken root had each publisher been required to own and operate such expensive equipment. However, the presence of even a limited amount of such equipment in commercial plants in a large metropolitan center created an economic situation which was favorable to the publisher with limited investment capital. Commercial printers who own such presses are constantly seeking to keep their presses running and in the past have bid competitively for the press work of community publishers. Over 80 percent of the community newspaper enterprises in the city of Chicago engage in this practice of subcontracting their press work. For many enterprises the practice of subcontracting press work fits in economically with typesetting and composition in the paper's offices, a series of technical processes which can be spread throughout the week.

Thus, in the more densely populated areas of the metropolitan area which grew up around new shopping districts the publisher-entrepreneur had to organize and contract for the various factors involved in periodical publication. Depending on his capital as well as on his temperament, the community newspaper entrepreneur could either establish or contract for the various factors of production he required. He could even contract for a circulation department by hiring a commercial circular distributing agency. With the exception of presswork, the tendency has naturally been in the opposite direction; as the publisher becomes more and more stable he seeks to organize his own factors of production and distribution rather than contract for them.

Whether the factors of production are subcontracted or purchased an important source of economic hardship for community newspapers are the ever increasing operating costs. Labor and material costs in the printing industry have increased steadily since the 1930's and appear to have remained relatively unaffected by the downturns in the business cycle.[14] The publisher typically looks forward to even higher operating costs since in all aspects of his operations he is presented with a variety of relatively uncontrollable fixed costs. His major problem continues to be labor costs as well as the supply and cost of paper, problems over which he has no control. Even the decision to raise advertising rates is a derivative one and not a step in which he holds the initiative. The publisher thereby develops a preoccupation with the "human" relations involved in his enterprise. He seeks to maneuver these factors so as to insure a continued and ever higher level of cooperation and coordination. One city chain publisher expressed the whole matter in a succinct fashion.

"We've got to work all the time to increase the dollar volume up and make the volume fit the rapidly increasing costs. Costs over which we have no control. . . . And we can't raise our rates to match it at all. We can't get the advertisers to appreciate these problems. That's why I'm constantly trying to control efficiency. That's the only thing I can do something about."

---

14. Kinter, C. V., *The Effect of the Business Cycle on the Newspaper Publishing Industry*, Chicago, 1945, p. 53.

The number of people required to produce a community newspaper varies from the extreme of the one- or two-man outfit to the largest establishments employing between 50 and 100 personnel exclusive of those engaged in the mechanical and production aspects. Both extremes are in the minority and are more likely to be found within densely populated city limits. In general the "typically small" organization employs some 4 to 8 persons. In the larger establishments, on the average, about 25 to 30 persons are employed. (All of these estimates exclude type-setting and the mechanical department personnel.) Depending upon the circulation, the number of editorial persons involved in a community newspaper tends to be equal regardless of the location of the newspaper. However, the city paper has a larger number of advertising personnel than have the suburban community papers. In part this reflects the greater competitiveness involved in producing advertising revenue, and in part the larger gross volume—though not necessarily profitability—of city community papers.

The varying size of the community newspaper can be measured by the annual volume of gross business. While the largest chains—those located in the more densely populated portions of the city—have an annual gross income approaching a million dollars, it is more likely that the gross volume of a moderate chain of newspapers will range from $100,000 to $500,000. Chains in the periphery of the metropolitan district may gross as low as $15,000–$25,000 annually. The independent city paper is likely to gross somewhere between $50,000 and $100,000 while the suburban independent may range as low as $5,000 to $15,000, although most frequently their annual gross income is in the neighborhood of $15,000 to $25,000.

Circulation Technique

Typically, the community newspaper is distributed on Wednesday or Thursday in order to give maximum support to the local business enterprises, since Friday and Saturday are the main shopping days in the satellite shopping district. As in other aspects of community newspaper business, publishers and circulation managers had to adopt traditional methods and promote new devices in order to circulate their papers. As a result, the industry is characterized by a wide variety of circulation techniques. Papers are circulated by carrier boy, commercial distributing agencies, or through the mails. Circulation ranges from fully paid to fully free.

But the community newspaper, especially in densely populated areas of the city, has come to be characterized by what is called "optional pay" circulation; this is sometimes referred to as "controlled circulation." The paper is delivered and the reader exercises the option of payment to the carrier boy. Delivery is made regardless of payment although periodic drives are undertaken to increase the percentage of paying readers.[15] This method of optional payment appears to be most effective and widespread in densely populated areas. In some few cases community newspapers employ commercial distributing agencies to circulate their editions. This results in a completely free distribution as far as the reader is concerned.

---

15. One device used to increase payment is to stop the distribution of the paper to nonpaying readers in a small sector of the circulation area for a period of two to three weeks. Resumed circulation usually results in a higher proportion of optional payment.

By contrast, in the suburban area, 90 percent of the papers are fully paid. This high proportion of paid circulation differentiates city from suburban community papers. The suburban papers rely largely on mail distribution and to a lesser extent on boy carriers since sparser settlement of residents makes the mails more economical.

In the years between 1910 and 1950, circulation method has undergone a marked change. A weekly paid circulation of 101,000 in 1910 comprised 89 percent of the city's total circulation. In 1950, however, 278,000 paid copies make up approximately one-third of the city's total circulation. Some of the free circulation arose in the Depression when competitive conditions and the demands of advertisers were for "100% coverage." Many community newspapers could do little but meet this demand if they were to remain in business.[16] However, the free circulation system and the optional payment system were devised earlier. These promotional devices were required to get a newspaper started in areas where both reader and advertiser had to be convinced. Today papers with paid circulation use these systems when new areas are opened up.

Since the Depression the community newspapers have shifted, albeit slowly, from free circulation to optional payment wherever possible. When this research was in process, a number of publishers were experimenting with total mail distribution which requires fully paid circulation; and there seems to be a trend in this direction. Increasing costs of production are forcing this change as a means of making the reader pay a higher proportion of the cost of production and distribution.

The carrier boy is a strange device. A well-organized, loyal

---

16. Allen, Charles L., *Free Circulation* (University, Louisiana: Louisiana State University Press, 1950), p. 24.

and effective cadre of carrier boys can enhance the success of the local community newspaper. However, developing a cadre of carrier boys does not simply involve financial investment; it also requires patience and promotion. Although the basic reward is a percentage of the collection, the boys are also motivated by non-financial and group rewards. The carrier boys are organized into teams and part of their payment is in coupons redeemable for sporting equipment, for goods has a higher value than money. The role of the carrier must be made to carry a certain amount of status. The carrier boy is generally recruited from the immediate area in which he will distribute papers. Frequently, the job is passed down from brother to brother in a family. The tradition of being a carrier boy is enhanced by the news columns of the community papers which from time to time report on the success of former local carrier boys in the business and professional world.

When the optional payment system is used, the publisher has another immediate and concrete indicator of the success of his paper. Variations in collections range from 30 to 60 percent of a typical route which may comprise from two to three blocks depending upon population density. In certain areas consistent payment as high as 80 percent has been recorded. Publishers are aware of the fact that the diligence of the carrier boy is an important factor in determining the amount of revenue to be produced from a given route. The records attest to the fact that variations in collection take place depending on how strongly the carrier is motivated to make collections beyond his guaranteed minimum salary. Variations in percentage of collections also take place between boys working the same route.

When evidence on collections is used to support readership claims, representatives of advertising agencies allege that the payment is made not for the paper but as a gift or favor to the carrier boy. Such claims are not supported by the findings of the readership aspects of this study. Interview data with three samples of community newspaper readers indicate quite conclusively that such motivation is generally absent and where it is present, persists for a few weeks at most.

Sources of Advertising Revenue

In the United States, all printed periodical media contain a high proportion of advertising to editorial content. The financial success of a daily or a weekly newspaper is dependent upon peculiar economic arrangements which are required to give the reader an exaggeratedly below-cost price for his single copy or his subscription. Neither the daily paper nor the community paper which sells its issues, makes any effort to bring subscription prices above the point of covering the white newsprint and the delivery costs. In fact, in 1950, the imbalance between these costs and the price of the printed media was in favor of the public buyers. Thus, almost 85 percent of the daily newspaper's gross revenue must come from advertising. For that portion of the community press which has a partly paid circulation, the percentage from advertising may be higher, but not markedly so.[17]

---

17. It is interesting to speculate as to why the sale of a newspaper at a price so far below the actual cost of production has come to be accepted as a standard. Practically every effort to modify these economic arrangements has failed. The attitude is present among the readership that they should not have to pay a high price for a publication which carries so much advertising. But this can hardly constitute an adequate explanation. Perhaps in a democracy, the social and political requirements for standardized behavior carry over into business which presses for as wide a circulation as possible regardless of the economic consequences. However, market explanations appear to be of crucial

The image of the community newspaper as a medium consisting completely or almost completely of advertisements is not correct. When the percentage of advertising of all types in the community newspaper is compared with the daily newspaper, the difference is slight. A content analysis of a representative sample of the community newspapers of the city of Chicago in 1949 revealed that 74 percent of the entire contents was devoted to advertising producing revenue. (See Table I (III)). A comparable sample of daily newspapers in Chicago contained 72.6 percent advertisements. Certain issues of daily newspapers issues exceeded the average for community newspapers. (The details of the content analysis are presented in Chapter III).

Nevertheless, the community newspaper's economic problems center around the inability of certain sectors of the local shopping center to provide a steady and sufficiently remunerative source of advertising revenue. Apart from the heavy fluctuations in numbers and wealth of retail establishments wrought by the business cycle, the reluctance and ambivalence many local merchants display towards advertising constitutes a perpetual source of insecurity for the community press. Getting display advertisements means a continual concentration on direct, face-to-face solicitation.

As a rule, most of the small local merchants have no con-

---

importance. The advertiser is desirous of offsetting the ever decreasing effects of advertising. Thus to maximize effectiveness, he seeks not only to extend circulation over crowded communities but to increase the actual amount of advertising. Technical considerations of production and distribution—rather than the social-psychological receptivity of the reader—are taken as limiting factors. The publisher, on the other hand, operates with a decreasing cost curve which places a premium on as large a circulation as possible. The most expedient way to maximize profit, therefore, is to cut subscription and single issue costs in order to increase circulation. This in turn creates pressure towards further and further dilution of the news columns with revenue producing advertisements—advertisements for which rates increase as circulation increases.

cept of a monthly, much less an annual, advertising budget; no set sum is specifically set aside for advertising purposes as is the case with most large-scale enterprises in America. Even in urban areas, the merchant's relationship with his customers is still to a large extent personalistic and this mitigates against the development of an all out "advertising consciousness." Continual solicitation, week by week, is required and frequently involves the chief salesmen or the publisher when large accounts are at stake.

As a result, community newspaper publishers complain endlessly about the difficulties they encounter in convincing the merchant that advertising pays. The advertising salesman has to seek to develop an understanding on the part of the merchant that advertising has to be related to merchandising and that long-term campaigns are required. A large city publisher who maintains that such attitudes are slowly being developed through the efforts of the community newspapers, spoke of difficulties that were encountered in the past:

"We used to run into this kind of attitude. Somebody would advertise an item for 16¢ and then stick it under the counter and wait to see how many people would come into the store and ask specifically for the product which they couldn't see. Then when it came to paying the bill—if they paid it—they would say, 'It was worth fifty dollars to convince myself that your advertisement ain't worth a good God damn'."

According to an estimate of this same publisher, as much as half of his advertising revenue comes from what he terms "prosperity advertising" in distinction to advertising which comes in routinely, "good times or bad times."

The branch location of the downtown department stores as well as chain outlets of national establishments operate on a more stable basis, and advertising space sold to the branch department stores represents a regular and lucrative source of revenue which helps the community newspaper to weather instabilities. Metropolitan advertising, principally from public utilities, is received in limited quantity by community newspapers from local and regional advertising agencies without direct solicitation.

National advertising is viewed as a still to be conquered frontier. The failure to receive what is considered a "fair" share of national advertising budgets is one of the main obsessions of the publishers of community newspapers. Some national advertising is obtained through tie-ins with local merchants who are given advertising budgets or allowances by national product organizations. Automobiles, radio equipment and home appliances are some of the national products advertised in this manner. National advertising when it is obtained direct from a national advertising agency, is usually the result of some particular local condition or personal connection for it is generally the policy of national advertising agencies, by and large, to avoid advertising in the community press.

Community newspaper publishers are constantly seeking to get more national advertisements. In many cities, including Chicago, selected community newspaper publishers have joined together to present a unified outlet to national advertisers. The goal of such arrangements is to be able to offer the advertiser city-wide or metropolitan area coverage. Two such organizations exist in Chicago: the Accredited Community Newspapers which includes four or five of the largest community newspaper organizations in the city, and The Chicago Suburban Quality Group which consists of fifteen wealthy suburban newspapers. Such arrangements are designed to simplify solicitation problems for it is well known that large advertising agencies prefer to deal with as few separate accounts as possible. A national organization, less than a decade old, known as Controlled Circulation Newspapers of America was founded as a trade association for all types of community newspapers and represents many of the larger publishers. The association views the national advertising problem as one of its main reasons for existence.

The failure of national advertising agencies to appropriate budgets to community newspaper media involves a complex of business procedures and attitudes. In the past, community newspaper publishers were not preoccupied with getting national advertising. They saw their economic frontiers right in the local community. In fact, they were subject to many pressures in the opposite direction since local advertisers frequently viewed national advertising as competing with their display space. The linking of national advertising to local retail outlets has helped to undercut such an attitude. Moreover, the stronger position of certain community newspapers no longer requires the publisher to be so sensitive to local merchant opposition to national advertising. Instead, the publisher is now able to take the offensive and point out to the local advertiser that national advertising is likely to cut down his lineage costs.

National advertisers fail to advertise in community newspapers because they are of the opinion that the community newspaper publishers cannot answer the crucial canons of advertising: "How many people get the paper?" and "How many read it?" In the past there have been enough marginal community newspaper "dogs," as they are known in the industry, to raise doubts about circulation figures. The refusal of the Audit Bureau of Circulation to audit community newspapers with any free circulation has not aided the position of the community newspaper publishers. (The A.B.C. methods which use press runs and cash receipts are ill adapted to the community press.) In the absence of extensive market research the national advertising world has looked askance at the question of readership, for it is assumed that those copies which are distributed free are not likely to be read. Moreover, actual decisions on allocating advertising budgets are based on the "milline rate," a mechanical cost formula indicating the charge of a line of advertising per thousand readers. It does not involve the appropriateness of the audience being reached from the point of view of the advertiser nor the probable impact or effectiveness of the advertisement.

Twenty leading media directors and space buyers in the Chicago area supply revealing attitudes on this subject. Their attitudes towards community newspapers were canvassed by a cooperative media director in a completely informal fashion because any sort of formal interview would not be likely to produce more than stereotyped responses. The responses gathered were tabulated both as to most frequent attitudes as well as which reasons were given first and thereby could be viewed as most important in their thinking. All twenty gave the unreliability of the circulation figures as the main reason for their low regard of the community newspapers. Nineteen gave this reason first. This response was almost automatic. They also expressed great skepticism about the character of the distributing facilities. One executive mentioned the army manual of organization which required 3 commissioned officers and 30 non-commissioned officers to supervise an infantry company of 300 men. Therefore he concluded that a specific community newspaper which employs 7 supervisors for 600 carriers was a defective organization. (He failed to elaborate on how distributing newspapers resembled warfare.)

The second most frequent reason for negative attitudes toward the community newspaper was the high cost (15). Duplication of existing media was cited by half of the group.

Thus, the three most frequently and readily given responses did not mention effectiveness or impact.

Although the data were gathered by a member of the advertising fraternity operating casually, only after these traditional canons had been acknowledged did a majority of the executives acknowledge their real feelings about community newspapers—feelings which are well known to the publisher of community newspapers. The majority of the advertising executives alleged that it did not enhance the prestige of the product to engage in community newspaper advertising. "An advertiser using a community newspaper to spread his message can expect the same consideration for his product that will be given to a classified ad in the same publication offering a baby's playpen for sale." To link a nationally advertised product with a baby's playpen appears to be injurious to the national product. By implication the executives also seemed to believe that community newspaper advertising would lower the prestige of their agencies.

The realization of this attitude by the community newspaper executives is neatly exemplified by a remark made by one as he addressed his fellow publishers in a recent convention:

"Because we don't drink and country club with that New York advertising bunch they think we're nobodies."

On another occasion, one publisher while discussing advertising with the author, blurted out:

"You're a college professor. You ought to know about these things. It's strictly a matter of social discrimination."

The data on community press readership collected in this study may perhaps be relevant for advertising agencies by indicating the types of information by which more rational decisions could made.

"Aggressive" salesmanship carries over into the classified advertising columns. More than half of the city enterprises report that a major proportion of their classified advertising lineage is solicited by telephone. About 25 percent of the city community newspapers practice telephone solicitation but are not dependent upon this form of salesmanship for the bulk of their classified ads. Another 20 percent do not engage in direct solicitation. Community newspapers in suburban areas rely much more heavily, if not almost exclusively, on voluntary classified advertisements.

A staff of young women who are located in the home office of the paper ingeniously track down all sorts of leads. One standard practice is to phone community residents who have placed classified advertisements in the daily newspapers a few days after the advertisement has appeared. If the transaction for which the advertisement was placed has not yet occurred, the telephone solicitor seeks to sell space in the local community newspaper. Since the classified ad solicitor is selling a more restricted "advertising area," the rate is likely to be cheaper; and for certain types of merchandise and transactions the closer accessibility of advertiser to potential purchaser makes the community newspaper a more effective medium than the daily newspaper. In addition to real estate, automobiles and employment notices, advertised items include household goods or items associated with the life cycle of the family. They are objects that might be handed down or bartered if personal contact permitted: baby carriages, bicycles, refrigerators, etc.

Solicitation techniques are financially profitable to the community newspaper but only in part explain the continued growth of classified advertisements over the last three decades. The sample of community newspapers studied indicates that the percentage of classified advertisements to all advertise-

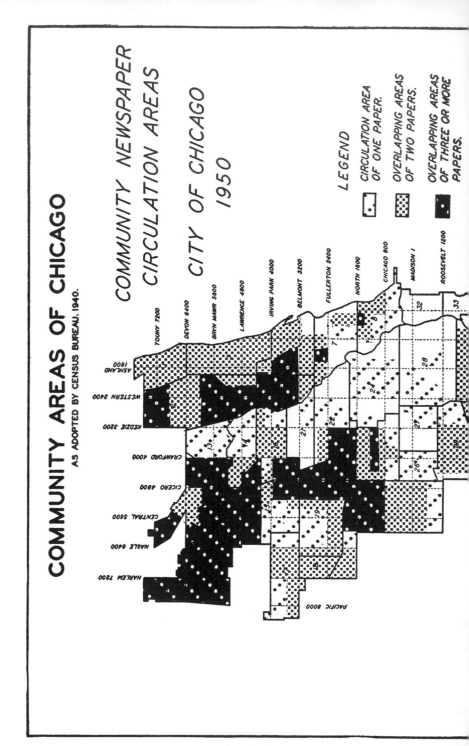

COMMUNITY AREAS OF CHICAGO

AS ADOPTED BY CENSUS BUREAU, 1940.

COMMUNITY NEWSPAPER CIRCULATION AREAS

CITY OF CHICAGO
1950

LEGEND

CIRCULATION AREA OF ONE PAPER.

OVERLAPPING AREAS OF TWO PAPERS.

OVERLAPPING AREAS OF THREE OR MORE PAPERS.

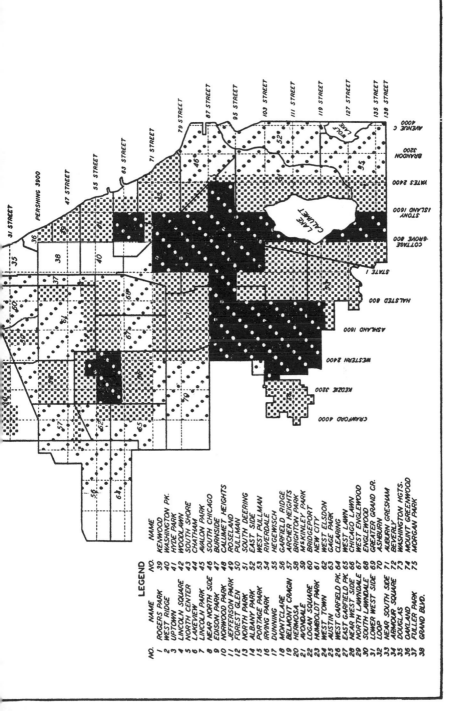

LEGEND

NO.	NAME	NO.	NAME
1	ROGERS PARK	39	KENWOOD
2	WEST RIDGE	40	WASHINGTON PK.
3	UPTOWN	41	HYDE PARK
4	LINCOLN SQUARE	42	WOODLAWN
5	NORTH CENTER	43	SOUTH SHORE
6	LAKEVIEW	44	CHATHAM
7	LINCOLN PARK	45	AVALON PARK
8	NEAR NORTH SIDE	46	SOUTH CHICAGO
9	EDISON PARK	47	BURNSIDE
10	NORWOOD PARK	48	CALUMET HEIGHTS
11	JEFFERSON PARK	49	ROSELAND
12	FOREST GLEN	50	PULLMAN
13	NORTH PARK	51	SOUTH DEERING
14	ALBANY PARK	52	EAST SIDE
15	PORTAGE PARK	53	WEST PULLMAN
16	IRVING PARK	54	RIVERDALE
17	DUNNING	55	HEGEWISCH
18	MONTCLARE	56	GARFIELD RIDGE
19	BELMONT CRAGIN	57	ARCHER HEIGHTS
20	HERMOSA	58	BRIGHTON PARK
21	AVONDALE	59	McKINLEY PARK
22	LOGAN SQUARE	60	BRIDGEPORT
23	HUMBOLDT PARK	61	NEW CITY
24	WEST TOWN	62	WEST ELSDON
25	AUSTIN	63	GAGE PARK
26	WEST GARFIELD PK.	64	CLEARING
27	EAST GARFIELD PK.	65	WEST LAWN
28	NEAR WEST SIDE	66	CHICAGO LAWN
29	NORTH LAWNDALE	67	WEST ENGLEWOOD
30	SOUTH LAWNDALE	68	ENGLEWOOD
31	LOWER WEST SIDE	69	GREATER GRAND CR.
32	LOOP	70	ASHBURN
33	NEAR SOUTH SIDE	71	AUBURN GRESHAM
34	ARMOUR SQUARE	72	BEVERLY
35	DOUGLAS	73	WASHINGTON HGTS.
36	OAKLAND	74	MOUNT GREENWOOD
37	FULLER PARK	75	MORGAN PARK
38	GRAND BLVD.		

ments rose from 8 percent in 1920 to 18.6 percent in 1949. Actual success of advertisements was influential as well as changed attitudes toward secondhand goods after the Great Depression.

Community newspaper publishers frequently point to their classified advertisements as one kind of direct proof of the impact of their papers. To them, response to classified advertisements is an immediate and demonstrable reaction in which none of the intangibles of "market research" claims of good will and long term confidence are involved. In fact, community newspapers have a larger proportion of their advertising space devoted to classified ads than does the daily press. Samplings of the community press indicate that about 18 percent of advertisement material is classified, while the daily newspaper average is closer to 10 percent. To men who are preoccupied with the concrete merchandising implications of their publication, this is taken as evidence of the "drawing power" of the community newspaper.

In selling advertising space the community newspaper is subject to strong specific competition. Competition comes from overlapping and competing community newspapers and the daily newspaper. Fully 20 percent of the area of the city is covered by more than one community newspaper. (See map, pp. 64-65.) In a few areas as many as three papers compete. Competition takes the form of sub rosa rate cutting, rebates and even contracts prohibiting advertising in competing papers. In the past, it has occurred that one community paper would steal another paper's advertising personnel who had a personal following or that advertising personnel would leave a newspaper and attempt to set up their own competing medium.

In Chicago, the community newspaper must also compete with the Metropolitan Section of The Chicago Tribune. The

Metropolitan Section is a special supplement published on Thursday and Sunday in five editions directed toward specific sectors of the metropolitan area. The advertising is geared to provide a specialized medium for the large stores in the various satellite shopping centers. The news content of each edition is a limited effort to duplicate community newspaper content in these areas. Nevertheless the Sunday edition (instituted in 1927) and the Thursday edition (1949) do not seem to have seriously hindered the growth of community newspapers.

The very smallest papers appear to be completely unaffected. "There's never an ad from these fellows around here in *The Tribune*," one publisher reported. "They're too small. It's not competition in any way, shape, size, or form." The main reason for the lack of success among more prosperous business outlets appears to be that the sectors covered by the various sections of the Metropolitan issue are geographically so broad that local merchants are forced to pay for the distribution of their advertising message to residents well beyond their shopping district. The apparently cheaper lineage per thousand circulation becomes meaningless when a larger circulation has to be bought than is required or worthwhile.

The prevailing public attitude of the local publisher towards such experiments is summed up by the following comment.

"Have you heard about Henry Luce's flop in Los Angeles? . . . He thought he could go around and buy up all the community newspapers out there and make one big shopper out of it. Well, when he did that the paper ceased being a community newspaper and he soon had to call it quits. It's the same thing with the Metropolitan Section of *The Tribune*. It's not very successful because they can't possibly cover the local community the way a small newspaper can. It's a pretty fictitious job in my opinion."

Economic Instability and the Consolidation Movement

All of the economic instabilities—the intense competition, the uncertainty of advertising revenue from local merchants, the ever-increasing operating costs—are reflected in the relatively short longevity of a great many community newspapers. Beginning with *Ayer's* listing for the year 1910 and taking only the listings for each succeeding fifth year up to 1950, we find that some 395 community newspapers were established in the Chicago metropolitan area during this period. Comparing this figure with the 181 metropolitan area community papers in existence in 1950 some idea of turnover can be gained. (Had an annual count been made for this same period and were it possible to include many community newspapers never listed in *Ayer's* directory, it is likely the figure would have been closer to 500). When this turnover is compared with that of other types of commercial enterprises in the United States the rate does not appear excessively high. Naturally a large proportion of defunct newspapers saw their demise during the 1930–35 depression years. However, even among papers begun after 1935 there seems to have been a noticeable death rate. Of 49 papers definitely known to have been started between the years 1935–40 in the metropolitan area some 19 (40%) were no longer in existence by 1950.

By contrast, many have enjoyed long and fairly prosperous existence. For example, of the 63 papers covered in our sample, 49 (almost 78%) have been in existence for 11 years or more. Twenty-one papers (33%) were in existence from 20 to 30 years, while 15 papers (almost 24%) had been in existence for more than 30 years. Thus, it seems that community newspapers which have succeeded in weathering a five to ten-year trial period are reasonably assured of continuing for many years to come, barring of course, economic catastrophes or radical alterations in the ecological structure of the metropolitan area.

Economic instability has led the owners of community newspapers to explore ways of lessening business risks. One response has been the rapid development of community newspaper chains since the mid 1920's. This development in the community press closely parallels that which has taken place in the daily press. The economic factors are roughly the same. The community newspaper chain is much less affected by fluctuations in advertising revenue of any single shopping center. By buying up competitors the chain is able to stabilize further its revenue. Finally, real economy results from centralized printing, editorial staffing, and management.

Some idea of the extent of chain growth in the community newspaper field can be gathered from the fact that, whereas in 1910, but 25 (30%) of the 82 metropolitan area community papers were owned by chain organizations, in 1930, 85 (51%) of 168 papers were so controlled. By 1950, although the number of community newspapers had increased to 181, 121 (87%) were under the control of chain organizations. The movement from predominantly independent to predominantly chain control applies equally to city and suburbs.[18]

18. So as to avoid attaching undue significance to these statistics, it must be pointed out that chain vs. independent status in itself does not necessarily constitute an accurate index of the economic power and wealth of the respective community newspaper organizations. Two paper chains were encountered which grossed considerably less than a well-situated independent. On the other hand, one two-paper chain circulating in Chicago is generally considered among the wealthiest community newspaper organizations in the metropolitan area. In estimating the wealth and power of the community newspaper, the extent

Publishers, when they expressed themselves on the subject, were in agreement that the trend towards consolidation and chain ownership would in all likelihood continue into the future. Chain publishers view the development as a necessary and rational means of combatting the chronically insecure economic position of certain community newspapers. Small publishers apprehensively witnessing the trend live in the hope that continued prosperity, good management, and the performance of services valued by the community will save them from being swallowed up or squeezed out by the large chain organizations.

Predictions are hazardous to make. Although the trends underlying consolidation are likely to continue, there is good reason to believe that the consolidation movement will continue at a rate less than that encountered in earlier periods. This is due to the success the movement has already had in the past and to the lessening benefits that can be derived from more consolidation. In any case, the technology of the community press makes for rather easy entrance into the field. Thereby, the present level of decentralization of the community press is likely to be maintained and to enhance the relevance of the medium at the local community level.

---

and wealth of the market area it covers and the density of its circulation within the area are important. While these factors do not correlate precisely with the number of papers a particular organization publishes, as a general rule a three-paper chain, for instance, does on the *average* represent a greater concentration of wealth and power than a two-paper chain, etc. Thus it is interesting to note that of the 181 community newspapers published in the metropolitan area in 1949, 60 papers (33%) were independently controlled, 25 papers (19%) were controlled by two- and three-paper chains, and 86 (48%) were controlled by chain organizations of four or more papers.

III

The Image
of the Community:
Content
for Consensus

On May 17, 1950 the *Bethel Park Bulletin* carried a headline
"Protest Chicago Transit Authority Treatment of Students."
For over a year the Chicago Transit System, operating under
new municipal ownership, had instituted a vast program of
modernization designed to increase the efficiency and solvency
of Chicago's public transportation. All these changes left the
West Bethel Park Parent-Teachers' Association unimpressed;
except that for them public ownership meant that they had a
greater right to protest. As a result of numerous protests, the
local alderman had been persuaded to convene a special meeting with transit authorities to hear the mothers' grievances.
The *Bethel Park Bulletin* printed in detail their bill of par-
ticulars—a revealing and candid testament of the local community view of the "real issues" of human relations involved
in operating the Chicago Transit Authority.

The mothers complained that "transit employees were coarse and unsympathetic in their treatment of students holding half-fare cards, frequently employing profane and obscene language in addressing them." The bus drivers "show no consideration for the safety of the children," frequently pulling away as students are running to catch them, or, while they are loading, leaving children hanging out of the doors. Moreover, there were long delays in issuing student tickets at the beginning of each semester and it was impossible to replace a lost or damaged half-fare card in a reasonable length of time.

This news story, which carries a concern for the details of daily existence reminiscent of "small-town journalism" is typical of those community newspaper items which have given credence to the contention that the community newspaper represents a survival of small town values. Community newspaper content involving the struggle against the individuating tendencies and impersonality of urban existence need not be viewed as a mere survival but rather as a continuing process of response to achieve human values the worth of which is not dependent on historical analogies. The item is typical of a central and underlying concern of community journalism, namely, the rights and privileges of the local community with respect to the larger metropolis. It also represents one of the limits to which the community press will go in supporting controversy. As we shall see, the maintenance of community consensus by the community press is built on the emphasis of common values rather than on the solution of conflicting values. This is a controversy which involves no conflict within the community, for the local community is in agreement about the welfare of its students. It is a controversy between the local community and an outside organization, the public bureaucracy.

A systematic content analysis of the community press was

required to investigate this and other such observations. Such an analysis was carried out within the framework of the basic hypothesis that the community newspaper participates in the process of integrating the individual into the urban social structure by assisting in the complex balance between local and non-local activities and identifications.

Related to this hypothesis is one contending that the content of the community newspaper is representative of a wide range of activities, values and aspirations present in the community which are not given expression in the daily press. The details of the content analysis were particularly designed to assist in investigating the following sub-hypotheses:

Community newspaper content supplies a flow of specific news to assist adjustment to the institutions and facilities of urban life and to interpret relevant external events to the local community in a meaningful and affectual context.

Community newspaper content is designed to help the individual orient himself in time and space in the local community by building and maintaining local traditions and local identifications.

Community newspaper content fashions the individual's integration into the social structure to the degree that the contents are designed to democratize prestige. Democratization of prestige is particularly relevant for local community leaders.

Community newspaper content is designed to emphasize values and interests on which there is a high level of consensus in the community. (Therefore analysis of its impact involves investigating how consensus is maintained or developed by the emphasis on areas of agreement rather than on the resolution of conflict.)

Routinely, all these content characteristics determine the limits within which the community press can create an impact in opposition to the tendencies toward segmentalization and impersonality of human relations in the urban community.

Moreover, all these content characteristics enhance the ability of the community press to create a specific impact in particular controversies or social situations in which fundamental values are involved or threatened.

In order to draw a comprehensive picture of the contents of the community press, a representative sample of fifty percent of the newspapers was subjected to systematic analysis.[1] The content analysis sought to highlight the manner in which the community press presented controversy and change. Moreover, it was central to the content analysis to chart the identifications of individuals and organizations described by the paper as being responsible either for maintenance of orderly development or disruption of the community and its values.[2]

The time period selected could be called "typical" in the sense that no extraordinary news events or peculiar local community conflicts were present. Four issues of each newspaper were selected from alternate weeks during the period March 15 to May 15, 1949, with the result that the contents described do not include any major political election. Only the last phases of a controversy concerning a municipal anti-discrimination ordinance for public housing fell into the sample. This

---

1. In order to insure representativesness of this fifty percent sample, the papers were classified into chain versus independents; large versus small papers in terms of circulation; eight sectors of the city. Within these stratification criteria, papers were selected at random.

2. See Appendix I—Content Analysis, for the full analytic code as well as some of the key rules for the content analysis. The adequacy of the content analysis is demonstrated by the data on reliability involved in the application of the most abstract coding categories. The reliability test shows that over ninety percent agreement was achieved between two analysts on such categories.

material was representative in the sense that it reflected one phase in the ongoing conflict over ethnic homogeneity in residential areas threatened by invasion. The treatment of some of the other major controversies is augmented through a more detailed "case history" approach.

In order to place the contents of the community press in a historical perspective comparable to the analysis of the growth of the community newspaper, a small sample of community newspapers for the years of 1920 and 1935 were analyzed with the same categories. These dates were selected so as to give a time span commensurate with the period of the community press growth and at the same time to represent years which were not characterized by marked economic disequilibrium. Four issues of the three major daily Chicago newspapers for the same period as the contemporary community newspaper sample were also included for comparative purposes. Finally, for further comparative purposes, a weekly newspaper published in Digby, Nova Scotia and of roughly the same format as the typical Chicago community newspaper was subjected to a similar content analysis. (Digby is a small, relatively isolated maritime community undergoing a technological revolution in its basic fishing industry and is under long-term study by a group of sociologists and anthropologists under the direction of Dr. Alexander Leighton of Cornell University.) [3]

The quantitative content analysis involved categorizing each textual item [4] and advertisement in terms of space devoted to the item, thematic content, and prominence (that is, location

---

3. The comparative results of the Digby content analysis are represented in the appropriate tables, but for purposes of readability, interpretations have been included as footnotes.

4. Text was defined to include headline space and photographs so as to encompass the entire contents of the paper.

in the paper as between a conspicuous and a non-conspicuous position). It was designed to make possible not only an accurate description of content, but to investigate the relationship of content to such considerations as the ecology of the circulation area or the type of ownership of the newspaper.

Format: Duplicate Model of the Daily Press

Most community newspapers are printed in the full size of the daily newspaper; of our sample only 5 were tabloids. In number of pages, the typical community newspaper falls far short of the daily newspaper. The average number of pages is approximately sixteen with a range from four to forty-eight. However, *if the daily newspaper is conceived of as having a format involving an allocation of space between advertising, news-features, and editorial matter, the community newspaper broadly conforms to this format.* In fact, one community newspaper as compared with the next—regardless of size, circulation, or type of ownership—conforms to this general format. (Table No. 1 (III).) Within this format, the community newspapers differentiate themselves from daily newspapers and to a much lesser extent differentiate themselves one from another.

TABLE NO. 1 (III)—*Format of the Community Press*
Percentage of Advertising Matter to Textual Matter

YEAR		ADVERTISEMENTS PERCENT
1920	Community sample	79.0
1935	Community sample	71.3
1949	Community sample	74.0
1949	Daily sample	72.6
1949	Digby sample	60.7

Distribution of Textual Matter

Percentage of News-Features to Editorial Matter

YEAR		NEWS-FEATURES PERCENT	EDI-TORIAL PERCENT	OTHER PERCENT
1920	Community sample	91.2	5.3	3.5
1935	Community sample	94.8	4.2	1.0
1949	Community sample	94.4	3.5	2.1
1949	Daily sample	93.4	5.2	1.4
1949	Digby sample	92.5	4.4	3.1

"Rigid" adherence to this format is in part a function of technological, economic considerations and postal regulations covering advertising for newspapers mailed under special rates. In another sense, adherence to this formula reflects an attitude of "inferiority" often encountered among the personnel of the local community press, as a result of which they seek to legitimate themselves by following the formula laid down by the more prestigeful daily newspapers.[5]

The more detailed content analysis underlines this reluctance or timidity of the community newspaper to be itself and openly create forms appropriate for its function. This, of course, is not only the curse of the small publisher but a widespread self conception besetting local leaders who believe that their worthwhileness is more dependent on emulating the "big time" than on intrinsic merits and gratifications.

Adherence to a formula in statistical terms and through historical trends, underlines the observations of those who have sought to understand the contents of the press not in terms of unique events but in terms of cultural uniformities. It is another example of the cultural uniformities that our society

5. In Digby, The Courier's monopoly position, and presumably other economic factors, reduce slightly the concentration of advertising material required. Nevertheless, even The Courier does not deviate much from the format of newspapers more generally.

has created which allow the individual entrepreneur and technician only a minimum of self-expression and self-differentiation.[6]

The community newspaper is frequently considered by daily newspaper publishers, the heads of advertising agencies and sophisticated critics of contemporary culture to be "all advertisements." The conclusions of the content analysis indicate that this is a case of distorted perception. Percentage-wise, the difference between the amount of advertising in the daily and the community newspaper is trivial; in fact, specific issues of the daily press contain a higher proportion of advertising.[7] The present balance between advertising and textual content in the community press had already been established by 1920, and therefore, community newspaper critics cannot claim that the community newspaper has just recently "reformed."

In contrast to such an appraisal, is the "image" held by those who actually read the community press. In our readership study with six hundred households in the three communities studied intensively, less than ten percent of all respondents—readers and non-readers combined—claimed that there were too many advertisements in their local community newspapers. While most felt that the amount of advertisements was all right, there was a minority (6.5 percent) who claimed that the newspaper had too few ads. Among non-readers, reasons given for indifference or hostility to the community press seldom involved the amount of advertising.[8]

---

6. David Riesman refers to this phenomenon as "marginal differentiation," in *The Lonely Crowd* (New Haven: Yale University Press, 1950).

7. This "image" is colored by the confusion that exists between the community newspaper and the shopping newspaper or guide which may consist exclusively of advertisements. In Chicago, at least, the shopping newspaper or "shopper" is extinct.

8. The details of these findings on impact are reported in Chapter V. "The Impact of Readership: Interest, Penetration and Imagery."

Focus of Attention

While the proportion of advertising matter is roughly equal in the daily and the community press, the geographical scope encompassed in the textual items of the community press is markedly different in that it concentrates heavily on contents which are local in scope. (Table No. 2 (III).)[9] Moreover, despite the fact that the basic format of the community newspaper in terms of balance between advertisements, news-features and editorials, had already been established by 1920, an historical trend in geographical scope emerges, which reflects a broadening focus of attention.

The historical comparison reveals a decline in the percentage of local news with a corresponding increase in news dealing with sectors of the city and with the city as a whole.

TABLE NO. 2 (III)—*Trends in Focus of Attention of the Community Press,** 1920–1949*

	1949 PERCENT	1935 PERCENT	1920 PERCENT	DIGBY PERCENT
Local-Implicit	49.6	49.5	46.9	27.0
Local-Explicit	25.8	29.2	45.9	57.2
Total Local	75.4	78.7	92.8	84.2
Sector of City	9.3	4.7	1.2	4.4
City-wide	14.8	9.9	2.3	. . .
State	3.1	2.5	1.5	1.2
National	3.4	.9	.5	10.0
International	.6	.1	.3	1.2
Non-classifiable	5.8	7.0	5.0	4.4

* Totals exceed 100 because of multiple entries.

9. An item is considered local in scope when the events described take place within the territory of one of the seventy-five local communities of Chicago in which the paper is published. Cf. Wirth, Louis and Bernert, Eleanor, *Local Community Fact Book* (Chicago: University of Chicago, 1949).

State, national and international news also increased but these increases are limited. Since it is an underlying hypothesis of this study that the community press serves to maintain the complex balance between local and non-local activities and identifications, these data indicate the relative persistence of the community press in maintaining a localistic focus of attention. The community newspaper has preserved its functions on behalf of the local community during the last three decades by limiting the degree to which it will broaden its horizons through the additional coverage of events of the larger metropolis which impinge on the local community. Advertising matter also refers mainly to local enterprise and when the advertisement centers about a nationally manufactured product local outlets are mentioned.[10]

In analyzing focus of attention, local items were classified as to whether *explicit* terms were employed to indicate the geographical context of the item or whether the geographical context was *implicit* in that no specific symbol of geographical identification was employed. Symbols of explicit local identification included the name of the community, or some such term as local community, local resident, and the like, beyond merely designating the individual's street address. A pronounced tendency to be more explicit about local referents might be assumed to indicate, among other things, a greater

---

10. The Digby paper has a more pronounced local focus of attention, one which is comparable to the local focus of attention of the Chicago papers around 1920. It would be interesting to have trend data on *The Courier's* focus of attention in order to chart its ability to maintain a local focus of attention as compared with the sample of urban community papers.

This comparison is not strictly accurate since those portions of the Chicago local community press which deal with sectors of the city were equated with portions of *The Courier* which deal with immediately adjoining communities. The city-wide category was not applicable for Digby. Therefore, if state (in the case of Digby, provincial), national, and international news is used as a measure of non-local focus of attention, Digby exceeds slightly the community newspaper average.

need on the part of the publisher to reaffirm the "independent" character and identity of the local community either for himself or for his audience.

The distinction between implicit and explicit local items thus permits some speculation about the manner in which local perspectives are rooted in the minds of the personnel producing community newspapers. In Table No. 3 (III), all local items, both implicit and explicit, are ranked in terms of the prominence accorded items of varying scope. Prominence is viewed at three levels; top prominence, the first two top stories on page one; middle prominence, all other stories on page one; and low prominence, stories throughout the rest of the paper.

TABLE NO. 3 (III)—*Local Forms of Attention by Prominence*

	TOP PROMINENCE PERCENT	MIDDLE PROMINENCE PERCENT	LOW PROMINENCE PERCENT
Local-Implicit	40.6	63.5	67.6
Local-Explicit	59.4	36.5	32.4
	100.0	100.0	100.0

There is a clear tendency for local-explicit stories to receive greater prominence than local-implicit stories. (The variation in prominence accorded to items of broader scope is not marked and presents no discernible patterns.) No particular type of subject matter seems accountable for this relationship. Instead, the story with explicit local symbols which receives the greater prominence can be viewed as a conscious effort to make manifest and impress local identifications, for unchallenged local identifications are more compatible with an implicit designation of the local community. The actual work procedures and outlook of the community newspaper editor as he selects and edits the contents of his paper throw light on this pattern.

Into the typical community newspaper office flows a steady stream of professional and amateur publicity releases about community and city news. The flow of publicity releases is greatly surpassed by personal and social news,—births, confirmations, engagements, weddings, deaths—which the readers submit. Routine arrangements are frequently made with local hospitals, churches, funeral parlors, photographers, etc. to augment this information. Telephoning to follow up tips and to cover the routine sources, e.g., the police blotter, substitutes for leg work.

All of these items are reworked into the editor's view of the local community. The routine flow of news into the offices of the community newspaper tends of course to alter the character of the editorial work from that of the daily metropolitan newspaper with its crush for "hot news." Nevertheless, each week the community editor is preoccupied with getting "the big story" of the week, or perhaps two such stories. The result is that these stories which receive top headline prominence are explicit in their reference to the local community because they are so clearly the result of conscious news collection.

Frequently some local event takes place, such as the opening of a new school or the installation of a new parking regulation. Elections, patriotic holidays and special events may fill the bill. At other times, the editor follows the traditional policy of the daily press in manufacturing a story.

Editorial specialization is obviously related to the size of the enterprise. In the largest units the editorial functions are handled as a miniature reflection of the daily metropolitan newspaper. However, in all but the largest organizations editorial personnel have usually to "double in brass." Reporting, rewriting, and makeup become merged into a single ongoing operation. In the very smallest organizations the publisher has to edit the newspaper as well as manage its finances. As the size of the staff increases, local meetings are covered, and finally meetings outside the community which have local relevance are included. Since the publisher and frequently many of the staff members are involved in local organizational life their activities in gathering the news can hardly be distinguished from their own local community participation.[11]

Developing and maintaining a community focus of attention involves utilization of community history, not only by specific items about local community history [12] but more frequently through a style of writing which proudly refers to the age of individuals or to the number of years an organization has been in local existence. Even routine announcements try to emphasize the stability and persistence of organizations and institutions, and all types of anniversaries are seized upon for this purpose. The most extreme form which this type of news coverage takes can be found in the special editions celebrating the historical anniversary of the local community or its newspaper. (The hundredth anniversary of Roseland, for example, was celebrated by a highly successful commercial promotion involving a sixty-four-page edition of the community paper carrying the banner headline "Roseland is One

---

11. Editorial operations among the network of community newspapers are developed to the point where an independent Community News Service is supported. The agency is privately owned and in the hands of a former community newspaper editor. It produces news to keep local community newspapers apprised of activities by the city council and central civic authorities which affect the local community. News is dispatched to newspapers by phone and special messenger. Over half of the city newspapers make use of the service.

12. The Atwater News carries a weekly feature on community history, but the more typical pattern is to publicize meetings of local historical societies and to print occasional stories about landmarks and anniversaries.

Hundred Years Old.") In part, the community editor is following the rules for journalism laid down by the daily press.

Aside from their news content, items which contain local explicit references are designed to reinforce local identifications which are being threatened by non-local influence. Interviews with community newspaper personnel raise the question as to whose identifications are being reinforced. Community journalism like all forms of mass communications is in part designed for the consumption of the original communicator. The editor, where he is distinct from the publisher, is frequently not a local resident and the big stories of the week in part serve the function of reassuring him of his own identifications and of the legitimacy of the type of journalism in which he is engaged.

Subject Matter of the Community Press

The predominantly local focus of attention in the community press results in a marked difference in the ratio of news to human interest features from that found in the daily press. *The community press overwhelmingly concentrates on news while in the daily press human interest features approximately equal the amount of news.* Certain types of events are news for both media but much of what is news in the local community newspaper is presented as human interest material in the daily newspaper. (Table No. 4 (III).) The community newspaper devotes a significant portion of its space to news of local individuals and organizations, and in a routine fashion represents a broad segment of those activities as they occur in the community. However, such items would get into the daily press only as a result of particularized selection because of human or dramatic interest rather than routine interest to readers. Thus, the community newspaper by its coverage reverses the trends and functions of the human interest feature story in the daily newspaper.[13]

TABLE NO. 4 (III)—*News-Feature-Editorial Space Distribution*

YEAR		NEWS %	FEA- TURE %	EDI- TORIAL %	OTHER %
1920	Community paper sample	83.2	8.0	5.3	3.5
1935	Community paper sample	88.4	6.4	4.2	1.0
1949	Community paper sample	86.9	7.5	3.5	2.1
1949	Daily newspaper sample	45.8	47.6	5.2	1.4
1949	Digby newspaper sample	86.8	5.7	4.4	3.1

More detailed analysis of how the community press rations its space indicates that in the typical community newspaper *social and personal news, local voluntary associations, municipal services, and voluntary community services,* receive the most space in that order. (See Table No. 5 (III).) When the dimension of prominence is introduced the rank order changes. *Municipal services* becomes first, *organized religion, business enterprise,* and *public affairs* exceeds *local voluntary associations,* and *social and personal news* in prominence. Clearly the integration of the local newspaper with the political party, business interests and the dominant churches spells success or failure for the paper, and community editors speak for and to the leaders of these groups. Again, the daily newspapers' definition of what constitutes newsworthiness and prominence is applied by the community editor. Since the readers' ranking of interest stress social and personal items (as measured by the readership survey) the editors compromise by filling the inside and less prominent portions of the paper with these items. The negligible amount of space

13. Helen M. Hughes, *Human Interest and the News* (Chicago: University of Chicago, 1940).

devoted to crime, accidents and natural disaster is reflective
of a desire to avoid the sensational approach of the daily
press.[14]

TABLE NO. 5 (III)—*Space Distribution of Subject Matter
in the Community Press*[15]

	COMMUNITY NEWSPAPER SAMPLE %	DIGBY %
Social and personal news	14.7	37.6
Local voluntary associations	13.1	9.7
Municipal services	13.0	13.4
Voluntary community services	10.5	5.9
Business enterprise	8.7	1.8
Organized religion	6.5	3.5
Sports	5.9	2.2
Public affairs	5.1	11.1
Amusement and entertainment	5.1	.1
Personal achievement	4.1	.5
Crime	2.2	.6
Accident or natural disaster	2.1	1.6
Community history	1.2	3.6
Political parties and political activities	.7	.5
Trade union activities	.1	. . .
Other, non-classifiable	7.0	7.9
	100.0	100.0

14. The subject matter categories for the Chicago community press were
applicable to the *Digby Courier*, but revealed a different emphasis in a related
pattern. The top three categories for Chicago, *social and personal, local voluntary associations*, and *municipal services* also predominate to a large extent in
The Courier. In turn, the low emphasis or almost complete absence of *crime,
accidents and natural disaster* and *politics* is common to both media. For both,
social and personal news constitutes the largest single category, but in *The
Courier* this emphasis is considerably greater reflecting a social structure in
which common acquaintance is more widespread.

15. *Social and personal* includes weddings, anniversaries, births and deaths;
municipal services refers to street cleaning, public transportation, crime and
accident control, school system, etc. and it includes items in which aldermen
are presented in connection with municipal services; *voluntary community
services* includes Red Cross, Community Chest, PTA and other welfare and

In terms of either total space or prominence municipal services receives more attention in the community press than business enterprise. In fact, the relative amount of space assigned to business affairs belies the contention of the community newspaper's overwhelming preoccupation with the source of its advertising revenue. Routinely, the community newspaper extends publicity to the meetings of businessmen's associations, to the election of their officers, to the purely business news of the community such as the opening of a new store and to the special programs undertaken by business organizations.

The appropriation of front page space for specially staged promotions in order to support local shopping is a practice that varies. Many community newspapers do not engage in such practices or if they do, they limit them to straight reporting. However, a number of papers follow the policy of encouraging occasional promotional stunts by business organizations and appropriating prominent publicity for such events.

Low Emphasis on Controversy

Examination of the allocation of space in the community press taken by itself might be misleading. Format, scope and subject matter can not obscure the *low emphasis on controversy in both news and editorial columns which characterizes the community press*. In Table 6 (III), space allotted in each textual item has been classified so as to designate whether a real controversy is involved, either originating in the columns of the newspaper or originating in the statements

community betterment activities not supported governmentally; *public affairs* includes city, state and national legislative and executive activities excluding those listed under municipal services; *political parties* is limited to party activities, party leaders and elections.

or activities of local individuals or organizations. The over-whelming bulk of non-advertising space is devoted to reports of routine activity and announcements and not to either change or controversy. Routine activity and announcements were classified under "no theme or issue involved." The changes in the local community could be classified under the category "expansion of community service, activity, or program," or those dealing with organizational achievements.[16] The emphasis on community and organization expansion and the absence of items involving contraction gives the community newspaper its "booster" quality. Less than five percent of the space was devoted to controversy in that it dealt with demands for or opposition to expansion of community services, activities, or programs, or involved larger political considerations.

TABLE NO. 6 (III)—*Consensus and Controversy in the Community Press*

Non-Controversial	PERCENT
No theme or issue involved	74.2
Expansion of community service, activity, or program	7.3
Contraction of community service, activity, or program	.1
Voluntary association undertakes, will undertake, fund raising campaign	4.0
Voluntary association engages in, will engage in, cultural event or program	7.6
Controversial	
Demand expansion of community service, activity, or program	2.0
Oppose expansion, maintenance of community activity, service, or program	.6
Support Fair Deal (not specified elsewhere)	.7
Oppose Fair Deal (not specified elsewhere)	.2
Other	3.3

16. E.g., "Voluntary association undertakes, will undertake fund raising campaign" and "voluntary association engages in, will engage in, cultural event or program."

Editorial matter, which has been defined as including public affairs, columns and letters to the editor, as well as editorials proper, reflects the same bias. In fact, community newspaper editorializing has the unique style of appearing to enter into controversy without really being controversial. The community newspaper feels under "journalistic" pressure to have editorializing content, but this runs counter to its normal position in the community. Thus, a portion of the so-called editorials are merely traditional appeals to community sentiment. In addition, by making use of selected letters to the editor, the paper can further relieve itself of the dilemma involved in expressing opinions.

However, where controversial material is presented, the tendency is clearcut to give it high prominence. Controversies which are most popular are those of the local community against the outside urban metropolis; there are few internal dissenters. Much controversy concerns better municipal facilities for the local community. Since the end of World War II, more significant have been those controversies involving opposition to public housing and thereby support of racial segregation and alleged maintenance of property values. Although the data gathered in the readership aspects of this study permit no direct observation, the implication emerges that the impact of the community newspaper on basic community issues is, in fact, a function of the normally low amount of controversial material in the columns of the community press, which enhances the impact of those items involving controversy.

Heroes of the Community Press

The bias of the community newspaper is more clear in terms of which individuals and organizations are represented as the leading "actors" and "agencies" in the community and what are their identifications, particularly their ethnic or religious identifications. Actors and agencies are the individuals and organizations involved or responsible for the events selected by the editor for publication. Data of this sort are relevant for indicating the middle class orientation of the community press. The audience for community newspapers would tend to condition content in this direction. Negro communities were not included in the sample, thereby eliminating a wide portion of the bottom of the social structure. Moreover, since the sample of papers subjected to content analysis was limited to the legal limits of the city, upper class groups, with the exception of certain enclaves within the city, were under-represented.

Table No. 7 (III) summarizes the frequency of mentions (or occurrences) of actors and agencies found in the contents of the community press. It elaborates the range of social groups and individuals involved in all areas of community life as mirrored by the community press.

Although the community press circulates in the areas where working class populations reside, mentions of labor unions are conspicuously absent, and in fact the isolated references to labor unions received low prominence. Although some of the publishers have a personal anti-organized labor bias, the community press generally is little concerned with the labor unions, partly because they are not organized on a geographical basis. Where unions are developing community oriented activities, the trade union publicists seem almost wholly to neglect community newspapers as potential sources of publicity.

Of the whole range of actors and agencies, there is a high concentration on various types of voluntary associations, with social, cultural, religious, and youth groups heading the list. Voluntary associations predominate over individuals (local residents) since even much of the social news involves associations.[17]

From Table No. 7 (III) the role of various types of voluntary associations in the change and development of the local community can be noted. *Youth and school groups* top the list and their expansion has become a frontier for community activity which can receive much publicity. The welfare of the young is a matter of relatively high consensus and a subject about which unabashed enthusiasm can be expressed.

The high mention of *churches and church groups* involves mainly routine news items. Clergymen *per se* in this sample, although the number of references were quite small, were presented generally in opposition to some new community development. Here the clergy appear as agents of other community interests, speaking to preserve the community.

Community councils also receive considerable coverage. Although their role frequently is to preserve property values, and thereby is largely negative, they attempt to represent themselves as either assisting or pressing for community developments by stressing the more positive aspects of their activities. By contrast, the older types of property improvement associations with their narrower concerns are less frequently found in the columns of the community press. When such organizations do appear, they are more forthright in that they are more likely to be found protesting rather than supporting, conserving rather than developing. Labor unions are completely unrepresented in these issues of community stability and change.

Mentions of actors and agencies of the city, state and na-

---

17. When an item referred to a voluntary association and listed individuals as being involved, the items were classified as in the appropriate voluntary association category; when an individual was identified by his voluntary associations the item was classified in the appropriate individual category.

TABLE NO. 7 (III)—*Actors and Agencies in the Community Press*

	TOTAL MENTIONS*	Total Non-Routine	NON-ROUTINE MENTIONS		
			Expansion	Demand Expansion	Oppose Expansion
Local social, cultural groups	899	28	18	9	1
Church groups	873	55	54	1	0
Clergymen	52	7	0	0	7
Total religious	925	62			
Alderman	50	30	15	10	5
City administration	589	201	180	19	2
State and Nat. govern.	172	26	15	10	1
Total Government	811	257			
Businessman	110	31	21	9	1
Business firm	484	114	103	8	2
Business association	103	20	8	11	1
Property owner groups	38	19	13	0	6
Total Business	735	184			
Youth Groups	667	70	63	2	0
School Groups	570	23	16	6	1
Fraternal Organizations	298	0	0	0	0
Community Councils	206	69	43	19	7
Political Parties	54	0	0	0	0
Labor Unions	13	0	0	0	0
Local Residents	2088	0			

* Both Routine and Non-Routine.

tional governments, although less frequent than voluntary associations, exceed in number references to business enterprise despite the close ties of business with the community press. As compared with the actors and agencies of government, attention to political parties and politics *per se*, throughout the year is not at a very high level. (There are only 54 such references for the non-election sample period.)

In fact, community newspapers today tend to present themselves as mainly independent in their political affiliations. Throughout the metropolitan area in recent years there has been a general movement towards self-designation of "independence." Even the small number of suburban papers which display a political affiliation usually display the prefix independent as well. This trend toward an apparent political independence is similar to the movement in the daily press throughout the country.[18] As a communications medium oriented around the interests of the local business and residential community, fear of alienating any wide sector of the business or readership clientele is a major factor in limiting political orientation.

Behind this apparent neutrality, the community newspaper is frequently aligned with the political parties and acts in mutual support.[19] It is at the alderman's level that the political juncture with the community newspaper operates, both in content and personal contacts. The political involvement is mirrored in the treatment accorded the alderman. The alderman is an important hero in the community newspaper and is presented less as a member of a particular party and more as a spokesman for the local community in getting its

18. Willey, Malcolm M., and Rice, Stuart A., *Communication Agencies and Social Life* (New York: McGraw-Hill, 1933), pp. 162-63.

19. A few publishers are directly involved in politics; two are ward committeemen and one is a leader in independent political action

fair share of municipal services.[20] This can clearly be seen from Table No. 7 (III) in which the alderman and the city administration with which he is associated are most frequently referred to in connection with non-routine news. Not only are they frequently associated with the expansion of community facilities and programs, but they are represented frequently as pressing for and making demands in behalf of the local community. Where opposition to the alderman exists it rarely manifests itself in unfavorable publicity. Support of a more outright nature takes the form of attributing to him responsibility for achieving some local improvement; for example, the *Uptown News* (September 6, 1950) ran a conspicuous headline "Devon Ave. Repaving Was Weber Dream," as an acknowledgment of the alderman's efforts. Frequently he is characterized with much color and dash and is occasionally photographed in action pose as he inspects community facilities or officiates at a ceremony.

Around election time commitment to politics *per se* naturally increases. For the bulk of the papers, in advance of election, notices of changes of polling places, registration, voting requirements, and other factual information receive attention. News stories about the election emphasize neutrality in the best journalistic tradition. A local figure running for high office is likely to receive a certain amount of added publicity regardless of political affiliations. When the paper seeks to give support to a candidate—and this varies from election to election—the procedure is not to give editorial endorsement but rather to give added publicity. For example, a congressman who is a favorite of the newspaper is photographed autographing a basketball at a Halloween party just

---

20. For this reason, the alderman was generally classified as an agent of government rather than of the political party except when he was acting as a political party leader.

before election. Or an alderman running for a county ticket position receives a special award from a women's auxiliary and gets a headline thereby.

In Chicago, the aldermanic elections are held in the spring apart from the general elections and here again community newspaper interest becomes marked. Since the alderman is crucial to such political tie-ups with community newspapers as exist, political bias in terms of disproportionate publicity for aldermanic candidates becomes most manifest during these elections.

In contrast to the alderman, the local businessman suffers somewhat as a hero in the community newspaper. The very fact that there are many business leaders in a community and only one or two aldermen gives the alderman a publicity advantage. Although the total number of references to all businessmen exceeded the number of references to aldermen, the aldermen invariably received top prominence billing. Businessmen and their firms and associations seem to be less often identified with expansion and development of the community than are the alderman and the city administration. Moreover, the businessman is generally not presented in a rounded community leadership position but rather as pursuing his economic interests. (It is, of course, easier to glamorize the opening of a new school than a remodelled store front.) When businessmen are presented as being involved in the role of community leaders, such as charity drives, the individuals involved are frequently employees in charge of public or community relations and are overshadowed by their organizational affiliations. Seldom if ever do the names of the most prominent businessmen of the metropolitan district appear in the columns of community newspapers. The community press is a world of successful local personalities in both business and politics.

THE IMAGE OF THE COMMUNITY

Symbols of Identification: Religious and Ethnic

Since the community press is strongly concerned with maintaining the current consensus, its presentation of religious identifications is socially important. According to some standards of democracy, the balance in emphasis in content among religious groups should reflect to some degree their actual concentration in the community. Therefore, each item, weighted by its length was classified on the basis of explicit symbols of religious identification, if any were present. Such symbols would include reference to Protestant, Catholic or Jewish denominational labels, or the proper names of religious institutions or organizations which could be clearly identified as to affiliation.

It is frequently contended, and documented to some degree, that minority group discrimination carries over into the mass media not only in that stereotypes are presented but also in that minorities receive limited attention (thereby perhaps contributing to the maintenance of stereotypes). However, religious groups might not be neglected in the community press, since with its decentralized ownership and narrower audience it was more likely to reflect actual religious group concentrations in the community. This was a specific application of the more general hypothesis that the community press reflected accurately a wide range of community values because it was not appealing to the widest possible audience. Moreover, if it were true that the community newspaper had a middle class bias, then Catholic and Jewish symbols of identification would be likely to find expression, since these groups within an urban center like Chicago constitute a wide portion of the middle class.

The content analysis tended to confirm these observations, for symbols of religious identification are presented without any noticeable discrimination although clearcut standards are difficult to construct. (See Table 8 (III).) This is especially borne out by the historical trend which indicates the marked emergence of minority religious symbols in the community

TABLE NO. 8 (III)—*Explicit Religious Symbols of Identification in the Community Press*

	1920 SAMPLE PERCENT	1949 SAMPLE PERCENT
Protestant	76.4	50.6
Catholic	18.6	30.4
Jewish	5.0	19.0
	100.0	100.0

press since the 1920's, reflecting not so much their rise in numerical ratio, which has not been great, but rather their social emergence. Jewish symbols, in fact, appear to be well represented, reflective of the complex issues involved in the high visibility of the Jews in an urban society. However, when the dimension of prominence is introduced, the presentation of Jewish symbols is found to decrease. Given a lack of clear norms to deal with in allocating prestige to Jewish symbols the result is perhaps an overpresentation of the number of Jewish symbols on the basis of their numerical proportion, but this presentation is—either consciously or unconsciously—"corrected" by allocating lower prominence to such symbols.

The lack of "discrimination" against religious minorities can also be traced to the personnel who run community newspapers. Community newspaper owners are over-representative of members of minority groups since the industry had its origin as a marginal enterprise and thereby attracted members of minority groups. (See Chapter VI, The Social Role of the Community Publisher: Agent of Personal and

Mass Communications.) Religious symbols of identification were found to be one of the few content characteristics of the community newspaper which were related to ownership. It seems as if ownership reflects the religious consciousness of the community, although it would be difficult to speak of community self-selection of community newspaper publishers and editors in terms of religion. Since the publishers are frequently members of minorities, they are minority conscious with the result that their papers reflect the differential concentrations of religious groupings.

Since the community press is in close contact with its readership, it is also sensitive to the aspirations of ethnic groups for publicity and recognition. With the decline of the foreign language newspaper the community press has taken over the function of disseminating ethnic news. And since the community press is generally direct and casual in tone, the existence of the ethnic groups is recognized as such without the embarrassment of a "brotherhood" outlook which would seek to obscure ethnic differences.

In the columns of certain of the community newspapers there is a constant flow of news items about ethnic fraternal and social organizations. In addition, the community press strongly supports special events among ethnic groups. Typical front-page banner headlines announcing such occasions are as follows:

Norwegians To Parade in Park. (*Northwesttown Booster*, May 11, 1949).

Croatians To Observe Two Day Centennial Celebration. (*The Calumet*, August 4, 1949).

Polish Americans Mark Constitution. (*The Logan Square News*, May 18, 1949).

Irish Folk Here Prepare St. Pat's Day Festivities. (*Auburn Parker*, March 10, 1949).

Preoccupation with ethnic affairs reflects the concentration of the ethnic group in the local community, and thereby permits the "glorification" of local community leaders. Ethnic activities frequently supply an opportunity for "neutral" political news, for in Chicago, Democratic party leaders are frequently in attendance and can be featured in the news report.

In contrast to fostering religious consensus, the community newspaper does not cross the color line. Maintenance of local autonomy and local consensus means, by and large, maintenance of racial segregation in residential matters. From the point of view of the publisher and his advertisers, racial segregation is required if the local satellite business district is to prosper economically. A minority of the community press could be viewed as being dedicated to non-discrimination in residential areas. These are frequently papers run by Catholic and Jewish publishers in areas where Negroes are not threatening invasion. Support for civil rights ranges from giving moderate publicity to inter-racial events to publicizing legislative and administrative action on behalf of civil rights.[21] Another portion, perhaps the largest number, avoid the problem entirely with the possible exception of giving a rare bit of vague publicity to civic unity activities. By implication, such newspapers stand ready to defend the community from invasion.

---

21. The range of attitudes on minority rights found in the community newspaper includes the position of two newspapers which for a short period followed the line of the Progressive Party. Typical of this position is the following news item:

"Dr. J. H. _____, pastor of _____ Church, declared that the greatest peril to democracy at the moment was from within the United States, rather than from Russia, when he spoke last week at the annual dinner of the Maxwell St. YMCA. He said that unless we grappled realistically with the problems of minority discrimination and second-class citizenship, we would continue to furnish grist for the Communists' propaganda mill." (May 19, 1949).

On the other hand, a minority of the papers are outspoken to varying degrees in their efforts to maintain ethnic segregation. As might be expected, these newspapers lie on the South Side of Chicago where pressure has been great for the expansion of the Black Belt. Ethnic relations runs as a thread through the contents of these papers. Some of Chicago's large metropolitan dailies have subscribed to the code which prevents race labelling in news stories; or substitute the word Southsider for Negro. However, segregationalist community newspapers merely continue to use race labelling in their headlines and stories. For example, the *Eastend Reporter* on March 16, 1949, headlined the story "Police Nab Hoods After Attack on Railworker Here. Arrest Three Negroes for Vicious Beating."

A series of fundamental assumptions about the undesirability of Negroes as neighbors relieve these newspapers of the necessity of being explicit when dealing with the question of ethnic invasion. Straightforward reprinting of news which in its origin was designed to aid minorities and to assist orderly residential mobility without regard to race is even practiced with the design to "remind" the reader of the ever-present threat. If necessary, the tactic involves the allocation of a great deal of prominent space and can be enhanced by a subtle twisting of the headline. For example, on August 6, 1949, the chairman of the Commission on Human Relations issued a statement about an anti-Negro disturbance in the Park Manor Community which had been quelled by effective police action. One paper ran the story under the headline: "Report Anti-Racial Situation Under Control in South Shore." Followed by the subhead: "Police Squelch Action Against Colored Family. Human Relations Commission Head Called Blue Coat Tactics Decisive." Here neutrality was little more than a sham, for the story received over a column and a half space, an amount allotted to few stories.

During the period of this study the State Legislature was debating the State FEPC bill while the city council debated the controversial Carey Ordinance which would have prevented segregation in housing erected on land assembled by the city's Land Clearance Commission. These legislative proposals, neither of which passed, provided the pro-segregation community newspapers with an opportunity to continue sham neutrality by extending wide coverage to these matters. The technique included describing the FEPC bill as one which was likely to pass because the State Legislature had to "cater to certain interests." Attention was also given to the activities of local improvement and property owners' associations which were fighting the Carey Ordinance.

Maintenance of Community Values

Maintenance of the local community through racial segregation implies opposition to public housing. Public housing, regardless of the economic and political implications involved, manifestly means that local residential areas will become the sites of large scale developments for those believed by many to be undesirable residents. Where Federal funds are involved, "undesirable" residents include Negroes because of the non-discriminatory provisions of federally subsidized projects.

At each step in the attempts to develop public housing in Chicago since the end of World War II, certain community newspapers have taken an oppositionalist stand. In fact, papers which usually avoid items referring to Negroes find the public housing issue suitable for coverage. They have reported opposition to the selection of specific housing sites particularly when these sites were in their own community areas. Late in 1950, emboldened by the successes of pressure on the city council which drastically limited public housing, anti-public housing groups began a campaign to have the public housing issue put up as a referendum. A number of important community newspapers devoted headline space to this campaign for a number of weeks. If the content analysis were repeated for 1950, the amount of controversial matter might be increased for certain periods, but only slightly since such issues fail to upset the basic format and focus of attention to any considerable extent.

While a minority of community newspapers are the leaders of opposition to public housing, many more, almost all, engage in publicizing activities designed to maintain property values and standards. The maintenance of an economic trading area to support the satellite shopping district requires fighting against the forces which tend to lower property values. Administrative action to fight illegal rooming houses, the removal of temporary veteran housing projects and trailers, and news about zoning ordinances, are all grist for this mill.

Local pride and a desire to maintain decent living conditions lead to a preoccupation with combatting the odors, the dirt, and the noise that beset the community. At times, complicated issues arise involving individual freedom versus the collective welfare; for example, the noisy auto horns of wedding parties.

Typical of such preoccupation was a story in *The East End Reporter* giving publicity to a police statement:

"We have no objection to wedding parties but there is a time and place for everything. These wedding parties . . . toot their horns loudly disturbing everybody. . . . They feel they have the same privileges as a funeral procession. . . . It is hoped that wedding parties will confine their noise making tactics within the confines of their home or the hall where they finally have their big celebration. Failure to cooperate may result in arrest."

Any slur on the local community is likely to bring forth responses in the community press which acts as the standard bearer of local pride. When *McCalls* published an article about one of Chicago's slums, the paper of the community involved printed headlines of protest and statements by leading community leaders. In addition to describing the residents as "honest, law-abiding, thrifty, industrious, home-loving, respectable and respected according to the merchants and business men who have daily contact with these residents" the paper pointed out that the area had seventeen savings and home loan associations, and two banks whose assets exceeded 163 million dollars.

In a similar fashion, community newspapers tend to appropriate for themselves a role as the enforcer of public morals. This reflects the publishers' sensitivity to his audience of householders beset with the complicated problems of socializing the young. The community newspaper publisher is not merely a commercial agent attempting to increase his profit without regard to the social consequences of his newspaper content. He is in too close contact with his clientele to be able to accomplish this; and he is aligned with the local community leaders who have a vested interest in promoting the respectability of the local community.

Stories about burning "crime" comic books, campaigns to foster respect for school property, and police drives against sex immorality are examples of concern for public morality. The community press warns its readers of confidence men, counterfeiters and "scheming crooks" who threaten the neighborhoods. Throughout the presentation of the community's efforts to enforce morals, the question arises as to which self-interest the community newspaper is really appealing. Is it desirous solely of maintaining public morality? Or since it is deprived of scandal does it at the same time seek an indirect way of appealing to the impulses which it cannot cater to directly?

News from beyond the Community

Although the amount of space devoted to national and international issues appears limited, the community press when it does concern itself with the state of the world develops the "local angle" with great sensitivity and speed. The international situation is described in terms that impinge directly on the lives of the local residents. The headlines and stories about the Korean war illustrate how external events are presented in terms of personalities rather than issues.

First, reactions to Korea in the community press were headlines early in July 1950 reporting the spurt in enlistments at local recruiting centers. The names and addresses of those who had volunteered were found in the columns of the community press, while the revival of the draft brought back the wartime practice of listing the names of inductees. On August 24, the *Rogers Park News* ran a headline "Rogers Park Boy Dies in Korea. First Casualty is Pfc. Hoffman." The story received banner headlines and contained a long sketch of the boy's local activities, hobbies and family. Soon thereafter community newspapers began to headline local civil defense plans. Since Chicago was designated as one of three cities for a mock air raid in September, the community press had a new type of copy with a "local angle."

Korean casualty lists no longer received streamer headlines but week after week community newspapers devoted full stories to the details and biography of local boys killed in action in Korea, men whose names were merely listed in the casualty reports of the daily press. Late in September 1950 stories began to appear about the return to the Chicago area of men who had been wounded in Korea. As plans for local civil defense developed and as special informational programs were required, items of news and information began to appear.

But the space devoted to events outside the horizons of the community is not taken up by international crises alone. (Table No. 2 (III).) Routinely, the community press selects from the total flow of "foreign" events those referring specifically to the local community and its welfare. A city survey on traffic hazards may be edited so that the portion dealing with the local community receives prominent attention. A debate in the State Legislature on the regulation of public utilities may be treated in the same manner. The local press supplies commercial news in its advertising; it also supplies the details of governmental and social welfare activities which though they arise outside of the community, find impact within it. Week after week the community press reports on old age benefits, unemployment insurance, health drives and governmental regulations and services. While the daily papers can report on main developments, the community press makes specific reference to the names and addresses of officials and agencies involved either in the specific community or nearby.

Content and Economic Control

The conclusions about community press content have emerged from the Chicago community press as a whole. Therefore, the question presents itself: To what extent can variations be found between papers which would require modification of these generalizations? A significant way to categorize newspapers is by type of ownership. Communications research has long been concerned with those problems of contemporary journalism which are held to be inexplicably bound up with economic control, in particular with the issue of chain versus independent ownership. It has long been a contention that chain ownership of daily newspapers is an evil and one that is constantly worsening. On the other hand, the counter-contention has been raised that newspapers operating under highly competitive conditions at times fail to achieve adequate standards. Since the community press is subject to the same consolidation trend as the daily press, economic ownership was investigated as it related to content.

Community newspapers are of three ownership types, large chains, large independents, and small independents.[22] In certain broad basic content characteristics, the variation between the different types of control was found to be less than the variation between papers operating under the same type of control formula. In particular, amount of advertising, format, and focus of attention between local and non-local items did not vary as between these groupings. There was a slight tendency for the chains and the large independents to have more items involving controversy and change. It might have been assumed that the large organizations would be "powerful" enough to be able to afford a markedly increased interest in these items, but it appears that the temperament of the publisher is just as crucial as economic control and stability in this regard.

However, there is a consistent variation between the subject matter of chain and independent papers in that chain news content is less community oriented, less intimate, and less personalized than the independents. As compared with independent newspapers, chains publish more items about business enterprise, more about accidents and about commercial amusements, less about organized religion, less social

---

22. In carrying out the actual analysis the three largest chains were each analyzed separately so that for particular purposes there were five groups of papers whose contents were being matched.

news, and fewer items about local voluntary associations. These differences place the chain community newspaper closer to the daily newspaper than the independent community newspaper. (Table No. 9 (III).) The broader focus

TABLE NO. 9 (III)—*Distribution of Subject Matter in the Community Press*

	CHAIN PAPERS %	LARGE INDEPENDENT %	SMALL INDEPENDENT %	DIGBY %
Social and personal	12.7	20.9	12.7	37.6
Local voluntary associations	11.5	15.4	16.3	9.7
Municipal Service	12.3	13.0	14.5	13.4
Voluntary commun. services	10.3	7.2	12.7	5.9
Business enterprise	12.0	3.4	7.2	1.8
Organized Religion	4.6	8.0	8.2	3.5
Sports	5.6	12.4	6.1	2.2
Public Affairs	6.6	3.1	3.1	11.1
Amusement and entertainment	6.0	.6	3.1	.1
Personal achievement	4.3	4.0	3.3	.5
Crime	2.6	1.8	1.6	.6
Accident or natural disaster	2.5	1.6	1.5	1.6
Community History	1.9	.5	.5	3.6
Political party, etc.	.5	1.0	.6	.5
Trade Union activities	.2	.1	.4	
Other	6.4	7.0	8.2	7.9
	100.0	100.0	100.0	100.0

of attention arises out of the broader scope of operations of the chain editors and publishers who have to deal with a broad sector of the city despite the fact that they seek to publish papers for specific communities. Chain newspapers invariably have some measure of centralization of editorial function and this centralization seems to bring with it a modification of news policy and degree of intimacy and personalization which makes the paper less community oriented despite all conscious efforts to the contrary.[23]

By comparison, the *Digby Courier*—the publication of an isolated small community—emphasizes even more intimate and more personalized content than the daily newspaper, the chain or the independent community newspaper. Thus, if the community newspaper is viewed as a communication which in the process of serving local community interests, resists the pressure toward impersonality, then the content of the *Digby Courier* constitutes a standard against which to judge the tendency toward impersonality in content in chain and independent papers. Nevertheless, the statistical measures do not adequately represent differences in patterns of content between these control groups, or for that matter, certain other major groupings into which the community press might be categorized.

All of the statistical aspects of content analysis have depended on systematic categories. The requirements for comparison produce categories which are essentially broad and in a sense lack detail. Moreover, most of the comparisons have been made between groups of papers rather than between individual papers. Comparisons between individual papers highlight some unique characteristics of individual papers, although the content analysis of the three papers whose readers were surveyed still revealed overwhelmingly more content

---

23. Standards for desirable performance are indeed difficult to establish and cannot be created merely on a priori grounds. A purely community orientation is not necessarily a sign of public service. The somewhat broader focus of attention of the chain newspapers perhaps indicated a sensitivity to the problems linking the local community to the larger metropolis. From this point of view, the independent newspapers may be considered as being over-committed to the local community.

similarities than differences. Nevertheless, the content of community newspapers is a much closer indicator of the social structure and value system of the various communities than these categories for comparative purposes can reveal. This should by no means be taken to refute the generalizations which these categories have produced. On the contrary, what is meant here is that differences in community history as well as real differences in community structure are mirrored in the community press, a tendency which differentiates one community from the next·and in a sense makes each community newspaper unique in tone or character. The narrower audiences to which the community press appeals tends to modify standardization. Pressure for evolving appeals which are designed for the widest possible population is less prevalent.

If the categories for content analysis were not drawn finely enough to highlight differences between individual newspapers, it must be remembered that the categories were conditioned by the requirements of fitting a description of community newspaper content to reader response. For this purpose, it was found that the categories were more than adequately refined.

IV

The Attributes
of Readership:
Family, Status,
and Community

The Research Design

One technique for gauging the impact of a continuing flow of communications such as the community press is to establish indices for the amount and forms of "readership." Once "readership" has been established, isolation of the social and psychological attributes of readers and non-readers becomes an initial step in making inferences as to the function and significance of the particular communications system.

Inferences from the attributes of "readership" must of necessity become an important research approach when the impact of a continuing flow of communications is under investigation. Investigation of psychological and social states before and after exposure to a sample of content is only of limited relevance because of the assumption that communication impact is gradual in conditioning human behavior. Repeated access to readers and non-readers over long periods of time is a partial substitute. Such a procedure was not possible within the scope of this research, but even if it were, such a research design would still leave unanswered many questions about communication impact. The interrelatedness of communication stimuli and other factors, as well as the impossibility of holding many crucial variables constant over a long period, would complicate the use of such an approach.

More precise and analytic estimates of impact can be developed by other research procedures. As an initial step, it is necessary to define readership in terms other than those of statistical units involving merely the amount of content to which the individual has exposed himself. To rely solely on exposure to the contents of a newspaper, even if it were possible to measure this precisely, would limit all subjective reactions to one level. It would assume that all who attend are emotionally and socially equipped to perceive in the same fashion and to the same degree. Reading is a social act involving a total response and it needs to be measured in those terms. Personal needs and the social context continually modify the stimuli to which the individual has exposed himself and thereby readership has to be defined in terms of the constituent elements of which this process is composed. To this end, readership was seen in terms of five constituent elements.

Exposure is defined as the amount of content to which the individual attends. However, exposure does not indicate the depth of the individual's involvement with the content to which he is attending. *Involvement* is defined as the degree of importance the individual attaches to the content in meeting his needs and interests. Although high involvement might increase exposure, a one-to-one association should not be assumed, for equal amounts of exposure may accompany different levels of involvement. Exposure, or amount of attention to content, does not indicate what specific types of content interest the reader. *Interest pattern,* therefore, describes the types of content (rather than the amount) within a communication system to which the reader attends. In addition, the reader has overall reactions to the medium per se and to its contents. These reactions constitute his *imagery* of the communication. Imagery can be defined as the verbalized responses to the communication flow which reflect to a lesser degree, reactions to specific content and, to a greater degree, more basic attitudes toward its overall format and character. Finally, *penetration* is defined as the conscious recall or remembrance of content to which the individual has exposed himself. Thus, readership in this study was conceived of as consisting of (a) exposure, (b) involvement, (c) interest pattern, (d) imagery, and (e) penetration.

These concepts aid in giving precision to the term "readership." As a second step, suitable concepts for describing the "readership" of the community press have to be related to relevant and precise categories for classifying and contrasting the social and psychological characteristics of readers and non-readers. In order to study the impact of the community press every effort was made to canvass and include discrete and objective indices of overt behavior which might be related to "readership." Such data were supplied by the individual respondent himself, by community leaders, community newspaper personnel, and local entrepreneurs. The data included items ranging from what the reader does when the paper is not delivered to his response to specific advertising campaigns. Interesting as such discrete and objective data might be, they could not become of crucial analytical importance since the respondent is only partially aware of his relevant motives and behavior. Of equal importance was the task of devising and employing indices which would permit locating the individual in the social and spatial structure of society and gauging accurately his subjective states in such a way as to be relevant for explaining his readership or non-readership.

In the past, sex, age, education, income, and occasionally occupation have been mainly used as key variables in communication research. These categories can be designated as "structural" categories as opposed to "dynamic" categories. As such they are significant in delimiting the communication problem but too often, unfortunately, they are overburdened as explanatory variables. They have limited relevance to basic hypotheses seeking to explain communication impact and social change. Since many of the basic hypotheses of this research involve social solidarity and community integration, explanatory categories designed to measure such social relations were required.

An interview and sample were constructed to conform to this research design which sought to investigate impact of an ongoing flow of communications through a single interview. In addition to maintaining rapport, great care had to be taken to prevent creating suspicion that the interview was simply a prelude to a "sales pitch" for the community newspaper. Reactions to the community newspaper itself were required and not reactions among the non-paying readers to the threat of being called upon to pay. This was complicated by the technical impossibility of knowing in advance whether the respondent paid or did not pay for his paper.

The commercial market research technique of presenting the respondent with an edition of the publication and leading him through the pages for comments on his reading habits and reactions was rejected. First, this technique greatly increases the likelihood that the respondent would attribute commercial motives to the interviewer. Second, although recollection of readership produces distortion, presentation of the publication greatly increases the manipulative and suggestive power of the interviewer. Third, many of our basic hypotheses did not involve the ability to remember reading a specific item as is required by a commercial survey. Instead, the interest of the study involved much broader and more basic terms of reference. Pretesting had indicated that to investigate *exposure, involvement, interest pattern,* and *imagery* required a broader interviewing approach which would emphasize total or gestalt-like reactions to community newspaper content. As for *penetration,* the unstimulated responses of the respondent were of central importance.

Fortunately, the data required for social and psychological attributes of readership and non-readership made possible the construction of an interview schedule oriented around family and community in which the community newspaper became only one, although a heavily emphasized, element.[1] Abreactions to the interview situation indicate that suspicion of commercial sponsorship was kept at a minimum.[2]

In constructing an appropriate sample a rationale was

---

1. See Appendix II—Readership Survey: Interview Schedule.
2. After a standardized approach which identified the interviewer and the sponsorship of the survey—the Chicago Community Inventory, a non-profit research organization—the interviewer described the survey's interest in local community problems. The interview itself opened with a series of personalized questions on the local community, its facilities, and the respondent's attitude toward them. The middle section dealt with the various dimensions of community newspaper "readership," as well as other media habits. The latter section involved not only background data and family data, but concluded with questions designed to probe topics involving political identifications and feelings of individual competence. The average length of the interviews was between twenty-five and thirty minutes.

evolved which resulted in selecting three communities from the seventy-five community areas in Chicago.[3] In selecting these communities the following criteria were taken into account: First, the communities should be within the legal limits of the city of Chicago since the investigation of highly urbanized areas was the basic research objective. This would direct the study toward those areas of the metropolitan district where the community newspapers are working under fewest advantages, and where the papers are most clearly not rural survivals. Second, the communities should reflect various levels in the development of their populations. Thus, the communities should represent respectively an old area, one in transition, and one still in the initial phases of growth. Third, they should be located at various distances from the center of the city. Fourth, the communities should reflect different socio-economic or prestige levels.

It was decided to limit the sampling to: (a) predominantly semi-skilled or working class—upper-lower class; (b) predominantly white collar and/or skilled—lower-middle class; and (c) predominantly professional, managerial, entrepreneurial —middle-middle to upper-middle class. The upper class was eliminated because the upper class is concentrated in a few small areas or has left the highly urbanized portion of the city. The very lowest—lower-lower class—was also eliminated because, in a city like Chicago, its inclusion would require sampling Negro areas. This was not considered advisable, since the Negro press is not organized on a community basis, although there are signs of the development of a Negro community press.

When these sampling criteria were applied to the seventy-five areas, a workable solution emerged. As the communities

---

3. See Wirth, Louis and Bernert, Eleanor, op. cit., for details of the method involved in establishing these community areas.

were ranked by any one of the three criteria, the other two in general revealed a crude pattern. The patterns rather typically reflected certain hypotheses which have been applied to the development of the ecological structure of the city, if the complicating factor of Negro migration were eliminated. The three types were: an old community whose residents were in the working class, which was located close to the center of the city (at least one ethnic transition had already taken place); a lower-middle class community of more recent origin in the middle of the city, which was in the process of transition; and finally, a recent or still developing middle-middle to upper-middle class community which was the furthest removed from the center of the city. These types hardly accounted for all the variations in communities, but this grouping made the sampling problem a manageable task.

The final selection of the communities falling within these types was based on characteristics of the community paper itself rather than the area. The community should be covered in its entirety by an *effective* community newspaper. To have an entire community covered would aid in the selection of respondents. More significantly, the contents of such a community newspaper would be oriented to the whole community rather than a portion of it. An effective community newspaper meant that the newspaper had been in existence between five and ten years. This did not necessarily mean that the most powerful, best edited and most influential papers would be included; to the contrary, this was not the result. (The paper covering the working-class area, for example, is one of modest profitability.) However, this did insure that specific historical accidents or other reasons for limited development of a community newspaper in a particular sector of a community would not hinder this phase of the research.

The working (upper-lower) class community has been

arbitrarily labelled for this study as Atwater (A); the white collar, skilled worker, salesman (lower-middle) class community as Bethel Park (B); and the white collar management, professional, and self-employed (middle-middle to upper-middle) class community as Carleton Manor (C). (Of course, these characterizations refer only to the most frequent class groupings within each community.) In each community a random sample of 200 households was selected.[4] Within each household the male and female heads were interviewed alternately, thereby producing a sample of 300 males and 300 females, or 100 males and 100 females from each community.[5] In addition, fifty community leaders were interviewed according to a modified schedule for comparative purposes.[6]

4. The details of the sampling procedure are set forth in Appendix II—Readership Survey: Sample of Respondents.

5. A brief historical and sociological description, plus certain socio-economic data for each community, is presented in Appendix III—Basic Data on Three Sample Communities. The data for 1930 and 1940 are based on U.S. Bureau of the Census Reports; the data for 1950 are based on the representative sampling of the three communities completed for the impact aspects of the study. Comparison of selected characteristics encountered in the sample with the 1940 census makes possible evaluation of the adequacy of the sampling procedure. For example, in two of the areas, where no building of any consequence took place during the decade, house type is very closely duplicated in the sample.

	Community A		Community B	
	1940 Census	*1950 Sample*	*1940 Census*	*1950 Sample*
Single	19.7	18.5	17.4	19.5
Two	36.2	36.0	41.4	44.5
Multiple	44.1	45.5	41.2	36.0

6. The definition of community leaders and the sampling procedures employed are set forth in Appendix II—Readership Survey: Sample of Respondents.

Index of Readership: Exposure and Involvement

The community newspaper is a communication system perceived by the respondent in the context of competition from other communication systems. The various dimensions of "readership" had to be translated into a research design which would incorporate the gestalt-like character of this perception. This implied the construction of a series of questions which would permit men and women to verbalize about their reading behavior in a way which was meaningful, and with a level of refinement no more detailed than that of their actual perceptions as revealed by the pretest. Of the five dimensions of "readership," both *exposure* and *involvement* were used in constructing one basic index.[7]

Exposure was measured by a series of questions asked after the subject of the community newspaper had been introduced and after the non-commercial character of the interview had been established. These questions made possible the ranking of readers on a continuum of *high* exposure, *middle* exposure and *low* or *non* exposure. In brief, *high* exposure meant weekly attention to the bulk of the paper; middle meant weekly attention to portions of the paper or less than weekly attention to the greater part of its content; while *low* exposure meant occasional attention to portions of the paper, glancing at the paper or no exposure at all. *Involvement* was measured by a series of questions designed to elicit the respondent's attitude toward the paper plus a particularly revealing question, namely, "Do you miss the paper when it

---

7. *Interest pattern* was analyzed separately, while both *penetration* and *imagery* were dimensions that were not amenable to index construction.

doesn't come?" These questions made possible the ranking of respondents in terms of *intense, average,* and *low* or *non* involvement. Of all the possible combinations of the exposure and involvement dimensions, four empirical types were found:

READERSHIP INDEX

	EXPOSURE			INVOLVEMENT		
	High	Middle	*Low* or Non	Intense	Average	*Low* or Non
Fans	X			X		
Regular Readers	X				X	
Partial Readers		X			X	
Non-Readers			X			X

Thus a single index was created, the internal consistency of which could be inferred from the small number of cases which had to be handled as exceptions. In all, considerably less than five percent of the cases represented variations from these combinations.[8]

Table No. 1 (IV) presents the distribution in the amount of readership found in the sample of 600 and among the 50 community leaders from these three communities.

The amount of community newspaper readers appears to be considerable although a definite minority of completely disinterested individuals is present. Eleven percent are fans, forty percent are regular readers, thirty-three are partial readers,

---

8. For example, in distinguishing partial readers from regular readers there were nine middle-exposure people who missed their community paper or who had strong attitudes toward it. The remaining deviates (19) from this crude "scale" were found among a small group who had high exposure but who either did not miss the paper or had no strong feelings toward it. These were arbitrarily classed with the partial readers since it was felt that they might be exaggerating the amount of their exposure.

TABLE NO. 1 (IV)—*Distribution of Community Newspaper Readership*

	COMMUNITY RESIDENTS		COMMUNITY LEADERS	
	No.	%	No.	%
Fans	69	11.0	8	16.0
Regular Readers	224	40.0	21	42.0
Partial Readers	199	33.0	17	34.0
Non-Readers	108	16.0	4	8.0
Total Number of Cases	600	100.0	50	100.0

and sixteen percent are non-readers. (The three community newspaper publishers when shown these results felt that such amounts of readership either equalled or exceeded their expectations. The criteria for selecting the three sample communities probably revealed a level of readership slightly higher than would be encountered in the city as a whole.)

Community leaders reveal a slightly higher community newspaper readership index than do community residents. Such a finding was expected and, in fact, there is good reason to believe from the details of community leaders' reading habits that community newspaper readership is an integral attribute of certain types of community leadership.[9] (Chapter VI, The Social Role of the Community Publisher: Agent of Personal and Mass Communications.)

The question arises whether this *exposure-involvement* readership index includes different *interest patterns* which

---

9. In the research design the procedure was employed of asking the respondent about the community newspaper reading habits of his spouse. (Where there was no spouse the respondent was asked about the eldest equivalent in the household.) A marked equality in the *total* distribution of exposure was reported by the respondents for themselves as compared with their reports about their spouses. This could be taken as an indirect measure of the adequacy of the interviewing techniques since in many cases individual respondents reported their reading habits as different from those of their spouses.

need to be differentiated before isolating the attributes of readers and non-readers. For example, do regular readers tend to read markedly different items from partial readers? Of course, the higher amounts of readership on the part of the fans would be reflected in a greater variety of interests. In particular, however, it was important to answer the question whether the partial readers had mainly a commercial interest while only the regular readers and fans had broader interest patterns. Although the fans had somewhat wider readership interests, the interests of the partial readers were not predominantly commercial. In fact, there was no clear-cut difference in interest patterns between the various levels of readership per se, and the proportion of men and women in the entire sample who read the paper just for the advertisements was less than three percent.

Finally, analyzing the attributes associated with community newspaper reading, it should be pointed out that the variation between the communities is slight and not statistically significant. (Table No. 2 (IV).)[10]

TABLE NO. 2 (IV)—*Distribution of Community Newspaper Readership by Community Area*

	ATWATER		BETHEL PARK		CARLETON MANOR	
	No.	%	No.	%	No.	%
Fans	31	15.5	20	10.0	18	9.0
Readers	72	36.0	84	42.0	68	34.0
Partial readers	63	31.5	61	30.5	75	37.5
Non-readers	34	17.0	35	17.5	39	19.5
	200		200		200	

10. Throughout the study when the Chi-square test was employed to determine the significance of attributes for the whole sample, differences of .01 confidence limit were considered as significant. Unless otherwise noted, a reported significant difference is at the .01 level.

The absence of significant differences in readership between communities simplifies the greater portion of the analysis of the attributes of readership which, in any case, is based on data gathered from individuals and must therefore be analyzed in terms of individuals.

Fundamentally, all social and psychological attributes of the individual respondents had of necessity to be related to the basic hypotheses linking the community press to the social processes by which the individual is integrated into urban social structure. In the local community, where the community press operates, the socialization of the next generation takes place, certain primary group relations are manifested, patterns of consumption are expressed and the mechanisms of politics are extant. Thus, if the community newspaper is an instrument—not necessarily out of conscious design—in opposition to the individuating tendencies of urbanism, it seems plausible that the attributes of readership could be put into two main groups reflecting social structure at the local community level.

First, the local community resident could be viewed as a member of a status and family group; and as such, indices of social and family cohesion should be related to community newspaper readership for such cohesion is a requisite to community orientation. Second, the local community resident in varying degrees participates in and identifies with the institutions and facilities of the local community; and as such, indices of greater community integration should be related to community newspaper readership.

Family and Status as Attributes of Readership

Examination of family composition and primary group aspects of family life revealed important and marked correlates of community press readership. In fact, effective and.cohesive families were correlates of the highest association. Status, as measured by a number of alternative approaches, had no explanatory values; unfortunately it was not possible to gather data on social mobility or mobility aspirations, measures which might have shown significant associations. Certain "structural" variables related to status, for example, sex and age, produced various significant differences in readership and assumed meaning as amplifying the central role of the family in the conditioning of local community orientations. Other "structural" variables failed to produce significant associations, or, as in the case of education, were of secondary explanatory value.

Family

Analyzing family structure is a complex task, especially since the formal data that could be gathered during the course of this study constitute only an indirect measure of family integration. Nevertheless, a number of different approaches reinforce each other.

Marital status itself revealed a significant association with readership since married householders are better readers than householders who are single. (Table No. 3 (IV).) Family structure is even more relevant. When the number of children is used as a measure of family structure a significant association with community newspaper readership emerges. It is difficult to determine whether a family with one child is still in the process of expansion or whether it is to be considered as completed. The completed one-child family would, of course, be less likely to be an effective family. However, the association of community newspaper readership and children emerges when groupings involving different numbers of children are employed. (Table No. 3 (IV).) Moreover, the association holds for the number of children at home.

The strong influence of family relations is highlighted when the reading habits of respondents from unbroken households (those with two parents) are related to the number of children in the household. Such families without children do not contain fans or regular community newspaper readers. With each additional child, readership increases sharply. The association between number of children in no-divorce households and community newspaper readership produced a Chi-square of 48.8 (coefficient of contingency .095), the highest encountered in the entire study.[11]

The underlying explanations are clear: children are not only the best neighbors in the community [12] but they lead their parents to neighborhood community participation and orientation. It is almost as if the children having become the socializers of their parents are aided in the process by the community newspaper which supplies the information and ideology relevant for the complexities of urban life. The community newspaper does not supply content for children; rather, it supplies content relevant for families grappling

---

11. The sample of community leaders—men and women with extremely high community orientations and higher community newspaper readership—displayed fewer childless marriages and had larger families than did the general sample of residents. (This difference could not be accounted for by the somewhat older age of the community leaders.)

12. Roper, Marion Wesley. *The City and the Primary Group.* University of Chicago, Chicago, 1935.

TABLE NO. 3 (IV)—*Attributes of Community Newspaper Readership*

Marital Status

	MARRIED		DIVORCED, WIDOWED		SINGLE		
	No.	%	No.	%	No.	%	TOTAL NO.
Fans	62	12.2	6	11.1	1	2.5	69
Readers	192	37.9	21	38.9	11	28.2	224
Partial Readers	171	33.7	16	29.6	12	30.8	199
Non-readers	82	16.2	11	20.4	15	38.5	108
	507		54		39		600

Children in Household *

	NONE		ONE		TWO		THREE OR MORE		
	No.	%	No.	%	No.	%	No.	%	TOTAL NO.
Fans	10	10.2	15	10.3	26	15.0	17	11.7	68
Readers	31	31.6	51	35.2	65	37.6	66	45.6	213
Partial Readers	34	34.7	52	35.9	53	30.6	48	33.1	187
Non-readers	23	23.5	27	18.6	29	16.8	14	9.6	93
	98		145		173		145		561

Children in Family
with Two Parents

	NONE		ONE		TWO OR MORE		
	No.	%	No.	%	No.	%	TOTAL NO.
Fans	0	0.0	14	10.7	40	13.8	54
Readers	0	0.0	45	34.4	120	41.6	165
Partial Readers	54	62.8	47	35.8	92	31.8	193
Non-readers	32	37.2	25	19.1	37	12.8	94
	86		131		289		506

* Includes divorced and widowed as well as married.

with the problems of child-rearing. When the families with children are examined more closely, the age of their children is found to be completely unrelated to community readership. In a sense, the children cast an advancing shadow which contributes to community orientations among the parents. As the children mature, these community orientations seem to persist not only in terms of the changing concrete involvements of the children in the community—community facilities, grammar and high school, marriage, and war experience of the children's friends—all of which make community news, but they persist after the children have left home.

The relationship between having children and community newspaper readership should not be attributed solely to the apparent functional requirements children create which the community newspaper helps to serve with concrete information and news. Having children and creating an effective family involves social psychological orientations reflective of the roots of personality. Thus, in future research it would seem relevant to investigate the link between personality dynamics linking the family oriented individual and community orientations.

Status

When families were identified in terms of total income and occupation of the head of the household, as in the cases of many other "structural" variables, no significant association was encountered. (Table No. 4 (IV).) Thus, readership remains unrelated to income when community area is held constant. Grouping occupations into three main categories revealed no statistical association; a low but statistically significant link appears only when the extremes of readership are compared with the extremes of occupational status. A specialized scale for status involving prestige ratings of occupation also failed to produce a significant association even though numerous other attributes were held constant.[13]

13. Prestige classes for this sample of respondents could be evolved from the body of data gathered by the National Opinion Research Center survey on occupational prestige. In this survey, a national sample expressed ratings of prestige attached to eighty professions and occupations. The ratings expressed by residents of metropolitan centers over one million were applied to the heads

TABLE NO. 4 (IV)—*Attributes of Community Newspaper Readership*

Income

	UNDER $50		$50-$75		$75-$100		OVER $100		NO	
	No.	%	No.	%	No.	%	No.	%	DATA	TOTAL
Fans	10	11.8	21	10.2	24	15.4	14	9.3	0	69
Readers	30	35.3	84	41.0	60	38.4	50	33.1	0	224
Partial Readers	25	29.4	68	33.2	44	28.2	59	39.1	3	199
Non-readers	20	23.5	32	15.6	28	18.0	28	18.5	0	108
	85		205		156		151		3	598

Occupation *

	SERVICE WORKERS	UN- SKILLED WORKERS	SEMI- SKILLED WORKERS	SKILLED FOREMEN	CLERK, ETC.	PROPRIE- TORS	PROFES- SIONAL
	%	%	%	%	%	%	%
Fans	13.0	3.4	8.4	12.1	15.9	8.3	14.7
Readers	43.5	44.9	42.7	42.8	31.6	41.7	11.8
Partial Readers	30.5	31.0	35.9	29.0	29.7	30.0	55.9
Non-readers	13.0	20.7	13.0	16.1	22.8	20.0	17.6
Number	(23)	(29)	(131)	(124)	(158)	(60)	(34)

* Students and No Data categories omitted.

Social Status

	LOWER- LOWER		UPPER- LOWER		LOWER- MIDDLE		UPPER- MIDDLE		NO	
	No.	%	No.	%	No.	%	No.	%	DATA	TOTAL
Fans	7	9.4	25	12.4	26	11.7	5	10.9	6	69
Readers	36	48.6	76	37.6	84	37.9	12	26.1	16	224
Partial Readers	18	24.3	73	36.1	72	32.4	19	41.3	17	199
Non-readers	13	17.7	28	13.9	40	18.0	10	21.7	17	108
	74		202		222		46		56	600

(Table No. 4 (IV).) Income, occupational structure and status in themselves reveal little about family cohesion or

of households in the sample. (Some arbitrary equivalents had to be made because the list of occupations was incomplete.) The ratings for each community supplied a crude means for delimiting prestige classes in terms of the social class scheme formulated by W. Lloyd Warner. This was done by preparing a frequency distribution for the six hundred classes and arbitrarily class divisions were drawn on the basis of natural breaks in the distribution and the generalized standards of this six-class system of analysis.

about community orientation, especially in the absence of
mobility data. Therefore, the lack of association between these
attributes might have been anticipated.

In the absence of mobility data, an effort was made to
relate social status more meaningfully to community structure by the following hypothesis: Men and women who are
either above or below the status norm of the community, and
thus can be presumed to be less integrated into the community, are less likely to be community newspaper readers
than those whose status approaches the norm for the community. Since the prestige rating scale employed made possible numerical values, the top and bottom fifteen percent
for each community were compared with the remainder of
the sample and *both* groups tended to be lower on the community newspaper readership index even though their
educational attainment "should" have put one group higher
and the other group lower on the readership index. When the
two deviational groups were combined and compared with
the rest of the sample, as between readers and non-readers,
a significant difference at almost .05 was obtained which indicated that social status when conceived in these terms is
likely to be more relevant.

Place of birth and level of education are relevant status
attributes of heads of households. Native-born individuals
might be more likely to be community newspaper readers
since the transition to American culture might hinder community integration. Moreover, the higher education associated with American nativity usually implies a greater pro-
pensity to read, other factors being equal.

The data reveal that place of birth of the respondent—in
Chicago, elsewhere in the U.S.A., or in Europe—is not asso-
ciated with the basic readership index. (Table No. 5 (IV).)
Likewise, amount of education is unrelated to the community

newspaper readership index as a whole. (Table No. 5 (IV).) Even when those who were educated abroad are compared with those who were educated in the United States, no link with community newspaper readership is present. However, by comparing the extremes in educational level, the college educated with the grade school, a significant association emerges in which the best educated tend to read less.[14]

Community press readership thus might tend to differ from the readership of many other types of printed material in that those with higher education are somewhat less interested in the community press. Education perhaps constitutes a degree of sophistication leading away from local orientations. The data on other attributes—occupation and social status—as well as on community identification, presented below, do not seem to support this contention strongly.

Finally, the family and its status position can be viewed in terms of sex- and age-grading. The tasks assigned to the woman, particularly as a purchaser, would orient her more to the local community, and certain years in the life cycle of the family should be more closely tied to the community. As was expected, women were more extensive readers than men. (Table No. 5 (IV).) However, the difference was not pronounced.[15] When fans were compared with non-readers, the influence of sex of the respondent emerges more sharply and in part accounts for the community newspaper publisher's

---

14. When length of residence, a key correlate of community newspaper readership, is held constant, educational differences in community newspaper readership become statistically insignificant. The extent of educational influence emerges when the sex of the respondent is held constant. Among the women, fans and regular readers tend to be more heavily concntrated at the lower educational levels (statistical significance is at the .05 level). For men, the difference in educational level is statistically significant at the .01 level with better educated men being poorer community newspaper readers.

15. The level of significance was only at the .05 level for the sample as a whole.

TABLE NO. 5 (IV)—*Attributes of Community Newspaper Readership*

Sex

	MALE No.	%	FEMALE No.	%	TOTAL NO.
Fans	30	10.0	39	13.0	69
Readers	100	33.3	124	41.3	224
Partial Readers	107	35.7	92	30.7	199
Non-Readers	63	21.0	45	15.0	108
	300		300		600

Age

	UNDER 29 No.	%	30-39 No.	%	40-49 No.	%	50-59 No.	%	60-OVER No.	%	NO DATA No.	TOTAL NO.
Fans	8	9.6	15	8.8	22	16.0	11	9.5	13	14.0		69
Readers	25	30.2	62	36.5	49	35.8	51	44.0	37	39.8		224
Partial Readers	29	34.9	60	35.3	48	35.1	36	31.0	26	28.0		199
Non-Readers	21	25.3	33	19.4	18	13.1	18	15.5	17	18.2	1	108
	83		170		137		116		93		1	600

Place of Birth

	CHICAGO No.	%	ELSE-WHERE U.S.A. No.	%	EUROPE No.	%	NO DATA No.	TOTAL NO.
Fans	35	10.7	23	14.4	11	9.9		69
Readers	128	39.3	50	31.3	45	40.1		224
Partial Readers	101	31.0	66	41.2	31	27.7	1	199
Non-Readers	62	19.0	21	13.1	25	22.3	1	108
	326		160		112		2	600

Education of Respondent

	GRADE SCHOOL No.	%	TEN YEARS No.	%	TWELVE YEARS No.	%	SOME COL. & COLLEGE No.	%	NO DATA No.	TOTAL NO.
Fans	30	13.1	8	8.4	19	10.7	11	11.6	1	69
Readers	103	45.0	34	35.4	62	35.0	24	25.3	1	224
Partial Readers	68	29.7	32	33.3	64	36.2	34	35.7	1	199
Non-Readers	28	12.2	22	22.9	32	18.1	26	27.4		108
	229		96		177		95		3	600

assumption that his paper appeals predominantly to women. Readership among housewives was significantly greater as compared to that of working wives.

This association is linked to the other indices of family cohesion which help to explain community readership. The importance of social role, rather than sex per se, can be seen from the fact that among the community leaders, those with strongest community ties, men tended to outread women.

The link between sex and community newspaper readership involves to some extent a self-confirming proposition. Since the publisher believes that the women's role orients them toward community preoccupations (shopping, child raising, etc.), they believe that they should slant their papers toward women's interests. (The content analysis hardly indicates that this imbalance is great.) However, there is also a modification in the "traditional" notion of the division of labor between men and women which implies not only that women develop broader orientations but also that men tend to assume certain social functions of women. Consequently men develop new community orientations (concerning child-raising and consumption) and the distinction between men's and women's interests is increasingly more difficult to make.

Age-grading revealed no straight-line associations with community newspaper readership although it seems reasonable to expect that later maturity might reflect a declining orientation to community life. (Table No. 3 (IV).) Viewing the life cycle of the 600 respondents in ten year periods, there is a tendency for greater readership in middle life. One association of statistical significance does emerge in that the group under 30 read less than the 40-49 age grouping. If this association appears spurious, it perhaps relates to previous data on family structure, and forthcoming data on community integration.

Community Integration as an Attribute of Readership

From a range of indices measuring community orientations, the evidence supports the hypothesis that greater community orientation on the part of the respondent is positively
related to more community press readership. However, reading of the community newspaper might be viewed as being
related to pseudo-community orientations—ersatz ideologies
designed to overcome isolation in the "big city"—without
realistic or meaningful counterparts in community behavior.
Therefore, not only did the indices of community integration
need to investigate identifications which might be suspect as
idealized expressions; in addition, emphasis had to be placed
on crucial phases of community-oriented behavior and participation. In examining these attributes of community participation, place of work, place of shopping, participation in
voluntary associations, neighbor contacts and the location of
friends, a definite pattern appears. Higher amounts of association with community readership are present as the indices
become more a measure of discretion and choice on the part
of the individual and therefore are more likely to reveal
genuine, as opposed to arbitrary and spurious orientations.

Length of Residence

In a metropolitan center which is constantly undergoing
growth and change, length of residence is a primary characteristic reflective of a wide range of motives and practices. A
longer period of residence, either in the community or in
the individual's present house, significantly increases reader-

TABLE NO. 6 (IV)—*Attributes of Community Newspaper Readership*

Length of Residence in Community

	UP TO 9 YEARS		10-19 YEARS		20 YRS. AND OVER		TOTAL NO.
	No.	%	No.	%	No.	%	
Fans	12	8.2	12	10.2	45	13.4	69
Readers	38	26.0	39	33.0	147	43.8	224
Partial Readers	58	39.8	40	33.9	101	30.0	199
Non-Readers	38	26.0	27	22.9	43	12.8	108
	146		118		336		600

Length of Residence in Present House

	UP TO 4 YEARS		5-14 YEARS		15 YRS. AND OVER		TOTAL NO.
	No.	%	No.	%	No.	%	
Fans	16	8.7	24	10.8	29	15.1	69
Readers	58	31.5	82	36.8	84	43.5	224
Partial Readers	67	36.4	75	33.6	57	29.5	199
Non-Readers	43	23.4	42	18.8	23	11.9	108
	184		223		193		600

Length of Residence in Present House

	LESS THAN 2 YEARS	2-4 YEARS	5-9 YEARS	10-14 YEARS	15-19 YEARS	20 YRS. AND OVER
Atwater						
Readers	7	12	26	13	7	39
Non-Readers	14	27	19	7	9	20
Bethel Park						
Readers	14	18	13	20	12	26
Non-Readers	16	22	22	12	9	16
Carleton Manor						
Readers	8	15	22	13	8	20
Non-Readers	18	13	38	19	7	19

ship. (Table No. 6 (IV).) Among the group of community leaders community residential stability acts in the same manner but to an even greater degree. In fact, a startling pattern of local stability of residence is presented by these community leaders. Almost one-third of the sample of fifty had resided in their present community for their entire life, with an average length of residence of over 22 years. While the three communities are probably more stable than the city as a whole, these data help to correct the image of big city "rootlessness" and indicate the degree to which community leadership is a function of residential stability.

The link between residential stability and community newspaper readership (and community integration) is hardly a one-to-one relationship. The pattern varies from community to community depending on historical and sociological circumstances. In general, after the first ten years, the chance of becoming a community newspaper reader seems to decrease. However, the effect of length of residence as a factor in community readership is highlighted when the number of children in the family is held constant. For families with two or more children, readership once the children are born increases less through years of residence than in families where there are no children or only one child. Thus, the children act as a catalyst in the process of community integration which is also possible through relatively long community residence.

Residential stability for the three communities varies; and the effect of residential stability within each community seems to vary. From Table No. 6 (IV), the balance between readers and non-readers in the three communities can be seen in terms of length of residence. In Atwater, a minimum number of years of residence, between five and nine years, is required before a majority of the respondents tend to become community newspaper readers. Atwater scores high on many indices of community solidarity and stands in opposition to the stereotype of the lower-class community where neighborhood relations are either absent or, if they exist, are only casual. The geographical isolation of the community plus the power of the Catholic Church with its separate educational system and its organizational affiliates have maintained community cohesion. The fact that the majority of the new residents are Catholic assist this process, although they are of different ethnic origin.

In Bethel Park, a slightly longer period of residence is required before the majority of respondents is likely to fall into the high readership class. Carleton Manor presents the most interesting case. In this middle-class community, for some residents integration and community newspaper readership emerges early, between two and four years of residence; these are the families with children of school age. For others the process takes many years. In fact, for this community area, the association between length of residence and readership hardly emerges and for certain years is reversed. The strong pull toward the Loop which arises despite actual distance not only out of the rapid transportation system but also out of employment and occupational patterns of husbands, is a factor in accounting for the lack of higher association between residential stability and community press readership.[16]

---

16. House type might also be considered as an attribute related to community newspaper readership. It is generally assumed that closer identification develops around one's own home than the impersonal multiple-dwelling unit and that the home owner has a larger stake in the community. It is also generally assumed that the period of residence in a multiple-dwelling unit is likely to be shorter. Single-family home owners therefore might be presumed to be better community newspaper readers than are residents of multiple-dwelling units. In these three communities no association was encountered between home ownership and readership. A statistically significant association (.05 level) was encountered between house type (single, double, multiple) and community newspaper readership. For these three communities, a range of attributes measuring community integration in the particular community is more fundamental in a sociological sense than is type of ownership of dwelling unit. No doubt for the city as a whole, more of an association between type of dwelling unit and community newspaper readership might be found,

Consumption and Work

Because of the wide extent of local shopping in the three communities, it was expected at the outset that an association would be found between shopping habits and community newspaper readership. However, when each community is treated separately, no tendency emerges for local shoppers to read the community newspaper more than do non-local shoppers; nor does holding education constant produce any differences.[17] Respondents were classified into those who shopped predominantly in the local community, those who shopped predominantly in the Loop and those who shopped in both centers. ("Shopping" was here defined as for clothes and furniture to distinguish such habits from routine purchases for food, etc.) This was no simple procedure and may not have been adequately achieved; it may, in fact, be a false distinction. In addition, shopping habits are behavior patterns over which the individual exercises some control, yet a wide range of arbitrary considerations enter in, such as transportation, work habits, availability of goods, which limit the usefulness of this measure.

Similarly, place of work was not found to be associated with community newspaper readership. Over fifteen percent of the sample worked either in the community area or in a community area immediately adjoining. A wide variety of factors enters into the respondents' place of work, over many of which the individual can exercise little or only nominal control. Thus, place of work does not constitute an important characteristic revealing community or non-community orientations.

---

but even here size of dwelling would be an indirect measure of more significant sociological attributes which can be ascertained more directly.

17. These data underline the conclusion at various points in the study that the community newspaper is not perceived as an "advertising sheet."

Voluntary Associations, Neighborhood Contacts, and Friends

In contrast to place of work and place of shopping, participation in local voluntary associations is somewhat more revealing of community orientations in that here the individual exercises greater power of decision. A positive association was established between readership and participation in local voluntary associations.[18] When church attendance was analyzed as a separate measure of local voluntary association participation, no difference in community readership was found as between Protestant, Catholic, and Jewish affiliation even though the Protestants were grouped into fundamentalist, middle, and high status denominations. Frequency of church attendance, however, which varied markedly between the three communities, was linked with community newspaper readership to a higher degree than was voluntary association membership.[19] Church attendance and community newspaper readership are further linked in that church attendance within the community tends to be associated with higher community newspaper readership

Neighborhood contacts and patterns of friendship are underlying indices of community integration and cohesion which involve individual choice to a considerable degree. With the separation of place of residence from place of work, it is increasingly assumed that work contacts become dominant in determining patterns of social contact. If this were the case, and it is probably so only for certain specialized upper-

---

18. The level of significance was .02; holding education constant does not alter the association.

19. Atwater, with its high readership, is a predominantly Catholic community with an extremely high regular church attendance. Carleton Manor is a mixed Protestant-Catholic community with lower church attendance. The Catholic hierarchy publishes a local Catholic publication which may in part account for the lower community newspaper interest. Bethel Park is also mixed Protestant and Catholic with the lowest church attendance.

middle and middle-middle class groups, social contacts in the neighborhood and in the community would measure orientations away from the place of work toward the place of residence and consumption.

Over seventy percent of the total sample reported regular visiting with their neighbors, neighbors usually implying residents in the immediate vicinity or on the block. Such visiting showed a statistical association with readership. Further probing was designed to determine in greater detail how much contact was actually involved. Rating men and women as to whether they had no or little contact, some contact, or much contact with neighbors seems more reflective of actual patterns of neighborhood contact than a dichotomy of visiting and non-visiting respondents and produced a high level of association with community newspaper readership. (Table No. 7 (IV).) The data indicate that as the length of residence increases so do neighborhood contacts but, as in the case of increased newspaper readership after the fifth year, the increases are less as compared to the first years of residence.

Men and women who had many of their friends in the community, as opposed to those having non-community patterns of friendship, produced the highest degree of association of the individual indices of community integration. When three of the individual measures of community integration—length of residence, contacts with neighbors and location of friends—are combined, an index of markedly higher association is produced (Table No. 7 (IV).)[20]

---

20. The amount of contact with neighbors and patterns of friendship vary from community to community, but the expected higher amount of contact among women in the community was not pronounced nor even statistically significant. In fact, in Atwater and Bethel Park, men have almost as much contact as do women, because of the strong role of local ethnic voluntary and veterans' associations which establish contacts that persist in the local neigh-

TABLE NO. 7 (IV)—*Attributes of Community Newspaper Readership*

Social Contact with Neighbors

	NONE		SOME		MUCH		NO	TOTAL
	No.	%	No.	%	No.	%	DATA	NO.
Fans	10	5.5	22	11.8	37	16.7	0	69
Readers	56	30.9	76	40.6	92	41.5	0	224
Partial Readers	67	37.1	59	31.6	63	28.3	10	199
Non-Readers	48	26.5	30	16.0	30	13.5	0	108
	181		187		222		10	600

Location of Friends

	HERE IN COMMUNITY		HERE AND OUTSIDE		OUTSIDE COMMUNITY		TOTAL NO.
	No.	%	No.	%	No.	%	
Fans	41	16.2	14	9.7	14	6.9	69
Readers	113	44.5	49	34.0	62	30.8	224
Partial Readers	72	28.3	55	38.2	72	35.6	199
Non-Readers	28	11.0	26	18.1	54	26.7	108
	254		144		202		600

Index of Community Integration

	LOW		MEDIUM		HIGH		TOTAL NO.
	No.	%	No.	%	No.	%	
Fans	5	6.0	35	9.4	29	20.0	69
Readers	21	25.0	131	35.4	72	49.7	224
Partial Readers	33	39.3	127	34.2	39	26.9	199
Non-Readers	25	29.7	78	21.0	5	3.4	108
	84		371		145		600

Community Identifications

The link of community press readership and behavior reflecting community integration made possible the analysis of community identifications not merely as an ideology independent of actual locally oriented practices. In fact, if strong community identifications did not relate to community news-

borhood. In Carleton Manor, professional and business men were more influenced in their social contacts by work contacts which tended to draw them away from the local community area.

paper readership in the light of the data set forth the measures of community identifications might themselves be doubtful. A range of indices was employed which involved over-all attitudes toward the local community as well as evaluation of specific aspects of community life. All of these showed significant association in varying amounts with community newspaper readership. (For examples, Table No. 8 (IV).) In

TABLE NO. 8 (IV)—*Attributes of Community Newspaper Readership*

Attitude toward Community

	LIKE IT		DISLIKE IT		TOTAL
	No.	%	No.	%	No.
Fans	67	12.8	2	2.7	69
Readers	204	38.8	20	26.7	224
Partial Readers	172	32.8	27	36.0	199
Non-Readers	82	15.6	26	34.6	108
	525		75		600

Community is "Real Home"

	YES		NO		OTHER		DON'T KNOW	TOTAL
	No.	%	No.	%	No.	%	No.	No.
Fans	63	13.0	2	3.0	3	7.1	1	69
Readers	194	40.0	18	26.8	11	26.2	1	224
Partial Readers	149	30.7	32	47.8	15	35.7	3	199
Non-Readers	79	16.3	15	22.4	13	31.0	1	108
	485		67		42		6	600

addition, the question, "Do you think of this community as your real home?" revealed the closest link with community newspaper readership among the measures of community identification, since it probably tapped underlying feelings most accurately. (Table No. 8 (IV).) Yet all these measures produced responses that were so heavily weighted on the side of high community identification that the projective aspects of the replies were even more relevant.

Some indication of what lies underneath this facade emerged when men and women were probed as to why they liked their local community. Among readers and non-readers, comments on the facilities of the local community were scattered at random and represent reasonable judgments to varying degrees. However, almost all of the men and women could be classified as to whether they were "people" oriented in their identifications; that is, gave answers about the people in the community, or whether they were oriented to "physical conditions"; that is, gave generalized or specific statements about the physical condition and appearance of the community. Typical of the first was:

"Everybody is very nice—honest neighbors—things can safely be left out of doors."

Typical of the second was:

"I like the neighborhood itself. It is neat and clean and there is good transportation."

Those who liked the community because of its "human resources" were more likely to be community newspaper readers than those who viewed the community in terms of its "physical resources." This held true for all communities, regardless of their actual physical conditions, for in each case the men and women were projecting their own values and needs.

V

The Impact
of Readership:
Interest,
Penetration,
and Imagery

The contents of the community newspaper are clearly tame by most literary standards for judging dramatic or melodramatic content. These contents, moreover, must run the gantlet of severe communications competition. Reactions that emerge are worthy of analysis if only because, given the competition to drown out the "feeble" signal of the community press, it is a question for some whether the readers retain any after-image at all. The proposition emerges, however, that the community newspaper's emphasis on community routines, low controversy and social ritual are the very characteristics which account for its readership.

If the theory of marginal utility is applied to communication research, the clarity and range of reactions to the community press indicate that various types of communications have markedly varying elasticity of demand. Data on the impact of the community press, if they fail to reveal anything else, underline the remarkable ability of the individual to select what he wants in his communication diet from the total flow of mass media; nevertheless, in an interview he may be limited in his ability to state what he would like to have more or less of. Self-selection is such a powerful defense that the balance between supply and demand is so altered that it is possible for the community press to be effective and penetrating.

However, self-selection as a concept is not limited merely to exposure, and thereby to the competition for exposure between the community press and the mass media. This can be seen from the fact that the community newspaper is not a competitor for mere exposure with the daily press, the radio, the magazine, the book or the public library.

Comparisons with daily newspaper readership were difficult because the interviews did not permit adequate analysis of the dimensions of daily newspaper readership. Except for a very small minority, all respondents claimed some amount of daily newspaper reading, while about fifty percent read two or more papers daily. Non-radio listeners were limited to five percent, 40 percent listening at least one hour per day, 30 percent at least two hours, while almost 25 percent reported three hours' listening per day. One-third of the sample did not read any magazines, while 70 percent never read books.

In general, greater exposure to each of these media does not produce lower exposure to the community newspaper, as measured by the basic readership index. Nor did sophistication of mass media habits, as measured by tastes in magazine readership, produce a negative association. If anything, the opposite is the case. Community newspaper fans, as compared with non-readers, tend to be more intense daily newspaper readers.[1] Television viewing was even more clearly associated with community newspaper readership.[2]

Self-selection has the broader meaning of referring to the ability of the individual to allow or not allow himself to react or be influenced. In these terms, the dimensions of *interest*, *penetration* and *imagery* are important. Analytic refinements, nevertheless, should not obscure the simple fact that the impact of community newspapers is conditioned by the smaller number of pages they contain and the relief this affords the readers who are overbombarded by the mass media.

Reader Interest and Content

Although the history of the community press and its economic organization clearly attest to its commercial origin, its management, in the process of seeking economic advancement, found themselves in close contact with those elements in the community seeking to maintain the existing consensus, or to modify it only gradually. Within the space allocated to text, the community press presents a wide range of activities and values not given expression in the daily press. Community press content, with its low quotient of controversy, produces a high level of readership. But uniformities in the background and outlook of the personnel as well as uniformities in the content which they produce, do not necessarily indicate that uniformities exist in communication impact. An

---

1. Significant at the .02 level.
2. Since the research was carried out during the initial phase of the rapid expansion of television, these data are not conclusive but probably indicate that both television-viewing and the community newspaper readership involve family orientation.

analysis, first of *interest* and *penetration*, and then of *imagery*, seeks to press more deeply into subjective meanings and psychological functions of the community newspaper. Only by an examination of these dimensions of readership can the newspaper be seen as a guide to elements of urban personality.

Specific reader interest and patterns of interests emerged from a series of direct questions which were employed after the level of the individual's exposure had been ascertained. The data are presented for each community area in Table No. 1 (V). Atwater's slightly higher readership accounts for the slightly greater interest in most types of content but it should be recalled that there was no clear-cut association between level of exposure-involvement and interest patterns. (See page 121).[3]

TABLE NO. 1 (V)—*Interest Patterns in the Three Community Newspapers*

| | PERCENT OF TOTAL SAMPLE | | | |
	Atwater %	Bethel Park %	Carleton Manor %	Total Sample
Ordinarily reads:				
Display advertisements	78.0	69.5	69.5	72.3
Classified advertisements	61.0	65.0	34.5	60.0
Community News	85.5	77.5	78.5	80.0
Social and Personal News	63.5	61.0	51.5	58.0
Church	61.0	42.0	53.5	52.1
Voluntary Associations ("Club")	43.5	25.5	37.5	35.3
Sports (Men Only)	57.0	42.0	33.0	43.8

3. Breakdown by sex further elaborates the higher interest of women in the community press. They outrank men in all categories, except for political matters in which their interest is markedly less. When area and sex are held constant, the lower readership of Carleton Manor's men of social, club and church news emerges and is reflective of the middle-middle class community whose men find their social contacts influenced by their work.

But the significance of *reader interest* depended on linking these findings to the content analysis data. On the content side, the analysis of the three newspapers for which readership was studied (presented in Table No. 9 (III)), was recast from the detailed categories into broader ones actually encountered in the pretest of readership. Relative weights were assigned so as to encompass the advertising material and thereby give a picture based upon the allocation of space of the communications stimuli presented to the reader. (Table No. 2 (V).)

TABLE NO. 2 (V)—*Divergence between Content and Interest*

		CONTENT PERCENT	ORDINARILY READ * PERCENT
Display Advertisements	61.5		72.3
Classified Advertisements	13.5		60.1
Total Advertisements		75.0	
Community News		10.5	80.5
Social and Personal News		5.0	58.6
Local Voluntary Associations		3.5	35.3
Sports		1.0	43.8 (men only)
Religion		.9	52.1
Others		4.1	. . .
		100.0	

* Percent of total sample.

One of the implications of this table is that the relative ranking of space and reader interest is high, thereby indicating a close, reciprocal interaction between publisher and audience. However, when considered in connection with other types of data, certain divergences appear.

The large amount of advertising material gains high readership, as does community news. However, the considerably decreased allocation of space to personal and social news is not accompanied by a corresponding decrease in level of interest. News of voluntary associations ("clubs") receives less attention than its relative space allocation would warrant. This is indicative of community press efforts to "support" and "push" local associations. Religious news presents a considerable divergence in that the minor allocation of religious news is accompanied by extensive readership; the same holds true for sports among men readers.

It cannot be argued that a direct parallel should exist between the editor's allocation of space and the amount of reader interest. This would be a mechanical approach for the existence of a specific interest does not necessarily mean that it can only be served by a major allocation of space. But the editor's allocations of space reflect his belief in the canon of daily journalism; this the content analysis has established. Yet editors and publishers are quite aware of the actual pattern of interest in their publications; this was established in interviews with them. Over half of them gave social and personal news as a dominant interest of the readers of the community; community news got almost as many choices, but frequently as a secondary interest. The remarks of one publisher represent a revealing view of the pattern of interest in the community press:

"The first thing they do when they get the paper is to turn to the inside pages and read the personals. Then after that they'll turn to the front page to see what stories we have on the leading page. Then after that they'll look inside again to read the classified ads; and finally they'll look at the displays."

What would happen if the community publisher went all out for social and personal items? (He would be unlikely to make such changes because of the need for legitimizing him-

self as a publisher.) His advertisers would undoubtedly feel
that the medium would be cheapened, as do national advertisers who currently look down on the community press.
But this study, viewed as a piece of market research, indicates
that increased emphasis in this direction might enhance
readership. However, there are reasons to believe that such
changes would not produce the desired result, but might be
in error. Conformity to a format of accepted journalism is
required for the interest of the readers as well as the publishers and advertisers. Regardless of their genuine interests in
the news of the community, readers want their interest in
"gossip" served in the false packaging of the more prestigeful
daily press. They seem to guard themselves against overindul-
gence in a practice which, if held within limits, is considered
keeping oneself legitimately informed, but which might de-
generate into an undesirable interest in scandal and cliquish-
ness.

Questions on specific reader interests supplied opportunities to probe for specific overt reactions which might be
traced to community newspaper content. Direct questioning
on overt reactions leaves much to be desired with regard to
the validity of the response because it may be projective of
underlying imagery. Readership of advertisements, both display and classified, was followed up by direct queries on the
use of such information by readers. The responses, which are,
of course, subject to inflation, are of considerable magnitude.
Over half of the total population claimed they obtain shopping information from display ads and well over one-third
made similar claims for classified ads.

Throughout the interviews men and women readers voluntarily gave a steady flow of specific examples of the relevance
of the community paper to their community routines. Associative comments were heavily characterized by a flavor of

concrete detail indicating the role of the community newspaper in supplying specific news to assist adjustment to the institutions and facilities of urban life.

Responses connected with church and voluntary associations figure prominently:

"It's a good paper and people miss it when it doesn't come. Our church would miss it very much. Our rummage sale is always advertised in the Bethel Park Bulletin." (56 year-old Bethel Park housewife who is a regular reader.)

"Keeps me in touch with the people I have to know in community work, especially the Red Cross." (56 year-old employed nurse and mother of two children, who resides in Carleton Manor.)

Especially in regard to advertisements, specific behavior was mentioned:

"I like looking for sales, particularly suit sales. I always look for sales. Right now I am looking for a piano in the classified ads and I got some good leads." (31 year-old Carleton Manor businessman who is a regular reader.)

The efforts of the community newspaper to supply news relevant to raising the young do not go unrewarded:

"I have an awful fit when it doesn't come. I depend on it especially for news for the children . . . I think it is very nice. Get all kinds of information for the benefit of the children. There was the notice recently of free ballet lessons at the community center and free singing lessons. The girls can take advantage of that." (50 year-old housewife with two daughters, 9 and 15, who is a fan of the *Northeast Advocate*.)

The paper may also be a guide to purely idiosyncratic behavior:

"I read obituaries and marriages especially. I'll check up if a neighbor has died, I'll make a special trip to them and say a prayer for them." (72 year-old retired contractor who resides in Bethel Park.)

Another group of respondents, although they did not mention specific, concrete examples, revealed a similar outlook:

"I get home and holler if I can't find it. I really like to read it. My wife hides it from me. I take it with me on my truck and read it at lunch time." (37 year-old Atwater truckdriver.)

"I can't wait until Wednesday comes to get it. If it doesn't come I miss it by six. If the boy hasn't brought it I feel a little lost. Up to 6 it's all right—I know the boy goes to school and by the time he gets out it's late. But after 6 I feel something missing, so I go out and start to look for him, for I feel something missing." (47 year-old Bethel Park housewife with three children.)

Attachment can, of course, involve merely staving off the alternative of boredom:

"Really I read it just to pass the time like when riding on the street car. You have to pull something out to read." (31 year-old mother of four children who works as a folding-box machine operator and lives in Atwater.)

It remained for the publishers themselves to supply an almost endless stream of documentation of the specific interests in their paper and in the concrete reactions generated by its contents. (Implications of these data are included in Chapter VI, The Social Role of the Community Publisher: Agent of Personal and Mass Communications.) For example:

"During the last war, the ———— plant out here had a new crop of vegetables that had to go into cans fast or they'd rot. . . . Well they came down to see if they could get some help. Well, they were referred over to me—Well they told me they had 275,000 cases of tomatoes that would rot if they didn't get into cans within a few days. . . . Well I looked at them and knew that they just were here because they wanted to save the money they had tied up in tomatoes. . . . They came to us for help but when they're doing advertising do we get any of it? No! But I told them I wouldn't want to do anything that would prevent their getting overseas to the boys in the Army. So I told them to have a man down at the Civilian Defense

Office on Thursday to take care of applications. They'd said they'd send a man down. So we printed a story on it. . . . They sent us some stuff they wanted us to print but we said we'll print the story our way . . . 'no experience necessary' they said—what in hell does that mean to the people out here? There's one thing we know—that's how to talk to the people in their own language. So we put in a story that said—anybody who can handle a paring knife . . . that's what we said. . . . Well we had to loan them 6 of our staff to help them with the applications. Out of about 2,000 people who applied by the time they got done they took on 600 people."

Patterns of Penetration

Similarities of interest between the readers of the three communities give way to striking differences in penetration of content. Such deviations would be expected since recall involves to a greater degree basic concerns and attitudes which can be related to the class level of the three sample communities, if not (in this study) to underlying personality structure. Penetration was measured by the crude index of remembrance of recent news about the community. A tabulation of the responses is presented in Table No. 3 (V); since the frequencies are too small for statistical analysis they are analyzed for the patterns which they suggest.

For the total sample, items of penetration, with the exception of the high mention of community history in Atwater, seem to follow the general pattern that the *type of content which received the most allocation of space is most frequently remembered.* For each community where penetration becomes more of a social projection reflecting local community concerns, interesting differences in penetration emerge.

Mention of municipal services varies directly with standard of living and social status; those that have the most and best services are most sensitized to the maintenance of what they have and to the acquisition of more. (Atwater lowest, 9 men-

TABLE NO. 3 (v)—*Penetration of Community Newspaper Content*

TYPES OF ITEMS RECALLED	ATWATER NO. OF MENTIONS	BETHEL PARK NO. OF MENTIONS	CARLTON MANOR NO. OF MENTIONS	TOTAL
Municipal Services				
School, parks	5	10	25	
Local improvements	4	7	13	
	9	17	38	64
Community History	61	0	1	62
Social and Personal	11	17	28	56
Voluntary Associations	14	10	16	40
Crime	16	4	11	31
Church	4	4	11	19
Public Housing Controv.	2	0	13	15
Politics	1	7	1	9
Other	9	15	8	32

tions; Bethel Park second, 17 mentions; and Carleton Manor highest, 28 mentions.) As would be expected, concern about schools presents much the same picture. By contrast, in the struggle for respectability which is common to all communities, lower-class Atwater remembers its crime news, an immediate and direct concern, more than do the other communities, despite the editor's attempt to minimize crime. It is striking to note that in Carleton Manor, which claimed the lowest readership of social and personal news, such items were remembered more frequently than in the other two lower-status communities. The need for false packaging in this regard seems to be important for this social stratum.

Bethel Park's more frequent mention of politics and Carleton Manor's recall of the public housing debate represent not only a variation in local concerns, but reflect variations in editorial emphasis in the content allocated to controversy.

The high penetration of community history in Atwater requires special explanation; at the time of the field study, Atwater was preparing to celebrate an historical anniversary and each week *The Atwater News* carried a special story of the Atwater of many years ago. Nevertheless, it would be easy to dismiss interest in community history, in a lower-class community such as Atwater, as a manipulative effort on the part of the editor, or an interest on the part of the reader, which is really a substitute of real identifications. Newness and modernization are too powerful preoccupations not to make interest in local history somewhat suspect. To some extent this may be true of Atwater's interest in its history. However, Atwater is too well organized and too well integrated to dismiss this preoccupation solely as a false manifestation of community cohesion.

Preoccupation with community history is compatible with interest in newness and modernization, for it is through the history of the community that standards are available to judge social change and personal achievement. Atwater's history is the history of its old horsedrawn fire engines which have been supplanted by new equipment; it is also the history of "local boys" who have made the "big time." The presentation of community history represents an attempt by the community newspaper to make available the peculiar view of history held by Americans in which history is not cherished for the values of history per se but as a criterion against which to measure "progress" in a self-congratulatory fashion.

The After-Image

Systematic investigation of *imagery*—reaction to format and content character in general—which persists after exposure is an approach to ascertaining subjective and psychological implications of the community press for its readers. Many of the specific questions on readership were designed to produce indirect and associative comments revealing imagery; therefore, analysis of the respondents' imagery depended on an analysis of all the data on readership.[4]

Four themes in general encompass the main elements of the image of the community press held by its *readers:*

1. The community press is generally perceived as an auxiliary not as a competing news source with the daily press (and tends to be viewed favorably because of its preoccupation with the details of the local community which are unreported in the daily press).

2. The community press is not generally perceived as a medium which is "commercialized."

3. The community press is not generally perceived as political or partisan but rather as an agent of community welfare and progress.

4. The community press is generally perceived as an extension of the reader's personal and social contacts because of its emphasis on news about voluntary associations and local social and personal news. As such, it constitutes a device for democratizing prestige, especially since there are few barriers

---

4. This procedure, at least guaranteed that the categories for analyzing imagery would include responses of all the respondents and not merely the most colorful responses.

to inserting personal or organizational news. For the majority, this function as an extension and reenforcement of social contacts which have real existence in the local community. Only for a minority does involvement with the news and personalities of the community press operate as a substitute gratification because of the individual's lack or paucity of social contacts in the local community. This proposition, as it applies to the urban community press, stands in contradistinction to the current view of the mass media which contends that significant portions of the mass media substitute for real social contact.

Non-readers, likewise, do not view the community press as overly commercial or politically partisan. Their non-readership arises mainly out of a lack of interest in the content and seldom evokes sharp criticism.

1. *The community newspaper is generally perceived as an auxiliary not as a competing news source with the daily press (and tends to be viewed favorably because of its preoccupation with the details of the local community which are unreported in the daily press).* When readers were asked whether the community newspaper devoted too little or too much news to the local community, the response was an acceptance by the majority (72.5 percent) of the present balance which overwhelmingly emphasizes local news and local orientations. (A quantitative content analysis of a three-month's sample of the community press in Chicago revealed that in 1949, 75.4 percent of the space dealt with local community affairs, 9.3 percent with sectors of the city, 14.8 percent with city-wide affairs, while the rest was concerned with state, national, and international affairs or was not classifiable.) However, when the present balance was questioned, criticism was almost all in the direction of demanding more local news (15.5 percent). The readers, fans, partial readers and glancers, all dis-

played interest in local news content while only a scattered few felt that too much attention was paid to local affairs.

The decision has to be made continually by the community newspaper editor as to how many events shall be selected from outside the limits of the community for publication in his paper. Interview data with editors indicate that, rather universally, the horizons of the editor are broader than those of his readers who tend to emphasize the purely local aspects of the community press.

Opinion was highly articulate among the readers about the distinct purpose a community newspaper serves:

"My goodness, the daily can't take the place of the paper in the community. They have two different functions; the community paper is the only way to keep up with the local area." (36 year-old taxi driver, resident of Carleton Manor.)

An occasional enthusiast even stated:

"You can learn all about your neighborhood. It is more important than the daily paper." (42 year-old housewife of Atwater.)

This image of community newspapers as a source of information lacking in the daily press, expressed in varying forms, was almost universal. Even the non-readers subscribed to it.

This image, together with the mass of examples of respondents on specific overt responses to content, support the proposition that the community newspaper assists adjustments to the institutions and facilities of urban life through the factual information it supplies. However, local news also has a purely symbolic effect. The phrase "keeps us informed," together with its often encountered variants, not only refers to information but has many overtones. The printed word has authority and still quite a bit of magic. Local news incorporates a strong feeling of local pride and personal respect which print enhances. Printing news in the local community paper, for all but those completely disenchanted, identifies and glorifies the persons and institutions reported. If the individual has any personal knowledge of these persons and institutions close at hand or any sense of identification with them, he in turn feels a sense of solidarity and cohesion well beyond merely being informed.

Moreover, community news consists of local news about events and people which the individual is in a better position to verify personally, directly or indirectly, than non-local news. The potentiality for verification is there, and this potentiality is a real factor in conditioning the reader's attitude and relation to the editor. In effect, many readers seem to attribute a higher degree of veracity and trust to community newspaper content than to daily newspaper content. The actual and potential confirmation of specific items casts a halo effect over the entire contents:

"There's more news in our neighborhood paper than in the big ones. And most is the truth too, not like the big papers—they print what they want." (27 year-old housewife of Atwater, with two children.)

"I think the Advocate is more important than the daily paper. Dailies are filled with lies and scandal." (53 year-old transit engineer, resident of Carleton Manor.)

Community newspaper readers do in effect make use of their closer ties in that errors in the community newspaper seldom go by unchallenged. Publishers are always complaining about the volume of complaints covering even apparently the most trivial errors.

2. *The community press is not generally perceived as a medium which is "commercialized."* The perception of commercialism in the case of the community newspaper would involve an image that the paper is merely published for profit, that it contains too many ads, and that it is guilty of a tone

of high pressure tactics, sharp practices and unbridled pursuit of business incentives. To the contrary, the advertising in the community newspaper generally is regarded with real interest and for many considered a genuine aid to daily living.

Previously it was reported that the community newspaper is frequently considered by daily newspaper publishers, the heads of advertising agencies and sophisticated critics of contemporary culture to be "all advertisements." The conclusions of the content analysis indicate that this is a case of distorted perception. Percentagewise, the difference between the amount of advertising in the daily and the community press is trivial; in fact, specific issues of the daily press contain a higher proportion of advertising. In contrast to such an appraisal, it also previously reported that of the six hundred respondents, less than 10 percent of all respondents (readers and non-readers combined) claimed that there were too many advertisements in their local community newspapers.

More positive indication of the lack of a "commercialized" image comes from the high interest among both men and women in display advertisements as an aid to shopping (51.5 percent) and in the classified advertisements as an aid to the respondent's own commercial transactions (37.6 percent).

Readers' beliefs as to why community newspapers are published supply a further clue to imagery. The following question was put to the readers: Did they believe the papers were published to develop community spirit, make a profit, or better community facilities? Only half said that their community newspaper was published to make profit. Getting better community facilities scored equally high while developing community spirit received more affirmative replies. The lack of a conception of the community newspaper as a "commercialized" vehicle seems reasonable in view of the positive attitude towards its content in general and to advertisements in particular. But attributing such altruistic motives to community newspaper publishers is difficult to understand. The fact that the powerful dailies appear more prosperous may help to condition such an image. The low emphasis on controversy and scandal, which arises from the reluctance of the community newspaper publisher to take a purely impersonal view of his content and "do anything for money," is apparently recognized by his readers and thus blocks the commercial image. But the readers surely are engaged in some self deception. They must have a powerful desire not to want to view all media of communication as commercialized and therefore untrustworthy. The community press does display some of the characteristics of non-economic incentives and practices; but this imagery is elaborated by the readers themselves.

3. *The community newspaper is not generally perceived as political or partisan but rather as an agent of community welfare and progress.* None of the three papers could be considered politically neutral. The quantitative content analysis revealed a low news coverage of politics and most limited editorializing. In a non-election period only about one percent of the content dealt explicitly with political party activities and five percent with public affairs material related to politics. However, many of the categories of content supply a vehicle of reporting the activities of local politicians and of offering "news" support to favored candidates in an apparently unpolitical tone. Thus in Atwater, the editor of the *Atwater News* supports the Democratic machine which, at the time of the study, had temporarily lost control of the central ward in the community to Polish Republican forces, and which was returned to office in the last elections. In Bethel Park, the publisher's independent stand confuses the issues, but he supports the Fair Deal and their local Democratic candidates.

The *Northeast Advocate* in Carleton Manor, over the issue of civil rights and public housing, has shifted from favoring traditional Democratic candidates to publicizing Republican candidates.

A small minority of politically alert readers were aware of the political forces at work and the subtle but influential support the papers give to favored candidates. In answer to the question "What does (the name of the paper) stand for in politics?" only 15.4 percent replied either Republican or Democratic. The overwhelming majority of the respondents gave answers which clearly indicated that they did not perceive of the paper in political terms ("it is impartial") or that they were disinterested in its politics.

Low political sensitivity led to the frequent expression of the incompatibility of politics and the community newspaper:

"They stand for progress in the community rather than for anything political." (42 year-old dry cleaner, resident of Carleton Manor.)

"They aren't political, they're a community paper." (22 year-old married laborer, resident of Atwater.)

In fact, politics stand as a threat to the appeal of the paper:

"You feel more intimate with local papers because big papers take sides in politics." (31 year-old resident of Carleton Manor.)

Such an underlying attitude toward the community newspaper was succinctly summarized by the comments of one reader:

"Well, it don't take stands for anything but whatever is in the interest of the community." (36 year-old pharmacist, resident of Carleton Manor.)

The extent of this attitude can be inferred from the fact that, despite the lack of an explicit political imagery, over fifty percent of the sample believed that one of the consequences of their community newspaper was to get better community facilities.

By contrast, among the politically alert, there was some tendency to express strong likes or dislikes for the political slant of the paper:

"That fellow . . . writes sensible editorials, I swear by them . . . In fact, I take them to the shop and pin them up for the fellows to see." (46 year-old machinist, resident of Bethel Park.)

"That's a grade school paper. I never look in there for news. I wish they would cease publishing it. It is vicious, always panning something . . ." (36 year-old housewife, resident of Carleton Manor.)

4. *The community newspaper is perceived generally as an extension of the reader's personal and social contacts because of its emphasis on news about local voluntary associations and local social and personal news. As such it constitutes a device for democratizing prestige.*

Thomas and Znaniecki in their analysis of the development of social cohesion among the peasants of Poland saw much of the contents of the Polish press operating in such a fashion:

"Now the psychological mechanism through which satisfaction of the social instinct is obtained in the wider community also consists in a large measure in supplementing actually experienced response and recognition by imagined response and recognition. The individual who sees his name or his contribution in print imagines the attitude of the readers and this has on him an effect attitudes would have." [5]

The significance of this proposition rests on the key phrase *supplementing actually experienced response and recognition by imagined response and recognition.* For Thomas and Znaniecki, actuality of social contact was requisite and conditioned the use of the press as an extension of primary group

---

5. Thomas, W. I., and Znaniecki, Florian, *The Polish Peasant*, Vol. 4, pp. 264-265.

relations as the basis of larger social cohesion. They did not examine the implication of mass media impact where primary group contacts did not exist. Under such conditions the content would be more likely to serve the individual as a substitute for actual contacts and therefore operate as a substitute gratification.

Therefore, in analyzing the image of the community press connected with social and personal news, a basic distinction was made. For one group, such content might serve as an extension and reinforcement of social contacts which have real existence. For another group, such content would serve as a substitute gratification in the absence of primary social contacts. The number for whom such community press content serves as a substitute, it seemed, would be small as compared with the first group. The community press here loses in the competitive struggle with the mass media, for it is not melodramatic enough to serve effectively the function of supplying phantasy and substitute gratifications. (The likelihood that the same person may get different gratification from different media must also be taken into account; this was beyond the scope of the present study.)

Relevant systematic evidence was difficult to gather for it involved the investigation of underlying motivations which are not readily apparent within the scope of the interview design employed. Nevertheless, much confirming evidence can be marshalled. First, though the reading of social and personal news was extensive, for a significant group there was no reading involvement at all. (Readership ranged from 51.5 percent in Carleton Manor to 61.0 percent in Atwater.) Readership by women exceeded readership by men, and women who read such content were more prone to volunteer their positive attitudes. Readership of social and personal news was associated with length of residence in the community. Even more relevant, such readership was associated with the extent of neighborhood contacts—more contact was linked to higher readership—indicating again that real participation conditioned interest in the social and personal news. Yet the question of distinguishing more precisely those whose readership was motivated by pseudo-involvement and substitute gratification required fuller analysis.

Pseudo-involvement or substitute gratification could best be identified in the instances where the respondent himself voluntarily attested to that fact in describing his reactions to and interests in social and personal news. One group claimed that they read the social and personal news and were strongly interested. Yet these individuals stated that they were unfamiliar or unacquainted with the people whose activities were reported, and thereby indicated pseudo-involvement.

"It's very neighborly even if you don't know the people; you know the streets and you can just about figure out which house they live in."

"I always look for names, maybe you do not know them, but you know they're neighbors."

"The socials are fine—I enjoy reading them even if I don't know the people."

By contrast are the comments highlighting the extension of real involvement:

"We are interested in the neighborhood—that's what it gives you . . . names of people we know. It always has something interesting in the ward, something the city paper hasn't got, you know, it gives the local news about stores and people. You know, about churches and activities in your ward. We're going to put in a notice of the birthday of our little daughter. . . ."

"I think the Northeast Advocate is a very nice paper, so many people you see in it that you know."

"The *Bethel Park Bulletin* is just as good as the Times paper. You don't read about the President's daughter or some prince. That gets tiresome. I like to read about the people I know."

In all, 14 cases were found in which readers clearly revealed themselves in the "substitute gratification" category in that they were interested in social and personal news without having acquaintance with those mentioned. The statements of 33 additional respondents were of such a character as to raise strong presumption of substitute gratification. Direct questioning would have put the respondent on the defensive and produced distortion, yet all the respondents who read the community press had equal opportunity during the probing to express themselves in this regard. Thus, it should hardly be assumed that all who had such attitudes revealed them, although it is quite likely that they did.

In any event, these "substitute gratification" cases are extremely revealing. They were distributed throughout the three communities, and their length of residence was roughly the same as that of the total sample. Nor were they characterized as falling into any particular social status group. Yet all but two had no or few contacts with their neighbors, seldom visited in the neighborhood, and in general claimed that their friends were located outside the community. The number of children in their households is also interesting. The families in which "substitute gratification" was found either had no children, or were, in a few cases, very large families with four or more children; these families were at variance with the family in which community newspaper readership generally was concentrated. Thus, marked deviations in primary group relations and the lack of community orientations led to the use of these social and personal items in the community press as a substitute gratification. It was impossible to investigate to what extent the community newspaper fans who are markedly integrated into the local community, still found substitute gratification in the other mass media; in particular those who boasted loudest of all the people they knew in the columns of the community press. (26 cases.)

An additional observation can be made regarding this imagery. Readership of social and personal news involves "equals." The individuals publicized are men and women quite similar to the reader. Associative remarks revealed not only an interest in the names of neighbors but also a preoccupation with the democratic aspects of prestige. Community social news is written with a bland flair not designed to create special distinction and was perceived in these terms. Easy accessibility to the columns of the paper was frequently mentioned as concrete proof of this point.

"Anyone who wants an item or picture in can get it by sending it in—no special group is a social elite." (56 year-old Carleton Manor contractor.)

Almost 10 percent of all respondents voluntarily mentioned some recent personal or family publicity in the community newspaper. The number who actually made use of the community newspaper facilities is difficult to describe as either large or small. But actual numbers are no more important than an image or ideology which is based on the widespread recognition of the potentialities for prestige which are available for each individual.

Democratization of prestige encompasses news and announcements not only of the various stages of the life cycle but also of death. In addition to a high interest in obituaries, the following attitude was repeatedly offered voluntarily:

"We don't get our names in the big papers even when we die; but the local paper prints everybody's death notice who wants it." (28 year-old Bethel Park pressman.)

"You can get news to be published in the *Atwater News* about deaths without having to pay for it and that's a good thing . . ." (42 year-old Atwater housewife.)

The Imagery of the Non-Reader

The imagery of the non-reader was more difficult to determine than that of the reader, if only because non-readers were more difficult to approach.[6]

Reasons given by the non-reader for his non-readership invariably centered around lack of interest in the contents. The amount of exposure of the non-readers of the community to the daily press, and radio was not strikingly different from the various types of community newspaper readers. Although the educational level of non-readers was somewhat higher, their other media interests hardly characterized them as highly sophisticated. As mentioned above, they did not generally consider their community newspapers as too commercial or too oriented toward advertising, although some held this view. Nor was there much open hostility toward the community press; most non-readers thought that community newspapers ought to be published. The fact of the matter was their imagery expressed their generalized lack of interest. Typical was the response of one woman:

"There's nothing in there that interests me. What's more the kids are all grown up so I don't buy it for them." (51 year-old Bethel Park widow.)

Commercial antagonism when present was usually mixed with a general negative affect toward the paper:

---

6. On the first call a higher proportion of readers than non-readers was encountered than for the sample as a whole; but the practice of making three calls eliminated this bias.

"There are too many ads, there is no news of interest to me; I don't care who gives parties or what is going on in the cabarets."

Lack of community identification figured prominently among reasons for non-readership:

"For those interested in their community it is all right to get news that you can't get in the dailies. Perhaps I would be more interested in the local paper if I lived in a community I felt was home." (26 year-old Carleton Manor electrical engineer.)

For some the newspapers in general were not relevant:

"I'm not much for newspapers. It's just a lot of troubles. This one kills this one and that one kills that one." (33 year-old Bethel Park seamstress.)

"I don't care for newspapers; they can't be relied on and they are poorly written." (48 year-old Army officer who resides in Carleton Manor.)

Non-readership also reflected changed interests:

"I lost interest in neighborhood news after my husband tried in vain to get people to do something for neighborhood improvement. He was block captain but the neighbors weren't interested, they weren't intelligent enough to be reasoned with." (35 year-old Atwater housewife.)

A fuller picture of non-readership was presented in the interview with a Carleton Manor businessman. He is a 41-year-old hardware store man who was born in Southern Illinois and who during eight years of residence in the community has prospered very well indeed. His attitude toward the community, he openly admits, is conditioned by the success of his business and his preference for privacy, but fundamentally he feels the community is dirty. The sewer system needs cleaning up, and there is a great need for better police protection because of the growth of a boys' gang in the nearby community. "If the police won't do something the organizations around here should." "The alderman is a fine man but is hampered by the sad political facts." He feels that most of the precinct captains are just a low grade "bunch of hangers-on." The sad political facts are that "politics is run by a bunch of would-be big shots and fixer-uppers," and therefore nothing will be done to improve the community.

His overwhelmingly negative attitude toward the *Northeast Advocate* persists despite his experiences with it as an advertising medium and despite the appearance of his picture in the paper when a local street improvement in the community was opened. He now only looks at the paper when he runs an advertisement, and that is rare. "I assume that there are people who are interested, especially if they themselves are involved. . . . But for me it is a lost cause."

He is in favor of community newspapers, but the *Northeast Advocate* covers too wide an area. "People around read the news, but a paper can't be run on vanity." "I don't know how much a community paper can serve, but they might try and handle this sewer problem." As far as he himself is concerned the paper does not have much influence, but "I might be mistaken, for it might have some influence." In short, he doesn't read it.

In summary, the findings based on the readership survey attest to the high impact of the urban community press on certain individuals. However, such impact cannot be traced merely to high exposure to its contents, if exposure is defined as the amount of content to which the reader gives his attention. The imagery of the community newspaper in the mind of its readers which is built on and in turn contributes to local social cohesion is a significant underlying element in accounting for its impact.

VI

The Social Role
of the
Community Publisher:
Agent of Personal and
Mass Communications

"Last week a young girl over on B—— Avenue committed suicide. She went over to the lake and jumped off the rocks. Of course it was in all the downtown papers right away and on the radio. In fact, the Hearst people ran a picture of her. Well, her mother calls me up on the telephone and says. 'Mr. O——, we've lived in the community for years and we don't want you to print anything about our girl.' This puts me in a hell of a spot. What kind of a newspaper man am I? I told her that all the downtown papers ran the story and her picture was even in the paper. Why shouldn't I print it if I'm a regular newspaper? And then she told me, 'It only counts for us if it's printed in the community paper.'

"Do you think that's the end of the story? No. I told her that we would have to print it if we were going to stay in business as a newspaper. Well then she went ahead and called up the advertising manager of one of the big department stores that advertises regularly with us. She told him the story and he of course sympathized with her. And what's more she's a good customer, I suppose. Then he called me up on the phone and started to bawl hell out of me, saying, Joe, don't be a scandal monger. Well, I explained the situation to him, told him how everybody else had printed it and what a spot I would be in if I didn't print it. Well this advertising man said, 'I can see you're in a spot. Go ahead and do whatever you want to, but be sure and tell the lady that I called up and squawked.' "—From an interview with a community newspaper publisher.

The community press is the product of a group of individual publishers who in the course of developing their enterprises have emerged as local leaders. By virtue of their occupation, they become subjected to the full impact of group pressures and social contradictions at work in the local community. By virtue of their occupation also, they become enmeshed in a wide network of contacts and roles in the community beyond the role of publisher.

If the community press is viewed as a communications system, it soon becomes evident that the social role of the men who operate it supplies a key for analyzing how the various elements of the system are interrelated. Communications research has tended to make a sharp distinction between mass communications and interpersonal (face to face) communications. But at every point in the operation of the local community newspaper its mass communication aspects are inextricably interrelated with the personal communications and social contacts which link the newspaper's personnel, the community leaders and the readership clientele. Without tracing the patterns of personal communications surrounding the community publisher in his various social roles it is impossible to judge the full range of the newspaper's functions, to understand the elements involved in fashioning its content, or to establish the quality of reader involvement and infer the character of local social cohesion.

These auxiliary patterns of personal communication are more easily observed for the community press than for the daily press where personal communications between the newspaper personnel, advertisers, key leadership groups, and others appear to be more difficult to analyze, although they are equally operative. No simple techniques for quantification of these patterns of personal communications are applicable, although in one newspaper office it was possible to record every incoming or outgoing communication of an interpersonal nature as a means of tracing community pressure on the paper and of analyzing community response to content. More fruitful were the data collected through interviews with the representative sample of publishers and editors in which personal contacts in the local community were probed.

In each of the three selected communities, the sample of community leaders also supplied data on their contacts with the community publishers and the use to which they put the community newspaper in their activities and organizations. These involvements of community leaders it was believed would clarify the blend between mass (formal) communications and interpersonal community contacts. Do community leaders speak to other community leaders through the community press, since the number of their contacts is too great to be maintained or managed by face to face communications? Are community leaders aided in their objectives in the local community through the community press?

Status Orientations

In general, the ability of a community newspaper publisher to perform his social role in the local community hinges directly on his social origin, his career line, and his self-conceptions. In most respects, he is not strikingly dissimilar from his readership clientele, and his social distance from his audience is slight compared to that of producers of most other forms of mass media. The data clearly indicate that community newspaper publishers are middle-class in origin, and that the management of a community paper is both an avenue of relative social mobility and a source of personal psychic gratification.

Using the best index available on class origins, namely father's occupation, 18 (50 percent) of the 36 community newspaper editors and publishers in the sample have fathers who fall in the occupational category of proprietors, managers or officials. Another 12 (33.3 percent) had fathers in occupational categories below that of proprietor-manager-official, and only 6 (16.7 percent) had fathers in the professional and semi-professional categories. Closer examination of the specific fathers' occupation points to their predominantly lower-middle class status.

Like their fathers, community newspaper men are still roughly of the middle class, although they have been somewhat upwardly mobile during their lifetime and today occupy higher status positions than did their parents. A comparison of the community newspapermen's occupation with that of their fathers, reveals that approximately 60 percent of them are in a higher occupational status. Approximately 23 percent are in the same status as their fathers and 16 percent are of a lower occupational status.[1]

The details of their career lines throw additional light on their heavy commitments to their enterprises and help to account for the reluctance of even the more successful to be drawn off into more large scale operations. These publishers have backgrounds which stress promotional activities rather than the broad skills normally connected with communications specialists. The largest number of publishers had backgrounds in advertising and general sales; fully eight of the eighteen publishers had such backgrounds.[2]

"I was an advertising man for a department store and I knew about community newspapers in my work. I met up with my partner K—— at that time. He was interested in starting a paper in this area and I went in with him."

"My interest in community newspapers developed I guess from the fact that I started out writing furniture copy. I suppose it was just a natural evolution from that. From writing copy I got into the selling end of it. I went to work for M—— (a community newspaper publisher) selling advertising. I worked for him about 10 or 12 years and then he went berserk. He was really a chump if there ever was one! There he had the best sales force you can imagine. They were being paid about a hundred to a hundred and twenty a week—this was along about 1935–36. Well, M—— got the crazy notion—he called the salesmen in and had a regular meeting. He told them the advertisers need us now, we don't have to chase after them. So there's no sense

---

1. The lower status than their fathers of some editors (as opposed to publishers) is due to the fact that their fathers were professional or semi-professional in background and these editors were still in process of formulating their careers. The Long Form of the Modified Index of Status Characteristics as developed by Lloyd Warner and his associates is the basis for making the comparison. McGuire, C., and Loeb, M., *Social Status, Peer Status and Social Mobility.* Committee on Human Development, University of Chicago, Chicago, 1949.

2. This stands in contrast to community newspaper publishers in the suburban sectors of the Chicago metropolitan district, most of whom entered their present occupation through the printing trades.

in keeping you fellows on. . . . Well, everybody got the general drift pretty quickly and they started quitting. In a couple of weeks he had only about 3 left out of his original 8 salesmen. . . . I quit at that time and just went out and started my own newspaper."

Three entered publishing through inheritance, only three more by way of editorial work, while one entered via the printing trades. The overall career lines of the remaining three city publishers defy a strict classification but these men might be termed as "promoters"; a former attorney, a personnel manager, and an entrepreneur in assorted business ventures. In short, they give the appearance of successful businessmen who will doggedly push ahead for the maintenance and development of their enterprises rather than shift to new enterprises if only because so much of their self-esteem is tied up with their achievements.[3]

In most other respects publishers are socially similar to the clientele of the communities in which they operate. Birth rate, divorce rate, family composition, and many other basic sociological variables of community newspapermen are typical of the urban middle class and hardly reflective of the stereotype of communications specialists of the largest mass media who are viewed as socially deviant. Their incomes are frequently higher than those of their clientele and they tend to have more formal education, but one hardly gathers the impression that wealth and education have developed strong

3. Previous studies of communications personnel underline the fact that successful newspaper reporters and correspondents came from families which were predominantly professional, or had what is loosely termed "white collar" parentage. The white collar and professional backgrounds have been pointed out as sources of broad conceptions of life careers and the skills required for artful verbalization. In contrast, the fathers of community newspaper personnel are predominantly small proprietors, skilled and semi-skilled workers. The comparative absence of such background traits among community newspapermen is a factor contributing to their gravitation to a locally oriented and small-scale medium of communication rather than the large metropolitan and the nationwide media.

barriers between them and the other community leaders or their clientele. For example, they do not exhibit the professional distance connected with medicine or law. The publisher in the central portion of the metropolitan area is more likely to be a member of a religious or ethnic minority, while a publisher out towards the periphery of the metropolitan district is more likely to be of native-born Protestant stock. The marginal character of the community press as an attraction to members of minority groups during the period of its development was discussed in Chapter II.

Community newspapermen were reared to an overwhelming extent in the Chicago metropolitan area. The heavy concentration of urban upbringing further belies the notion that the community press is a creature of men who are attempting to adjust a small-town outlook to localized portions of the metropolis. To the contrary, these men are urbanites and as such are not characterized by the extensive feelings of latent or underlying antipathy for big city life so frequently encountered among those communications specialists who spent their childhood in rural areas or small towns and who have gravitated toward the urban metropolis.

Upward social mobility arising from the successful management of a community newspaper does imply the development of some social distance from the readers. There is some tendency for community newspaper publishers over the years to move their residence to areas outside the communities in which their newspapers circulate. But it is the wide range of daily contacts in the local community, with businessmen, with members of voluntary associations, with politicians, and purely personal contacts, which fashion the social role of the publisher. It is clear that his initial ties arose out of the commercial requirements of his enterprise and have spread out into organizational, political and fraternal circles.

Personal Contacts in the Local Community

The community newspaper publisher, regardless of the size of his organization, is expected to maintain fairly close and personalistic ties with local businessmen. Yet because of the nature of his services, he occupies a special position among them. As a member of the local business fraternity, he is constantly soliciting its advertising and working hand in hand with its members in major business promotions. Even if his organization is much larger than the usual one, the fact that so many of his business relationships are anchored in the context of a business *fraternity*, prevents him from personally ignoring an even small-to-moderate advertising account. As a result, a strain is evident in the degree to which the size of his organization warrants his setting up administrative and social barriers to direct contact with his advertiser clientele, and the extent to which he can effectively do so. Although finding it necessary to maintain these personalistic connections, the more successful publishers are prone to feel somewhat abused at having to withstand more pressure than they imagine men of similar wealth in other businesses do.

The personal relations between publisher and businessmen are frequently colored by underlying attitudes of ambivalence among many local advertisers toward the community paper. On the one hand, local advertisers recognize the need for a community newspaper, while on the other hand, they frequently resent it, and are prone to deride it as just "small-time stuff." Although the large publishers might possibly consider this an adequate characterization of most community papers, they naturally resent this attitude, and regard it as a severe affront in view of the wealth and size of their own enterprises. The publishers indicate that segments of their advertiser clientele (although not necessarily only those with large accounts), feel they have a right to dictate policy and other matters to the publisher. This too excites the prestige anxieties of the more successful publishers. In an area where advertisers are concentrated within a few blocks and are well organized they can put more pressure on the publisher than in an area in which they are scattered throughout the entire community.

Since publishers are sensitive about their business status and independence, one response is to seek to minimize business news in their columns without fundamentally alienating any advertiser. The results of the content analysis indicate the relative success that has been achived by many publishers, although a minority are more compromising. Moreover, national advertising, with its impersonal contacts with advertisers becomes a much desired objective. Apart from the increased revenue which would accrue to the community newspaper industry should it eventually secure greater amounts of national advertising, this advertising would serve the additional function of bestowing a cultural symbol of legitimacy upon the controllers of the medium. Among the more successful publishers, as men with incomes generally well in excess of $25,000, whose businesses gross between half a million and a million, and who initiate and actively engage in numerous public undertakings of a disinterested character, they naturally desire to be looked upon as *respectable* men of achievement. These successful publishers are, moreover, continuously seeking to disassociate themselves from the less "legitimate" segments of the industry, without, at the same time, destroying the distinction of the community newspaper as a medium devoted to the intensive *local* coverage of a market area.

The desire for respectability and prestige as well as pressure to keep the community viable soon draws the publishers into a wide range of community activities and voluntary associations. In all these organizations, the publisher is usually looked upon as a promoter and a man with special talents. Local community councils and centers, planning and improvement associations, local civic welfare leagues are typical of the organizations in which the key personnel of the community newspaper participates. Aside from almost universal membership in local business and fraternal organizations, the majority of the publishers and editors in the city indicate membership in one or more of the local civic organizations while some are involved in literally a "dozen." For local organizations, the community press functions as the major formal media of local communications. In addition to the constant flow of publicity releases into the office of the community newspaper, personal contact and pressure on editor and publisher for more publicity is ever present, and impossible to divert to underlings.

Obviously, this pressure is a source of gratification for publisher and editor both. On the one hand, it permits them to remark of the publicity seekers, "they are mostly selfish. They are out to make a name for themselves and they want all the publicity possible." On the other hand, community newspaper personnel see themselves as adjudicating among local voluntary organizations for publicity and thereby for public support. One publisher commented:

"They are all pretty much taken up with themselves and think that their activity is the most important, to the exclusion of everything else. From this angle, a newspaper is the most·important organization in the community because it judges what party or group's activities is the most beneficial. It acts like a judge deciding a case when it has to decide which group gets how much space in the paper. . . ."

Local organizations initiating activities and campaigns frequently call upon the newspaper for advice and assistance, since awareness of the local community enables its publisher to act as a kind of public relations counselor.

All of these contacts tend to give the community publisher a perhaps exaggerated view of his importance. Given the struggles for economic survival, it is understandable that a city publisher would boast:

"You know, I think that if it weren't for the fact that community newspapers exist to give them help they could not do their jobs at all."

Moreover, the community publisher is constantly sponsoring community-conscious programs which put him in wide contact with local residents. Although these activities benefit the commercial operation of the newspaper, and are often so planned, they frequently develop an independent existence as far as the self-respect and well-being of the local community are concerned.

"Right now we're in the middle of arranging a swim carnival. It's a yearly affair; it's due next Thursday and everybody's busy on it. . . . Then, we have fishing contests for the kids. . . . Right now, we're running a . . . beauty contest, too. We have had cooking schools. . . . Then we run soft-ball and basketball meets. . . . We're going to have a parade on wheels contest too. That is something like a soap box derby except that it's mostly baby buggies."

While not all of the community newspapers engage in as many or as varied a group of activities, most papers at one time or another throughout the year sponsor some local programs or campaigns. For the promotionally minded publisher, the success of these events is a source of great satisfaction, for in addition to the financial benefits it helps establish his friendly reputation in the local community.

But, in his contacts with the local political parties, the publisher's formal status is projected most significantly into the social organization of the local community. Armed with the columns of his newspaper which give a peculiar "unpolitical" publicity to political personalities, he obtains wide access to the political forces of the local community.[4] In this process he makes use of his network of friends and contacts to represent local interests to politicians and to municipal government officials. At the same time, he attempts to remain "independent." One chain publisher said:

"We're neither Democratic or Republican. . . . We ride with the one we think is best. And we jump down their throat if something's wrong. . . . Generally, we're able to accomplish what we set out to do. We've made friends with both sides. We've given both sides space in the paper and we've gotten things done by both sides."

Thus, the community newspaper publisher is able to exercise influence in the solution of various local problems such as traffic control, crime suppression, garbage collection, playground facilities, school construction and the like.

Basically, the community newspaper publisher does not regard it desirable to be constantly crusading, and he limits the use of his news columns to bring about direct pressure. This is not the result of "economic control" but rather of his own feelings of community pride and because he believes in the power of personal contact. The following comment of an editor of a chain of papers is typical of how community newspaper personnel view their role in guiding the activities of the municipal agencies in the community:

"We get things done partly through the material that appears in the paper or through contacts with the police and the aldermen. . . . The reporters on their regular beats, most of them know the police—the police reporter, especially—and the aldermen, and they'll mention some problem to them. Sometimes we can solve a problem even before

---

4. See Chapter III, The Image of the Local Community: Content for Consensus.

it appears before the public as a problem. . . . Sometimes, too, we'll bring the attention of the aldermen to problems they didn't know of. . . ."

Another editor put it in these terms:

"On streets, for example, too, we work pretty closely with the alderman. We don't just print something about it and let it go. We contact him when somebody calls in and tells us or we find a street needs work. We keep a check on it and if it isn't done in a reasonable amount of time we'll come out with a good spread on it."

Since the paper's news columns must function as a final sanction, the community newspaper is far from successful in its own terms in performing these various political service functions for the local community. Political expedience is just as often the rule as the exception. An editor of a chain of papers located in the city sums up:

". . . You take a problem like sewerage—there's a lot that goes on behind the scenes that you can't do anything about. For example, if there's a Republican alderman in, he can't get anything done by the Democratic administration. . . . They feel it'll be to his credit. We realize that but we have to keep plugging the problem anyway, try to do the best we can."

This process leads to the development of a kind of "watchdog" mentality. Among larger community newspapers, publishers become outspokenly boastful about their own influence:

"I think the alderman out here is very close to his people. . . . I think the reason for that is because he has the ———— /community newspaper/ in the community. The alderman realizes he is being watched. . . . I think politicians are very sensitive. When a problem comes up he'll consult with other aldermen, with the people in their ward, and so on. . . . I think if it weren't for the ———— /community newspaper/ they'd probably relax like politicians usually do and not do very much at all. As it is, however, we attend the council meetings and we notice what they do and we report that in the paper and the people get to know about it, so they have to be on their toes. . . ."

As a result of the high accessibility of the publisher and his enterprise, the community newspaper, like the local alderman's office, becomes an information and advice bureau. Community newspaper personnel usually adopt a sympathetic and cooperative attitude toward local residents who are extremely prone to make inquiries although little is done openly to encourage such inquiries. The daily press with its well staffed information bureaus serves a similar function only the character of the requests is somewhat different. Local residents inquire for information on such matters as licenses, old age assistance, unemployment benefits, etc., and are referred to the proper local or governmental agency. The remarks of one editor gives an indication of the flow of queries which come in daily:

"They call up and ask us all sorts of questions. . . . A merchant called yesterday and asked what we knew about the financial reputation of an auxiliary that wanted to get a hundred dollars worth of equipment on credit. One man called me and asked me if I knew the Whtie Sox had been rained out. . . . They think we have a special information bureau."

It is not unusual for publishers to find themselves involved in requests of a more intimate nature, and to be asked to assume the role of an unprofessional social welfare agency.

"The readers bring in personal problems. For example, I had an old lady here whose son refused to support her. . . . Well, we told her what steps to take to get some action or referred her to people who could take care of the matter. Then we have cases where people have quarrels with their neighbors and they come in here and tell us about them. . . . Sometimes we have to duck out from under, they're so petty. . . . But other times we try to take a hand or get something done because the quarrels are serious and may affect more than just a few neighbors." [5]

All of these points of contact in the local community serve to augment the integrative role of the community publisher in the community. The personal contacts the community newspaper publisher has with businessmen, aldermen, and community leaders create the milieu in which the publisher operates and condition the content that appears in his paper. These personal contacts help to develop an institutionalized aversion on the part of the community newspaper publishers toward incurring the bad will of any section of their clientele and also to account for their inhibitions in the pursuit of a vigorous editorial policy. Moreover, as mentioned above, the publisher is prone to rely on his contacts to achieve an editorial objective. Of course, the threats of reduced advertising and reduced circulation are basic and cannot be separated from the publisher's social role in the local community. Rationalizations for editorial passivity are readily available. "Nonpartisanship," "giving both sides a break," "presenting both sides of the issue in the news columns and letting the public make up its own mind," "being constructive and not knocking anyone unnecessarily," are expressions much more frequently reiterated than claims of editorial independence and outspokenness.

---

5. Services rendered by the community newspaper, especially in lower-class areas, border on those rendered by the lawyer and general fixer. One publisher, while being interviewed, pointed to a box containing dollar bills:

"That's money turned in to pay fines on traffic violations. The general set up is that tickets are turned in with the proper amount of the fine plus approximately $1.50 fee for the person taking the ticket down. We know he has to go back to the end of the line each time; he just can't hand in all the tickets at once . . . You can see the law is discriminating for the poor man; he just can't take half a day off and go down and pay his fine. The rich man can easily send his lawyer down for him . . . The poor man just can't. That's why we have this service."

The extreme in this point of view was articulated by a publisher who spoke of partisanship as being old-fashioned, a part of an immoderate era long since past:

"We give both Democrats and Republicans an even break. The days when a publisher reared himself up on his hind legs and yelled that the fellow down the block had holes in his head are over. You've got to be more moderate and constructive in your editorial policy in this day and age. Nowadays, your readers and your staff make up editorial policy. It's very unwise to do it entirely by yourself."

But if the publisher and his editor are convinced that community opinion is unified in support of a specific objective, their presentation can become quite blatant.

The definition of legitimate news as well as the content of editorials is fashioned by continual social pressures. The range and detail of the pressures to which the publisher is subjected by community leaders and by his readership clientele is striking evidence of the existing social cohesion which is threatened by certain types of content. Editors and publishers constantly relate instances of socially disapproved behavior in the local community which they are asked to suppress. Frequently the items suppressed do not relate to central political issues but rather to gossip which the local community feels is inappropriate in the columns of the community newspaper but which nevertheless makes up a great deal of local conversation. A typical incident was related by the editor of a community newspaper:

"Not so long ago, I was downtown at police headquarters and they brought in a woman—she didn't have anything on—they'd picked her up and brought her in. She was drunk and just playing, I guess. Anyway, they teased her and said the reporters from the papers were there and they'd spread the story all over the dailies. But she said to me, 'I don't care if you do put it in all the papers, but don't put it in the ——— (community newspaper) where all my friends can read it!'"

Interaction with Community Leaders

Community leaders' contacts with and attitudes toward the community press supply additional information on the network of interlocking patterns of personal and mass communications in the local community. Their particular roles in the community lead them to make special use of the community press and to be in a position to judge its effectiveness to some degree. Though their opinions may be more informed than those of the representative cross-section samples of the three communities, in part they are still projective images which are in themselves important measures of the function of the local community newspaper. Readership among this group, described in Chapter IV, was higher than among the population at large with only 8 percent who could be classified as non-readers; moreover, among these readers interests were more specific and less related to advertising. Since only fifty community leaders were interviewed, the results are presented without measures of statistical significance but as suggestive case material.

Personal contact between the community newspaper publishers in the three sample areas and the group of fifty community leaders was extensive. Twenty out of the fifty community leaders were personally acquainted with the publisher of their local paper, with personal acquaintance implying more than superficial contact. Although the pattern varied from community to community, those who were personally acquainted tended to be politicians, businessmen, institutional leaders, and the clergy. Women officers of the PTA generally were unacquainted with the publisher and if this group is eliminated from the sample, the number of personally acquainted rises to over 60 percent of the sample. Carleton Manor, the smallest community with the least crystallized leadership (especially male leadership), revealed the least amount of personal contact between community leaders and the publisher of the *Northeast Advocate*. Personal contact, of course, did not necessarily imply friendliness toward the community newspaper publisher. In fact, attitudes toward the publisher were reflective of the underlying schisms in social stratification and politics in the three local communities.

The value of the attitudes of community leaders was enhanced since they were more articulate and more critical of press content, despite the fact that 90 percent of them had seen their names recently in their community paper. Only a few of the community leaders displayed either coolness or indifference to the publicity extended them in the local community press. Although the majority clearly revealed favorable over-all attitudes, under specific probing many tended to be outspoken in wanting more local news of their community and by inferring that more news about their activities and organizations would be an aid to their leadership positions. In general, the belief that their particular community newspaper had much influence in the community markedly outweighed scepticism in this regard, with variation, of course, between communities. Respondents usually rated the paper in their community as being more effective when they were speaking about its significance for their own organization than when they were expressing their opinion about the paper in general.

Atwater and the Atwater News: The *Atwater News* represents the case of a publisher's reaction to community contacts and economic instability which have led the paper to assume a position of studied neutrality and "community service" colored only by the most subdued political overtones.

Atwater, which has the highest amount of readership, found its leadership divided about the influence of the paper. In good measure this was conditioned by the community leaders' personal attitudes toward the new publisher who had not yet been integrated into the community. Their responses are a striking indication of the closeness of the mass and interpersonal aspects of the community newspaper as a communications system. Moreover, in Atwater, community life and attitudes toward the community paper reflect the schism between the dominant Catholic group and the Protestant minority and between the Polish and Irish ethnic circles.

The *Atwater News* was founded in 1935 by a dress manufacturer who went bankrupt in the depression. Atwater was without its own newspaper at that time except for some neighboring papers circulating sporadically at the edges of the community. The new publisher succeeded in establishing a small but profitable venture, through hard work and personal activity in the network of local organizations. By 1949, when he died of a heart attack, he had become a figure of local prominence and had earned for himself the reputation of a "real gentleman." His deviant political outlook became at times a point of friction though it hardly seems to have undermined his position. This ex-dress manufacturer became a Wallace supporter and permitted Progressive Party publicity to appear in his news columns. Catholic priests took to their pulpits and denounced him until finally peace was restored.

The circulation manager for the original publisher persuaded his brother to assume ownership and, together with a third brother, an advertising staff of three, and two editorial workers, they operate the enterprise on a family management basis. Today the *Atwater News* is a ten- to twelve-page full size weekly which carries beneath its banner the slogan "Non-

Partisan Independent Newspaper." Some 65 boy carriers distribute approximately 20,000 copies on an optional pay basis.

The new publisher, aged 34, of East European Jewish parentage, was born and raised in an adjoining community, and prior to his present position had no editorial or publication experience. His occupational career began when he left high school in order to drive a taxicab. He sold shoes, worked for the WPA, and finally became established in the dry goods business while at the same time completing high school at night. After his Army service, he completed junior college and was studying at Roosevelt College when he purchased the *Atwater News*. Since then he has sought to equip himself better for his new role by taking college courses in abnormal psychology and journalism.

His efforts are devoted to office management and selling advertising. Being relatively new in the enterprise, he sees his main task as "keeping on an even keel." Since the business community is not a wealthy one, the publisher is engaged in a struggle to maintain an adequate flow of revenue. Although the former level of prosperity has not been achieved, the new management seems to have passed the transitional phase. Among other activities, his promotional talents have been directed toward developing a lottery as a circulation booster.

The publisher's editorial control is mainly negative and designed to insure that no crusades or controversies are created. Editorial control means avoiding the race issue although the editor is personally liberal. Atwater, because of its natural barriers, has avoided Negro in-migration for many years and its residents are in agreement about keeping the status quo. Editorial control also involves the important issue of public housing. During the initial gambits of a debate in the City Council on local implementation of federal public

housing, the publisher avoided taking a stand. The deterio-
rated condition of parts of the community and apparent
retail business sentiment in support of a proposed housing
site which would attract new residents led the publisher to
take a mild stand in favor of public housing. The reaction
from the property owners' association and the residents was
sharp since the proposed housing was to be unsegregated, and
the community preferred no public housing to interracial
housing.

All of these pressures have led the publisher to feel that his
paper "exists on account of the advertisers, but that is not
its sole purpose." "There are other things we can do in the
community . . . but I guess we're conformists . . . we have to
conform or we're put out of business . . . It's more evolution
rather than revolution . . . We have to go along with things."

On the positive side, however, editorial control means
standing up for the morality of the community, especially
since Atwater is an upper-lower class community and wants
respectability very much.

"Well here's another case. One day a policeman walked in here.
I knew him from before. And he started to ask me not to print a
particular story. This was a story we got from the Community News
Service to the effect that some girl had been raped. He said the story
was true but it hadn't happened in Atwater. He said the girl had
been taken out of Atwater and then been raped. He was afraid it
would reflect on the people around here. They had nothing to do with
it at all, he said. Just because both of them came from this area didn't
mean that it happened here. . . ."

To carry out his policies, the new publisher brought in a
new chief editorialist, a 22-year-old woman University graduate. Her job consists mainly in editing the news releases
brought into the office and "covering" the one or two big
stories each week.

"I was just looking for a job. . . . It's wonderful. I edited the magazine at school and I thought this would be dull. . . . But it's fascinating" (almost gushing). "It's amazing the hold the paper has over the people in the neighborhood. . . . It's not like the *Woburn Call* /community newspaper for the district in which she lives/. They wait for the paper to come out. . . . If they move they get on the subscription list. . . ."

The community newspaper in her own area is meaningless in its impact upon her. But to edit a paper for another, even a lower-class community, is a temporary thrill. In expressing her attitude as to what could be done to help solve the problems of the community, she answered, "Well, there are a lot of vacant lots but there's nothing being done about them. Even letting the kids play on them—even without putting up equipment would be a big help. . . . I'd like to do a big campaign on the playground." But the new publisher felt that such a "crusade," unless handled gingerly, would create more problems for him than it would solve. The taboos on race relations problems create a source of friction for her. But these editorial restrictions seem to be of little relevance in numbering her days with the *Atwater News*. The enthusiasm of the outsider wears off, and the social and cultural differences remain. Soon after the interview, the humanist drifted out of Atwater to be replaced by an older newspaper man relaxing between jobs, and predisposed to the formula of community journalism.

Typical of the reactions of leading businessmen to the reorganized *Atwater News* was that of a 37-year-old native-born resident of Atwater of Polish Catholic descent who, although trained in law, spends most of his time in real estate and in savings and home loan enterprises. He appeared to be a hard-driven, hard-bitten community organizer with plenty of ambition and political connections. Regular and careful reading of the *Atwater News* keeps him informed of the activities of local organizations and "the politicians." However, he declared that the paper fails to print enough local news for his taste. "It ought to show the community what we are striving for. It does, but not enough."

The alderman, a Republican of Polish descent, temporarily assumed power in the last election when the Democratic organization traditionally in the hands of the small minority of old Irish residents failed to adjust its ticket to the new ethnic composition of Atwater. (In the election just after the completion of the field study, power returned to the Democratic organization.) He is bitter about the *Atwater News* since he feels the publisher slights him personally and does not give Republicans in general all the space they deserve. Nevertheless, he reads the paper assiduously. "I read all the events in the ward which might affect me. I read the social items so that I can know to whom I have to send telegrams of congratulations; it keeps me in touch with community events." The alderman's Irish ward committeeman is also an avid reader who considers the *Atwater News* "a fine paper, except for its political slant." He told the interviewer, in a confidential tone of voice, that the alderman could "hurt it" by telling people not to read it but he would not "because of the goodness of his heart."

Atwater's civic improvement association is run by a 51-year-old insurance salesman, resident of the area for 11 years, who devotes most of his spare time attempting to better the community. He describes the community as a place which he likes "for many reasons":

"It's a community of family people, home-owning folks, who have lived here all of their lives. They have a good record as tax payers and with the ration board during the war. (He was on the ration board.)

People are God fearing, middle and slightly lower class, but not too high nor not too low."

He reads all the news about the activities of local voluntary associations since he is constantly seeking to mobilize them in his civic betterment campaigns. Although he is a local community enthusiast, he is shrewd, hard-headed, and realistic, and this attitude is borne out in his appraisal of the *Atwater News*. When asked about its influence he said he was uncertain. "People around here are pretty set in their ways to be influenced by a paper." Yet, in his opinion, it "helps keep people and organizations aware of the meetings and helps groups keep in touch with each other." As an organization man he is sensitized to the paper's role in aiding him in his network of voluntary association contacts.

Atwater has a boys' club, a Salvation Army, and a settlement house. The attitude of the leader of the boys' club, who is beset by the almost insoluble problems of juvenile delinquency, is a mixture of the cynicism and eternal hope so frequently encountered in the professional social worker. A resident of the community for twelve years, he reads the paper in order to keep informed about "goings on." Initially in the interview he stated that the *Atwater News* had little influence "as far as swaying the people." But in the course of the interview, as he spoke of his own work, he remarked on the publisher's cooperation with local groups and with his own institution. He claimed that it created a "better understanding for his agency" and that he sends in news regularly and hopefully, looking forward to the time when the paper would have more influence in solving the problems of the community.

In Atwater, the Catholic clergy are powerful community leaders. Their attitude toward the paper, to the degree that it is revealed, is simple and straightforward. It provides a useful way to announce church activities; its other functions seem of little interest to the clergy and are almost resented by them. The Lutheran pastor, who feels frozen out of At-water communal life, is quite disinterested in the local community paper and its publisher.

Religious factionalism mirrors itself in the parent educational organizations and in turn affects attitudes towards the newspaper. Mrs. S——, mother of seven children, who has lived for 24 years in Atwater, is president of one of the dominant Catholic mothers' groups and has been active in community affairs for many years. Atwater is a place, in her words, "without a caste." The area is really home to her, although she is upset about the possibility of "colored coming in." "I don't believe in prejudice, just in separation and everybody having their own." She reads the paper regularly for news of people she knows. Frequently she sees her name and that of her organization and quite regularly those of her friends in the paper. On the whole, her attitudes are favorable. Yet she feels in her enthusiasm that the paper could "drum up things which are needed, such as playgrounds and stop lights."

By contrast, the president of the local Parent-Teachers Association, a Congregationalist who has lived most of her life in Atwater, and is the mother of two children, feels that the *Atwater News* pays too much attention to national groups, which, after just a bit of probing, she identified as Polish. Although she reads the paper regularly and likes to see the names of her friends in it, she feels that her organization is not getting sufficient coverage. Factionalism among mothers' groups is not merely limited to the Protestant-Catholic axis but exists among the Catholic women as well. The Irish women display intense rivalry at the new social dominance of the Polish women who have assumed organizational leadership and who as a result are garnering local community newspaper publicity.

The commnunity newspaper not only serves existing leadership but also emergent leadership. In a lower-class community such as Atwater, commandership of a veteran's organization is a significant post. Commander of one of the posts is a 35-year-old production foreman who has lived in Atwater most of his life. He is a man of considerable organizational ambition, although his position in the community is as yet hardly established. He reads the community newspaper and describes it as a "very good paper." "You get to look for it, and I raise hell if it doesn't show up." The paper is a means of keeping track of his many friends and of keeping posted about the activities and publicity of other veterans' organizations.

The news stories which his organization has submitted are invariably printed, although too often on the last page in his opinion. He feels such news is very important in keeping members informed of post activities. Despite these remarks, when asked whether the paper had much influence in the community, he answered, "not much right now because the publisher is not too well known as yet."

Bethel Park and the *Bethel Park Bulletin*: The *Bethel Park Bulletin*, by contrast, was more generally described as an effective and influential paper even on the part of those community leaders who might have disagreed with its relatively outspoken editorial policy. In fact, of the three communities, the strongest sense of social solidarity between community leaders and community newspaper publisher was expressed in Bethel Park. Over 25 years of continuous contact in the community, a long record of public service, plus this publisher's genial personality have enhanced the impact of his publication.

The *Bethel Park Bulletin*, a 16- to 18-page weekly, is one edition of a 23-paper chain, which grew as a result of the remarkable editorial and promotional skill of its publisher. A native-born Chicagoan, he proudly claims that he started his crusading journalistic career as a boy of eight when he edited a grammar school publication.

"When I was in sixth grade we were protesting the dismissal of our school principal. We went over to visit old man ———— (a political science professor at the University of Chicago). I went over with a girl from the eighth grade. We went into a room, a 5x7 room piled up to the ceiling with books and papers. He put his hand on me and told me, 'Now we'll straighten this whole thing out; don't get so excited, fat boy'."

By the time he became a sophomore at Northwestern University's undergraduate school of journalism, in addition to working on *The Daily Northwestern*, he was editor of a small suburban weekly. He secured the job from the owner of the printing plant which produced his college paper. Here, he started learning community politics, for by attending all the town meetings and making use of the columns of the paper, he succeeded in establishing a town library. In between jobs he took a copyreading course at the Hearst newspapers which consisted of working for nothing on the copy desk at night.

When in 1926 his employer decided to buy out the *Bethel Park Bulletin* and convert it into a community paper from an advertising newspaper owned by a group of department stores, he became editor of the new venture. Soon he found himself a partner and over the years, the *Bethel Park Bulletin* became the keystone paper of a chain of community newspapers with a total circulation of over 160,000 and a staff of over 170 people, including 70 men in the mechanical department.[6] The chain is organized in three groups, each of which has its own central editorial offices, its own managing editor and advertising director.

His daily routine is hardly a leisurely one, for in addition to maintaining close supervision over this complex enterprise he has risen to a position of city-wide and national organizational leadership. His remarks about a page from his appointment book describe a constant flow of contacts and meetings on which he thrives:

"At 10:30, I made a long call on a big advertiser who had been somewhat hostile to community newspapers. Then at 12 noon I picked up an auto dealer and we drove to the auto show . . . and went on the air for fifteen minutes . . . it was North Side Day yesterday at the show. Of course I kept putting in plugs for the *Bulletin*. It was about 2:30 when I got back to the *Bulletin* offices and stayed there until about five. First I checked over the figures on the week's deposits and then I took care of editorial problems. I wrote an editorial and blue-penciled a couple of stories. About five o'clock, I talked with a delegation from a local organization who were planning a civic drive, and then squeezed in a conference with one of my managing editors. I left the office for the plant where I spent two more hours checking advertising schedules, and warning the night staff to watch out for certain things going on through the night . . . you know, everytime I wake up in the morning I have just the slightest feeling that something happened during the night that's going to make for more problems. After supper, I dashed to a surprise party for a well-known radio announcer. I went home after it and fell asleep reading papers and magazines. Another day might be the same or it might be different (closes notebook)."

He failed to add that throughout the daily routine he is subjected to a continual series of phone calls and short interruptions by members of his staff, for all have access to him since he has a profound distrust of remote and bureaucratic execu-

---

6. During World War II, an overseas edition for a number of communities was published which had a circulation of over 4,000 copies.

tives. He feels that since he is engaged in producing a "live newspaper" and not in mass production, rigid routines would be a fatal barrier for his staff.

This publisher has mastered the business intricacies of the industry and is constantly pressing for new promotional devices and financing arrangements to strengthen his newspapers and get additional advertising revenue. He has pioneered in cooperative arrangements in raising standards, especially reporting accurate circulation figures, and is at present head of the national community newspaper association's sub-committee on auditing procedures. As he describes the complexity of his chain, it is apparent that he is a man who gathers satisfaction from the effective financial functioning of his organization, for this organization makes him a self-reliant journalist.

As a journalist, he produces each week a front page column for all his papers. He is one of the most outspoken community newspaper publishers in the country and recently won the Herrick Award of the NEA, "for interpreting Americanism and Democracy." Politically he claims to be an independent, which implies support of both Democrats and Republicans. Crusading for him runs the whole gamut from local community improvements to national politics. It involves not so much editorial comment but news coverage for organizations and individuals engaged in local improvement and social action.

"All these things around here—these schools, highways, and playgrounds. They don't mean anything to you but I can remember waging campaigns, fighting to get improvements. See this main street? We had some fight to get it repaved . . . now that building on the right, it was half-completed for many years—an ugly sight, we kept shouting to have it pulled down but the city fathers finally did something and had it finished."

In addition to membership in a wide range of community and city organizations typical of a community newspaper editor, he has become trustee and finally chairman of the Board of Trustees of a local university and has served as national officer of an independent political action organization.

He is involved in community newspapers with a deep passion, but with the modesty that frequently accompanies real success:

> "I have come to realize that we really run our papers for the readers. We are not like the big papers, and in the struggle to run our papers we get to see the problems and we fight to solve them. This business grows on us, but we can, we hope, make the big boys recognize the problems of the local communities in Chicago."

The managing editor who carries out the publisher's detailed directives for the group of which the *Bethel Park Bulletin* is a member is typical of the mixture of business and editorial talents found so frequently to be successful in the industry. He is a forty-year-old native of Chicago, with academic training in journalism. He made his first contact with the chain in 1933 while working for a small retail advertising agency in the local community. Since then he has worked in all phases of the business until he became managing editor. Quiet and soft-spoken, he is an editor with a great deal of self-respect for his newspapers and their content. He feels that "the *Bulletin* is considered a leader in this community," and for him this implies that the paper should avoid being a scandal-monger or an expose sheet just to build reader-interest. The resources at his disposal make it possible for him to assign staff to go out and dig up news, check leads and get the information necessary to produce a well-rounded paper. As managing editor, he looks back nostalgically at the contact he once had with the community when he was a reporter out covering stories and had closer contacts with the local community.

Bethel Park's business leaders, all of whom are well acquainted with the publisher and his staff, are of two types: (1) older business leaders who, having prospered for many years in the community, view with some concern the changes in the community, and (2) newer businessmen who are managers in the local branches of downtown department stores or chain stores in the local community and who are more detached in their attitudes toward the local community.

Representative of the older type is a prosperous and socially influential local merchant of Swedish extraction who has been active in many local organizations and served as president of local fraternal organizations. Bethel Park, so far as he is concerned, is divided into two sections, the north end of the community, in which he lives, and which he describes as a fine, stable, residential area; and the south end, which is just "not as good." He reads the paper "to see what's going on in the community." For him the paper has plenty of influence, especially with the low income groups, and therefore carries plenty of weight in certain parts of the community and with the politicians who "appreciate it very much." Despite his disagreement with some of the paper's editorials, he is a booster of the *Bethel Park Bulletin*, because of all the publicity his organizations get, which has the effect, in his words, "of helping make the membership self-conscious and thus work hard."

Another example of this type of leader is a rather prominent State Street lawyer who, since he has lived all of his life in Bethel Park, is much concerned with its problems. Even before the interview touched on the *Bethel Park Bulletin* he lauded the paper for its effective role in the fight with the Chicago Transit Authority. During his lifetime he has been president or active in practically all the organizations of any influence in the community. But now he sees the community in terms of his friends who unfortunately are either dying off or slowly moving out of the community. "The calibre of the people has decreased, morally and educationally, and what's more the businessmen are now beginning to live outside the community. The neighborhood has not progressed mainly because there has been no building over the last twenty-five years." His extremely positive attitude towards the paper is colored by its efforts to support him in improving the community.

By contrast, the vice-manager of one of the large department store branches in the local community and president of the local businessmen's association after only three and one-half years with the department store, represents the new type of businessman who is developing in the local community.

His attitude toward the community newspaper was conditioned initially by his advertising connections with it and the fact that he is struggling to maintain a hard-boiled unsentimental attitude towards community affairs. As president of the businessmen's association, a position which he enjoys considerably, he now sees his name quite regularly in the paper and he finds himself involved on numerous delegations and on many local improvement projects. In this role, his attitude toward the paper and the local community seems to be broadening if only because, as he reported, he finds frequently that advance publicity eases these tasks, especially when calling on other community leaders for support.

In addition to the network of politicians, fraternal leaders, officers of Parent-Teachers Associations and the like, the clergy play a crucial role in the communal life of Bethel Park. Their reactions ranged from that of an orthodox Protestant minister who, although he feels that the *Bulletin* is fair to all the churches in the community, expressed a general suspiciousness about church publicity. "Putting the church in front of the public" as he described it, was neither useful or even desirable. On the other hand, another minister, active in Chicago church circles and a powerful community leader, when asked whether the newspaper was an aid to his organization declared, "It acts as a tuning instrument for the membership so they don't feel obscure; it (publicity) is a reward for the individuals and makes people aware of the church." His remarks were not mere promotional ideology for he spelled out the problems and the implications of mobilizing public opinion in support of community life with great realism and expertness.

Carleton Manor and the Northeast Advocate: In Carleton Manor, community pressures coincide with the preoccupation of the Northeast Advocate to maintain the status quo, particularly its property values and its social and ethnic composition. Nonetheless, the contacts between many local community leaders and the personnel of the paper tended to be limited and formal. The smallness of Carleton Manor, and the lack of geographical isolation tended to prevent the development of a clearly differentiated leadership group. Thus, the link between personal and mass communications in this particular community was least well developed and most difficult to trace. Carleton Manor was only one of the communities in which the Northeast Advocate circulated, with the result that community leaders were somewhat remote from the main center of the paper's operations. In the communities which bordered on the main satellite business districts of the area in which the Advocate circulated, community leadership was closely associated with the publisher and his staff.

The present publisher of the Northeast Advocate is an influential community leader who has been associated for over thirty years with a larger community paper of which this is an offshoot. Today his control is purely nominal, for younger men on the staff have taken over responsibility.

Before World War I, when the main satellite business district near Carleton Manor was developing, the local community newspaper serving this district was closely tied to a small printing firm. By purchasing the print shop the present publisher found the antecedent of his present enterprise already in existence and as a result he was in the newspaper business. He was a printer of Irish Catholic parentage, native to the district, who was seeking a business of his own. It was, as he puts it, "just a chain of accidents" that got him into the community newspaper business. Since then the paper has flourished and grown steadily in circulation and wealth. The *Northeast Advocate* as a separate edition was founded in 1935, and today circulates as a 16- to 18-page weekly in Carleton Manor. Some 90 employees (11 editorial, 32 mechanical, 30 advertising and circulation) produce 96,000 copies for the parent paper with its many editions, plus 44,000 for the *Northeast Advocate*. A large crew of carrier boys distribute the paper on an optional pay basis.

This publisher looks back with great satisfaction at the struggle involved in developing his profitable enterprise. "I suppose I'm sort of coasting." His attitudes have been modified so that the promotional outlook has vanished, for he knows that his enterprise is efficient and effective. "Take our classified ads . . . people say they're much more efficient than the daily newspaper ads are. I've had real estate men volunteer the information that they've listed items both with us and with the daily newspapers and they get far more results with us."

The growth of his paper, and his effective personality have

put him in a position of community leadership and prestige. For many years he held public offices as a member of the Democratic Party. Today the paper's traditional allegiance has been altered because of municipal politics and community issues, particularly with regard to public housing and civil rights. In addition to membership in a number of business and fraternal organizations, this publisher has been president of a planning association which has been a powerful influence in fashioning the growth and development of a wide sector of Chicago. It has acted as a political focal point in numerous legislative and administrative conflicts involved in attempting to maintain the present character of the area and in opposing public housing.

Active management has been turned over to a long-standing employee of the firm who entered from the editorial side of the business. He is a 45-year-old Catholic of business parentage, born in Toledo, who started in Chicago community newspaper work around 1930 after graduating as a journalism major from a large midwestern Catholic university. After a number of jobs, he went to work for his present employer. His main concerns center around increasing advertising volume and keeping operating costs down. He is a devoted booster of the sectors of the city in which his papers circulate and of the areas now undergoing expansion in which he looks forward toward increased circulation. Yet his apprehension of the changing conditions in the area surrounding the main office and in the original satellite district on which the paper is dependent is hard to disguise:

"D—here is about the best place in the city for good living. Everything that's necessary is here . . . shops, theaters, good transportation . . . and so on. There's a master plan for the whole area . . . and there's no reason in the world why it can't remain a good place in which to live."

In operating his community newspaper he has developed a strong conviction about its social implications:

"Oh well, the paper is the *sine qua non* of action on anything that is of a widespread community nature. . . . For instance, during the war, the daily papers could blab their heads off about the war bond drive and they couldn't do any good. . . . The people feel the daily paper is remote . . . it's off there somewhere. But when we took up the cudgel, people took immediate interest in the bond drive. . . . The downtown statesmen could see it that way."

Like the publisher of the paper, his position has thrown him into numerous community activities; during the war he was head of a Civilian Defense Unit. A great deal of his energy still goes into mobilizing community projects.

"Don't give us the credit of altruism. We feel a good healthy community is not only a good thing in itself, but it's a damned good basis to make a buck and if the community starts to deteriorate . . . well then, we start to deteriorate too. . . . Your basis of livelihood starts melting away."

The chief of the editorial department is a highly competent journalist, aged 48, who came up through the ranks of the newspaper business without benefit of formal journalism training. Born in downstate Illinois of Protestant, skilled worker parentage, his professional experience was typical for a metropolitan newspaperman. In the early thirties he joined the paper via its radio station and has been with the paper ever since.

Today he considers himself the "active editor." When he was interviewed about his work, he reflected:

"I'd say that I spent half of my time talking, discussing something. People come in and I'll spend some time with them . . . or a member of the staff wants to know something about an angle . . . well the other 50 percent I spend editing—some writing but very little of that unless there is something which is completely out of line and then I'll rewrite it completely myself."

Although he reports that he "is in touch with the paper and the influences brought to bear on both the paper and the community," policy formation seems to rest largely with the publisher.

The editor expressed his outlook toward the paper openly and freely:

"We try to be small-time (pause) a small oh, how can I put it. . . . Small time isn't what I mean. We try to be intimate with the readers. . . . You know the small things that might never see the light of day. Of course that isn't all. I said the paper was a molder of public opinion . . . some people dislike the paper, but we try to maintain an open door policy . . . by that I mean this door is always open for anybody to come in and tell us what they think. We try to run a friendly paper."

He has resisted efforts to become involved in community activities, frequently declining speaking engagements, although he has been active in local fraternal life.

In Carleton Manor local leadership rests in the hands of the political leaders, the clergy, and the socially and organizationally active women. Catholic and Protestant differences express themselves in the social life of the community and around the issues of the PTA.

Both the Republican alderman and ward committeeman read the paper avidly. In the alderman's words, he reads for his "business as ward alderman. . . . It tells me what's going on and I get a survey of the week's activities." His name appears regularly and the paper sees to it that his activities in the city council are well covered. Editorially, he sees eye to eye with the *Northeast Advocate* and is on close terms with the top personnel of the paper.

The Protestant clergy in the community receive regular coverage for their churches and regard it as useful. The Catholic clergy are rather indifferent to the paper in part because the diocese publishes its own periodical.

The various women's groups, including the PTA, turn in publicity weekly which, together with local social items, are important topics of conversation. But in the case of the clergy and the women's group leaders, direct contacts with the *Northeast Advocate* are rather limited. There is a distinct feeling that since the paper covers an area larger than Carleton Manor, it really does not serve community needs. In this middle-class community the lack of emphasis on Carleton Manor as a symbol of identification is relevant in generating this attitude regardless of reader interest in specific types of content.

The patterns of interaction between the publisher, his staff, his advertisers, community leaders, and his readers serve as indicators of the social structure and cohesion existing in the local community. The three communities studied represent variations in class and ethnic lines; but despite these differences common roles for the community newspaper publisher tend to emerge, which are conditioned by the social functions and decision-making process operative at the community level.

VII

The Social Dimensions
of the Local
Community

The urban community press, in the light of the findings of this study, has a wide audience and a discernible impact. As such, its significance as an approach to the local community is more than a research assumption. The contents of the community press, the social attributes of its readers, and the social role of its publishers when viewed as elements of a communications system make possible inferences about social cohesion in the urban metropolis. In such a process of synthesis, the interpretative conclusions are likely to outrun the data at hand and become rather speculative because of the complexity of the task of understanding the urban community.

The analysis of the community press if it reveals nothing else indicates that significant proportions of the residents of the urban metropolis are not "rootless" individuals. Counter-trends to large-scale organization continually develop which modify the impact of technological impersonalization and make possible the gratification of individual needs in the local community. This is a crude statement. Ultimately, the task at hand is to emerge with a theoretical "model" of the local community. Such a "model" will present a meaningful analysis of the complexities of the local community and point the way toward constructive support of those mechanisms and institutions which maintain social cohesion.

In moving toward such a "model" or generalized description of the local urban community, three basic social dimensions of analysis are required, similar to those relevant for analyzing most social systems;[1] (a) the motivational involvements and gratifications (or non-gratifications) connected with community residence, (b) the social organization of the local community, and (c) the resultant patterns and mechanisms of social control on the local community level.[2]

---

1. See Talcott Parsons, *The Social System* (Glencoe, Ill.: The Free Press, 1951), for an elaborated frame of reference for analyzing social systems.

2. Moreover, it is necessary to delimit the "spatial" boundaries of the local community in order to differentiate community research from certain other types of social system analysis. Social scientists have charted the historical boundaries of the local community and plotted "natural" areas on the basis of location of industry, commerce, transportation and residence. The community areas employed in this research were derived in large measure through such a procedure. The residents' subjective definition of the "spatial" boundaries of the community are also required.

In addition, the residents' estimates of the prestige or status position of their community as compared with adjoining and nonadjoining communities are relevant. These rankings are crucial since the mechanisms of social stratification in the metropolis involve not only sensitivity about economic class but also consciousness about the status of one's community.

Motivational Involvement in the Local Community

On the one extreme, the present sample reveals that there is a minority of residents (non-readers; 16 per cent) for whom the community press had no meaning and who can be presumed to have practically no commitment or involvement in the community regardless of the amount of their use of local facilities. These individuals are most likely to constitute the "rootless" individuals on whom community social controls have little or no effect. On the other hand, there is another minority (fans; 11 per cent) who find themselves heavily involved with the local community and who are most likely therefore to respond to the pressure of the local community. For the remainder varying levels of involvement emerge.

Interpersonal contacts around the use of local facilities and not mere use of local facilities mold these commitments and involvements. The most direct way in which the social organization of the local community seems to serve these individual needs and motives hinges on its ability to serve the primary group requirements of child-rearing. The local community functions as a community particularly around the needs of its most conspicuous consumers—the children—as the data of this research attest.

Thus, family cohesion becomes central for understanding the inner dynamics of local community involvement since it seems more explanatory than the age, education, income and other such characteristics of the residents. Involvement, within a given community, seems hardly to be associated with attributes such as renters vs. home owners, or single family dwellers vs. multiple dwelling unit residents. Length of residence increases community involvement, but here again children act as catalysts in the process.

Community involvement is also linked, but to a lesser degree, to primary group attachments outside of the family, but rooted in the local community. There can be no doubt that given the same community facilities there is a level of involvement which reflects an underlying personality orientation, left unmeasured by the instruments of this research. A clue to the influence of these personality variables can be seen in the fact that community orientation was concentrated in those individuals who perceived their local community in terms of its human "resources" as compared with those who were preoccupied with its physical "resources."

In any case, it is difficult to designate the frequency of these personalized contacts as being considerable or inconsiderable. By what standards are we to judge the fact that within these "typical" three urbanized communities drawing on all strata of the metropolis over two-thirds of the families had social contacts with their immediate neighbors? How easily could these contacts be broken? Perhaps more relevant are some of the consequences of these contacts and involvements. The data at hand indicated that where stable primary groups existed in the local community the community press tended to operate as an extension of real social contacts. Where these contacts were absent the contents of the community press operated merely as a substitute for contact, and thereby negated the impact of the community press in developing local social cohesion. The role of these primary group contacts and involvements which conditioned the impact of the community press certainly seems relevant to other sources of symbolism as well as participation in local voluntary associations.

Social scientific efforts to analyze community involvement have been dominated by a typology involving a sharp distinction between those individuals who display local community orientation and those who are reputed to have a broader or metropolitan outlook.[3] At numerous points, the data at hand question the advisability of considering urban personality in these sharply opposing terms.

The study of community involvement and orientations by means of the community press seems to highlight a developmental view of the distinction between "community" orientation and "metropolitan" orientation. Local orientations for some broaden out to include wider needs and perspectives, but which do not necessarily eliminate local orientations, although a predominant balance between the two can be discerned. It is as if the individual had the opportunity to make use of community facilities but he augments the satisfaction of his needs by making use of non-community facilities and thereby creating metropolitan orientations. The balance between the two varies from community to community, as can be seen between Atwater, Bethel Park and Carleton Manor. Yet, for the bulk of the sample population, the use of local facilities is impressive and has a significance that wider and broader orientations and identifications do not destroy automatically. It is hardly a case of either one or the other. For the bulk of the population, it is a matter of relative commitment. How else could one explain that, by and large, community newspaper readership is compatible with high levels

---

3. Such a dichotomy often implies either a hidden value judgment of the social desirability of the metropolitan outlook, or, on the other hand, a judgment of nostalgia for a return to some sort of rural-type community orientation.

of exposure to broader mass media? This does not deny that a small group may, because of occupation or specialized life experiences, develop metropolitan orientations without local identifications. It would be a grave error to view this group as typifying the balance between community and metropolitan involvement.

The Social Organization of the Local Community

The analysis of the community press as a communications system reveals immediately some of the complexities of the process by which the individual and his primary-group affiliations are integrated into the large-scale organization of the urban metropolis. It reveals that despite the growth of mass communications and large-scale organization most individuals are not living in a "mass society" in which they are directly linked to the major agencies of concentrated social and political power. Rather, the growth of large-scale organization has been accompanied by a proliferation of intermediate haphazard-like social arrangements and communication patterns. The local urban community appears to be a complex of social interactions which tends to identify a local elite and local institutionalized patterns for controlling social change. The community press is but one institution that stands intermediate between the individual and the major institutions of the metropolis; and the publisher is but one of the members of this intermediate elite.

In power terms, the scope of this elite and the significance of its actions are obviously limited by the character of the decision-making process that finds a context on the local level.

This local elite is composed of business, political, religious, voluntary association, and professional community leaders. At first glance it might appear that they constitute a network of individuals whose significance arises out of their hierarchical position midway between top metropolitan leadership and the bulk of the population whose consensus is required for collective action. In this view, interpersonal connections among community elite within a given community or group of communities do not loom significantly and the local elites are considered merely as agents rather than effective leaders.

This view of local leadership is conditioned by the lack of clear-cut correspondence between the geographical limits of the community and the geographical limits of the leaders' social influence. But this is an erroneous view of community leadership. The pattern of group leadership that emerges around the community press and its operations highlights a clear-cut pattern of interpersonal contact among local leaders within the community. The various institutions and associations which penetrate into the local community have no manifest geographical homogeneity or unity. Nevertheless, the lateral interactions of the local leadership within the geographical limits of the local community have a definite pattern which contributes to the self-consciousness and power of these local leaders. This process can be understood better only through prolonged participant observation which social scientists seldom undertake.

Moreover, community leadership does seem strikingly associated with residential stability. It is worthwhile noting the degree to which community leaders display residential stability (twenty years or over at the same address), again in contradistinction to the view of the urban community as a "rootless" mass. Beyond this simple fact, the social personality and the social techniques of local leaders remain to be investigated. The level of community management that this study probed uncovered again and again the effort at adjudication of conflict by emphasis on areas of common agreement and the postponement of disagreement. The role of the community newspaper in the political life of the community with its curious non-partisanship reflects this approach and makes it more difficult to uncover the realities of political conflict.

Today, local community organization is perhaps most threatened in precisely those areas where the socially articulate leaders of the community are in the process of departure or are unable to replace themselves. The development of social absenteeism, as the process can be called, need not be viewed as inevitable, for it does get altered, slowed or temporarily stopped.

The removal of leadership with strong community identifications through the process of social absenteeism can develop to the point where ultimately profound changes in local politics take place with most unfortunate implications. In a city such as Chicago, social absenteeism in certain traditional Democratic wards, located near the center of the city, with lower-class constituencies has fundamentally weakened the Democratic party organization. The ward organizations have been weakened to the point where the wards have suddenly turned Republican. This shift hardly represents the normal and desirable workings of the two-party system. These wards have not turned to traditional Republicanism for the working class elements of these depressed local communities are not expressing a political allegiance to the platform of the national Republican party. They have been forced and intimidated into support of a Republican machine so completely weakened through absenteeism that it fell easy prey to the underworld and a new kind of hoodlumism in politics.

Social absenteeism expresses itself in a variegated set of problems in the local community less dramatic than the collapse of traditional political institutions of the most depressed areas. Social absenteeism affects the public educational and social welfare system and even the religious institutions, although religious hierarchies are more aware of the need to act to offset these effects.

Because of the wide variety of functions which gravitate to a community publisher, he operates as a limited counterforce to social absenteeism. In those areas where social absenteeism is less of a problem, the publisher's role seems to be one of galvanizing the local leaders to collective action. Community publishers are self-conscious men because of the kinds of life experiences which have led them into their enterprises and which they have had in operating their enterprises. The peculiar skills of the publisher and the role he plays in seeking to adjust conflicting interests sensitizes him to the evolving trends in the local community. Economic interests, of course, condition his outlook. Nevertheless, he is less reluctant to accept the inevitability of adverse changes and more prone to press for desired change than the members of the business community. His promotional background and in part his quasi-intellectual outlook are here at work.[4]

---

4. One cannot help contrasting the publisher and the editor of the community newspaper with those types of mass media specialists who for some reason or other seem to be beset by ever-increasing amounts of self-hatred and cynicism. Even the highest priced movie scenario writer develops these attitudes which involve not only a contempt for the self but a contempt for the audience. The factors involved are complex, but a comparison with the community newspaper publisher and editor reveals at least one striking difference. There can be no doubt that the community publisher has some sense of inferiority about his position and his limited economic achievement. But this hardly constitutes the basis for self-hate and cynicism. He has too many specific and concrete gratifications from his activities; he has too much direct evidence of the response to his medium to feel isolated and self-deprecatory.

In particular, no group is more sensitive to the political and economic inequalities inherent in the present trends toward suburbanization than the urban community newspaper publishers. The divergence between the long established political boundaries and the changing patterns of population in a metropolitan area such as Chicago seems to increase continuously. Throughout the research, specific problems of social action took meaning in this overriding political context. The metropolis is an outgrowth of a machine technology which made possible large concentrations of population. While the distribution of commerce and transportation conditioned the form and location of the residential community, political boundaries seemed to coordinate, or discoordinate, social adaptations to these movements. The outmoded character of the legal limits of the urban metropolis is a striking case of a basically discoordinating element of local social organization.

It is not within the power of the community press to have a central role in altering these administrative and political trends. Yet if politicians in the near future seek to deal with this fundamental issue, either through boundary changes, new forms of political representation or new taxation basis, the community press—both in Chicago and throughout the entire country—constitutes an important resource for clarification and action.

Social Control at the Local Community Level

Social control at all levels involves the clash between individual motives and effective social organization. The code of ethics for operating a community newspaper is a skeleton of the social attitudes and group pressures that are operative in most collective actions at the local community level.

Much research which has been concerned with community social control implies that, as one moves from the center of the metropolis outward, the rates of "disorganization" decreased. The rates usually refer to crime, insanity and similar indices. Regardless of the validity of these particular findings, it is doubtful whether these differential rates measure variation in effective and overall social control. For example, if, in the case of crime, the definition was broadened to include white collar crime, would these straight-line relationships still hold true? Probably not. Extremely "disorganized" areas exist in the shadow of the central business districts and adjoining the inner belt of industry. But there hardly seems to exist a clear body of data to link well-defined measures of "disorganization" to types of community areas for the metropolitan district as a whole.[5]

There is no reason to believe that the community press increases in readership or significance with removal from the center of the city. By inference, moreover, analysis of the community press indicates that, as between the three sample communities, location from the center of the city is not a distinguishing indicator of the level of community social control. Family cohesion and primary group contacts seemed more relevant for predisposing an individual toward the acceptance of the community's controlling institutions and associations. There can, however, be no doubt that income and class mold the forms and technique of these institutions and associations as well as condition the outlook of community leadership. This does not carry the implication that lower

---

5. The more relevant problem seems to be to account for the different types and modes of deviant behavior as between community areas.

income and lower status mean less social control from these sources but rather different norms of control.

The range of collective action which involves the community newspaper—from blood bank campaigns to support for police action—grows out of the leadership position and contacts of the publisher. But, in addition to collective action, social control involves the quest for respectability and morality. The ideology of the community newspaper, and of many other community institutions, seeks to present appropriate symbols of respectability and morality to those who have such motives. Yet for that substantial minority who seek anonymity, avoidance of community involvement and its consequent controls requires little effort.

Local social controls assume particular meaning when a link between these controls and the norms of the larger society can be established. The decisions made in the local community are of limited consequence for the "big" political issues of the moment; yet the motivational commitment toward the local community is certain to bear some relationship to the individual's orientation to the "politics" of the larger community.

In this context, a final hypothesis is presented. Individuals who display high local identifications are people who are likely to display higher political competence than those who have low or no local identification. This hypothesis is presented in its most general form; a minority who are "over-identified" in the local community might display low political competence, while on the other end of the continuum a minority with low community identification might display high political competence derived from ideological considerations. But leaving aside these sub-groups, should political competence correlate with community newspaper readership some light might be thrown on compatibility of local autonomy and local identification and the requirements of the larger political process.

Those portions of the readership survey which dealt with local community affairs included indirect questions on the individual's contacts and estimates of his local precinct captain, alderman and ward organization. Specific questions involved the problems of the local community and the capabilities of the political offices and officers to deal with these concrete issues. These questions were not designed to determine whether the respondent was a "Democrat," a "Republican" or an "Independent," but rather to probe his trust in and reliance on politics. They produced a flow of material revealing underlying attitudes toward the political process and made possible inferences about self-conceptions of competence in this area. For example, the following respondent leaves no doubt about his own low competence in politics:

"I think it's all the bunk. I'm a Democrat. I been a Democrat for years. If Truman runs again I don't think I'll vote for him. I don't think the little persons can do anything. The politicians may start out all right but they end up the same—corrupt. They can't help it. You need someone to rule. Everyone can't be for himself."

Regardless of the respondents' political affiliation, relative confidence in the effectiveness and honesty of local politics— projective measures of personal political competence—tended to be associated with high community newspaper readership. However, in the case of the political parties the association was larger and more statistically significant than for precinct captains.

These conclusions point to the ambiguities of the social roots of political agreement in the urban local community. Social scientists and reformers are frequently preoccupied with the political type whose competence is operative without a sense of specific local community identification. Indispensable as such individuals are for politics, it is likely that in the near future such individuals alone cannot maintain or strengthen the basis of democratic organization in a metropolis such as Chicago. To the contrary, further weakening of local community identifications is inextricably bound up with the growth of even greater anti-democratic potential among the rank and file residents than now besets the urban community.

An issue of social and political control which had mobilized a great deal of local community interest is that of federally supported public housing. This study was initiated before the outbreak of the hostilities in Korea, in a period in which a great deal of attention was being expended on the problems of developing new communities and the redeveloping of old ones. Since this was a period of full employment, it was understandable that urban development and redevelopment would be a fundamental concern. Conceptions of local autonomy and local community, which have so long been the basis of democratic organization, were subjected to a searching criticism on a very pragmatic basis.

Each community newspaper has implicit rules as to the role it intends to play in fashioning the real estate composition of its local community. This, of course, depends on whether the newspaper is confronted realistically with the urban development and redevelopment problems in its own area, or whether it deals with the problem in terms of principle. In general, the community press in the Chicago area has been in opposition to federally supported public housing including some in a most outspoken fashion. Moreover, because of parochialism the local community and its community newspaper, it was felt by certain critics, were likely, in fact certain, to have created undemocratic standards for residence, particularly with respect to ethnic composition.

This issue can be considered a key to understanding the "manipulative" aspects of community journalism, for underneath the issue is the fear of altering the ethnic and racial composition of the community. Systematic attitude data is not available on public housing, but there is enough data on ethnic and racial attitudes in metropolitan areas to indicate that often the community press reflects rather than molds attitudes in its opposition to unsegregated public housing.

Therefore, for these same critics of the community press, democratic objectives frequently implied the elimination of local community autonomy if urban redevelopment and residential mobility were to be guaranteed. To justify such an attack on a traditional preconception of the democratic process, they frequently argued that, in effect, the local community no longer exists or could never possibly exist in an urban community. In this view, much is made of the "artificial" attempts to stimulate local autonomy in a world in which local autonomy has been rendered meaningless.[6]

But a solution to the dilemma between local autonomy and freedom of residential mobility is not possible by denying the power of the local orientations that persist in the metropolitan community—the mass of evidence to which this study contributes is too great to be denied. Although the elimination of segregation is a basic and fundamental democratic value its achievement through the destruction of local

---

6. The rhetoric with which these matters concerning the ethnic composition of the local community are discussed in the columns of the community press at times makes use of "factual" reportage of events which are designed to remind the resident of the local community of the "collective danger." (See p. 87.) Perhaps the criticism leveled at the community press in this area arises from the fact that the majority tend to avoid the issue, and thereby they fail to discharge their social responsibility. It is a matter of individual discretion to judge the community press by this standard. Such a point of view also fails to recognize that at times it is constructive to engage in deliberate avoidance of a problem if that makes possible a desired solution whereas recognition would prevent the solution.

autonomy would be undesirable. The destruction of all local community autonomy and all sense of local identification would seem to lead the individual as indicated previously to a sense of personal incompetence which can only result in an even greater anti-democratic potential than is present today.

The Community of "Limited Liability"

The findings of this study call into question theoretical formulations which see the local community merely in the time perspective of a historical shift from "gemeinschaft" (simple—intimate) social forms to "gesellschaft" (complex—indirect) social forms.

The analysis of the collapse or survival of postulated earlier and simpler social arrangements in the urban community eliminates much significant data on how community social controls operate. This observation has become increasingly evident to social scientists who are interested in the workings of power and voluntary association in the local community. The large-scale organization of the urban community hardly eliminates the necessity of theoretical analysis of the networks of intimate and cohesive social relations which supply the basis of collective action on the local community level. In a fundamental sense, the contemporary balance and interrelations between "gemeinschaft" and "gesellschaft" social forms in the local community are as relevant as estimates of long-term trends. (All too frequently, these estimates of the long-term trends in gemeinschaft merely focus on the formal aspects of social organization.)

Recent theoretical reorientations have sought to free the

concepts and definitions of the sociology of the urban community from the limitations linked to the bias of implied value premises. The disrepute in which the concept "disorganization" has fallen in certain types of sociological writings is reflective of this issue.[7]

It seems appropriate to point out that the generalized description of the urban residential community implied by this research is a community of "limited liability." Our community is clearly not one of completely bureaucratized and impersonalized attachments. In varying degrees, the local community resident has a current psychological and social investment in his local community. In varying degrees, use of local facilities is accompanied by community orientations. The extent and character of these attachments are in good measure linked to the individual resident's predispositions and acts. Raising a family and, to a lesser extent, length of residence and local social contacts predispose him to an acceptance of local community institutions and social controls. In the process, purely "rational" and "instrumental" relations are modified. In this regard, individuals vary in the extreme; some are more capable (or have more need) than others of developing these orientations.

But, in all cases, these attachments are limited in the amount of social and psychological investment they represent. Thus, the notion of a community of "limited liability" emerges. (The term is viewed as similar in many aspects to the individual's commitment of "limited liability" in economic affairs.) The individual, responding to the general cultural norms, is likely to demand more from his community

7. Robert Merton in his theoretical work *Social Theory and Social Structure* (Glencoe, Ill.: Free Press, 1949) seeks to deal explicitly with this problem. A careful reading of Thomas and Znaniecki's *The Polish Peasant* will indicate that even earlier, when these authors used the term "disorganization," they were not oblivious to the value implications of from the term.

than he will invest. But more significantly, his relation to the community is such—his investment is such—that when the community fails to serve his needs, he will withdraw. Withdrawal implies either departure from the local community or merely lack of involvement. Withdrawal to some extent takes place with individual aging. More often it accompanies changes in the ethnic or social composition of the community. For some the withdrawal is slight since the original investment was slight or non-existent. Finally the point of withdrawal may vary from community to community, from class to class, from ethnic group to ethnic group; but for each individual there is a point at which he cuts off his losses. Seldom is the investment so great that the individual is permanently committed to a community that cannot cater to his needs.[8]

Thus, in summary, the dimensions of the local community point towards emerging social change in the largest metropolitan districts. Motives for community orientation center around the family with its gravitational pull toward the community and to a lesser extent around other primary group contacts. Within a specific local community, significant

---

8. Such a view of the community eliminates the necessity of employing the orientations of small and isolated community research where frequency of personal acquaintance is viewed as the basis of social stratification. The common indices of frequency of contact are mostly misleading for analyzing these local interlocking directorates. In the urban community, influential contacts do not necessarily require high frequency of contact. Models of influence based on the observation by social anthropologists of small isolated communities hardly reflect the social realities of the urban metropolis, where "rational" and "instrumental" considerations mold elites into power blocs.

Into the "limited liability" conceptualization can also be built dimensions of indirect social control involving the mass media, as well as the leadership and power relations of the local community. From this general orientation, the sharp distinction between mass communications and interpersonal communications research begins to fade. Instead analysis of the interrelated patterns of mass communications and personal communications in the context of a particular social structure becomes more relevant.

aspects of social organization operate without respect to socio-economic status, although deviations (both higher or lower) from the status norms of the community tend to some degree to interfere with community cohesion. Local leadership functions in a social milieu of apparent rationalistic interpersonal contacts but these contacts are surrounded by a network of purely personalistic relations. Local leadership also involves a heavy emphasis on non-partisanship, which is in effect an emphasis on the perpetuation of the status quo. Compromise is the general theme except when fundamental values in the community are impinged by external threats.

The resulting balance of social control at the local community level is one which leaves relatively untouched only a minority of residents, heavily involves another perhaps smaller group in the community, and creates varying degrees of involvement for the bulk of the residents. Many of these elements are indicative of socially adaptive mechanisms seeking and struggling to modify the impact of industrialism and large-scale organization on the local community. This perspective eliminates the necessity of overemphasizing the impersonalized aspects of urban personality and thereby the character of social manipulation in the local community can be seen in its proper limits.

VIII

The Future of the Community Press

After three decades of growth, the community press has been established as a sound business venture. This was possible as a result of the decentralization of the central business district combined with technological innovations in the printing trades. Changes in publishing technology and in the economics of the local community will be prime factors in accounting for future trends for these elements supply the limiting factors within which the publisher as an entrepreneur must operate.

Contentwise, the distinctive aspects of the community press relate to the division of labor in supplying news which has grown up between the daily and the community press. This division of labor which is likely to persist in the near future extends beyond that of information and news. The community newspaper presents a content which is low in controversy and thereby affords stark relief from the "noise" of the daily press, and the other mass media. Moreover, it extends prestige to those individuals who are without influence or reputation and who by their sheer numbers are excluded from the columns of the daily press. This hardly implies that all local residents are involved; rather there is a reversal of emphasis.

The extensive reader interest in the community press is related to family attributes and community orientations, and trends in these factors are certain to influence the viability of the community press. In turn, the degree to which the community press contributes to the maintenance of family solidarity and community cohesion is less certain, although clearly operative. Moreover, the impact of the community press is conditioned by the imagery of its audience which sees the contents in a non-commercialized, non-partisan perspective. This imagery contributes to a willingness to accept the validity and trustworthiness of its message. Careful management by community newspaper publishers can help maintain this audience perspective. Finally, the community newspaper is characterized by a network of personal communications which surrounds its formal and mass character. This network not only influences its contents but also increases credibility and impact.

The social role of the publisher as an entrepreneur of advertising space and a spokesman on behalf of the local community, makes possible the day-by-day functioning of the community press. The pressures brought to bear on the publisher and the elements the publisher can mobilize for community action have frequently been viewed as those linked with real estate and property interests. This is a stereotype, which, like all stereotypes, has some important basis in reality. It would be more accurate to describe the social role of the publisher as tending to extend into a wider range of community interests. This trend which seems likely to continue has served to enhance the position of the community press.

Fundamentally, the viability of the community press, like any other mass media, is linked to the "economics" of production and distribution. To date, the technology of the community press has been tied to the linotype and the rotary press. The present rising cost levels, when compounded with the ever-increasing shortage of newsprint, contain potentials for weakening the economic position of the community press. The community press in the past has been able to deal with increasing costs by increasing circulation and advertising rates. There are, of course, limits to such adjustments, although the last decade has seen a steady rise in national income and therefore in the allocations of advertising revenue.[1]

The community press also displays a strong tendency away from "free" circulation and even from "optional pay," to full payment and subscription. This trend reflects the increasing costs of production which force publishers to pass on to their readers at least the cost of the white paper and circulation facilities, a formula which is standard for the daily press. In the last decade, the publishers have been more secure in their sense of the adequacy of their product and their ability to attract and maintain a readership which will bear these costs.

Nevertheless, economic weakness may develop from the inability of the community press to adapt to new technological changes. This seems to be a peculiar observation for an industry whose growth and success was characterized by great flexibility and ingenuity in achieving its self-interests. The development of various types of new photographic printing processes seems to hold the greatest economic possibilities

---

1. Strangely enough during periods of business fluctuation in which merchants feel a temporary decline in revenues, advertising expenditures have increased. Advertising becomes a means of dealing with temporary fluctuations in the level of retail business. Long-term downward trends must, however, spell marked contraction of advertising revenue for community newspapers.

of expansion in the community newspaper field.[2] Estimates have been made of the decrease in costs of production of the three sample papers of this study if they were to introduce modernized composition and presswork facilities.[3] Reduction in costs is both a function of the number of pages and the number of copies published; more pages and more copies, in general, result in increased savings when the new technology is introduced. The saving ranges from about twelve per cent in the case of small papers to almost forty per cent for larger community newspapers.

Nevertheless, where such processes have been introduced, it has usually been in areas where new newspapers are being established rather than in converting old-type rotary-type operations to new reproductive techniques. Usually this has taken place in new communities, especially in suburbs, and has hardly affected the bulk of the urban community press. In addition to reluctance to experiment as long as reasonable profits are assured by present techniques, opposition to change is also fostered by unionized printers.

A widespread feeling exists among publishers that both advertisers and readers would react negatively to the newer forms of printing, especially since this would make the community press look less like the daily press. Such an attitude, of course, is clear testament to the persistence of the sense of inferiority among the community publishers with respect to

---

2. Community newspapers can modernize either by (a) maintaining their present linotype setting facilities and introducing photo-offset procedures for printing their publications or by (b) substituting new typesetting facilities which do not employ metal molds but are based on typewriter principles and printing by means of photo-offset procedures. The latter technique represents substantial savings in operation.

3. The estimates were made by John Malone, noted newspaper economist, of the University of Chicago, after careful examination of the available data. The introduction of photo-offset technology has the effect of cutting down slightly the number of words per column inch, of increasing the number of pictures and drawings that can be employed and in altering to some degree the format and typography of the paper.

the daily newspaper publisher. There is little discussion of the possibility that by further distinguishing themselves from the daily press the community press might increase its audience rather than decrease it.

In like manner, there has been little interest on the part of community newspaper publishers to experiment with market research. This is, in part, due to the high costs involved; in part, it is due to the perspective of advertisers in the urban community press who look directly to their sales figures and their profit statements for the basis on which to make decisions about advertising expenditures.[4]

All in all, the various factors that enter into productions of the community newspaper tend to produce an equilibrium similar to that encountered in the daily press. Entrance into the field by new units is progressively more difficult. Increasingly, the community publisher needs more revenue from his readers, and an increasingly larger proportion of revenue must now come from classified as compared to display advertisements. These requirements imply sufficient organizational ability and resources to permit the development of a paying

---

4. It is of course difficult to estimate whether the impact of market research is a function of the actual validity of the findings or the peculiar prestige accorded these findings in certain circles. The community newspaper industry's reluctance to make use of market research arises partly out of its presumed belief that the techniques of market research are not applicable in this case. The findings of this study when they first became known to community newspaper publishers aroused interest as to the possibility of a national audit which would certify to national advertisers production, distribution and readership of the community press. At two national conventions of community newspaper publishers this topic was of central concern, especially since representatives of national advertising agencies were outspoken about the failure of community newspaper publishers to establish audit procedures.

Collective action has been slow in emerging. Differences of opinion in the industry not only have to be overcome but the development of market research would introduce a new and imponderable factor in the industry which must be carefully weighed. Preoccupation with national shortages of newsprint has of course de-emphasized interest. Publishers are once more in a seller's market and therefore are less concerned with this issue.

readership which will also make use of the paper's classified advertisements. It is no longer possible for a publisher to get the support of a group of merchants and thereby guarantee himself the financial base for his enterprise. Population growth in the last decade has assisted most community publishers, although with considerable variation. Community publishers at the periphery of the legal limits of the city or in suburban areas have of course experienced the most marked growth. But increases in circulation without adequate increased advertising revenue are not profitable and do not represent real growth of a newspaper. However, the decentralization movement of retail business outlets seems to be continuing and even accelerating with resultant increases both in display and classified advertisements. (On the other hand, it is not difficult to see a point at which the metropolitan newspapers might adapt their techniques through specialized editions to sections of the city in order to recapture this revenue.)

No single economic factor is as significant for the future stability and development of the media as a realistic appraisal of community newspapers by national advertising agencies. Even a slight increased allocation of national advertising budgets to the community press would result in a significant difference in the stability and growth of the industry. The community press through cooperative arrangements has eliminated the administrative difficulties involved in placing national advertising in numerous decentralized outlets. Although type of circulation bears no relation to readership or impact, the decline of the free circulation aspects of the community press ought to alter national advertising agencies' practices in utilizing the community press.

Nevertheless, the managers of national advertising revenue have been slow to recognize the relevance of community newspapers for their commercial objectives. Commercial self-interest of large-scale merchandisers requires the specialized audience of the community press. Moreover, the current interest of national business and industrial organizations in meeting their long-term social responsibilities in community relations should contribute to a reappraisal of national advertising in the community press.

The future of the urban community press involves the viability of its economic arrangements; it involves also the persistence of the needs which the community press now meets. The current decentralization trend of the central business district is likely to continue to strengthen the economic basis of a wide segment of the community press. Likewise, this decentralization trend probably means the persistence and strengthening of local community needs, although the dynamics of community change will certainly produce casualties.[5]

Today we are in a period of crisis. Social cohesion grounded in local community integration supplies an important ingredient for mobilizing our human resources. Social cohesion, whether it be in an army or in a local community, means, in effect, the existence of a communications system by means of which individuals are oriented towards group action. As during World War II, it will become more and more apparent that the "big" mass media are less and less relevant for guiding the vast array of community-based activities required for national security if only because of their generality. The urban community press will become an object of interest to all sorts of organizers and executives. The current effectiveness of the urban community press can be utilized only if it is able to strengthen its decentralized roots and to maintain its current perspective of a predominantly community focus of attention.

---

5. There are signs that in carefully planned areas of urban redevelopment the community press is strengthened.

Appendix

I. Content Analysis

A. Procedures for Applying Content Analysis Categories

The content analysis employed the individual news story, feature story or editorial as the basic unit of analysis. The individual item constituted both the unit of analysis and the context unit. Each item was recorded in terms of column inch length. The contents of a community newspaper, for the purposes of this analysis, were divided into three categories: 1) printed text, 2) advertising, 3) miscellaneous.

The printed text was defined to include news stories, features, announcements, letters to the editor, editorials, etc. Pictures were treated as textual material. Headline space was measured as part of the text to which the headline was linked. Advertising included all types: display, classified, public service, and self promotion. Under miscellaneous, there were those items which could not be treated by content analysis, such as mastheads, crossword puzzles, etc. The content analysis encompassed all the printed text and for some content dimension the advertising was analyzed. Data on the reliability of the content analysis schema were present previously on page 74.

B. Content Analysis Categories
for Textual Material

Each item was analyzed in terms of the following dimensions:

a. Space	e. Subject matter
b. Type of item	f. Theme or issue
c. Prominence	g. Major individual or agency
d. Scope	h. Identifications

SPACE MEASUREMENT

The following space categories were employed:

Less than 1 inch	6-7
1-2	7-9
2-3	9-12
3-4	12-15
4-5	15-20
5-6	20 and over

TYPE OF ITEM

Care had to be employed in classifying the items into news, human interest, features, editorials. Since the delimitations were viewed in terms of the special news problems of the community newspaper, the following definitions were employed:

1. News: factual reports (these include all factual reports regardless of the importance of item if the item is designed to report on the occurrence, past or future, of some event).

2. Human interest: items designed to dramatize routine events or, on the other hand, items which assume affectual value because of their strangeness, uniqueness, etc.

3. Features: items dealing with home economics, cultural materials, commercial entertainment and nite life.

4. Other

PROMINENCE

Prominence was defined in terms of three levels:

1. Top two stories on page one.
2. All other material on page one.
3. All other pages.

SCOPE

Scope was defined as the geographical area in which the events described in the item take place:

1. Local community—implicit designation of the local community —in which newspaper circulates

2. Local community—explicit designation of neighborhood, community, specific community area—in which newspaper circulates

3. Sector of city (with which newspaper is identified)
4. City-wide
5. State
6. National
7. International
8. Not classifiable

SUBJECT MATTER

1. Public housing
2. Street cleaning and clean up campaigns
3. Public transportation
4. Crime and accident control
5. School system, libraries
6. Parks
7. Public Health Service
8. Educational (PTA)
9. Inter-group
10. Community Chest
11. Other
12. Business enterprise activities
13. Political party activities
14. Public affairs (not specified elsewhere)
15. Trade union activities
16. Organized religion

SUBJECT MATTER—contd.

17. Crime
18. Accident and natural disaster
19. Local social organization activity
20. Local cultural organizations activity
21. Fraternal organizations
22. Veterans organizations, patriotic organizations, ROTC
23. Patriotic celebrations
24. Social and society news, including weddings, anniversaries, deaths
25. Personal achievements, including education
26. Amusements and entertainment news
27. "Women" features
28. Community history
29. Self promotion
30. Other
31. Sports
32. Light, water, public utilities

THEMES

1. No issue of theme involved —routine report
2. Service, activity expanded, is expanding or to be expanded (new program launched)
3. Service, activity, contracted, is contracting or to be contracted
4. Demand service, activity expand or maintained
5. Oppose expansion, maintenance of service or activity
6. Organization will undertake, or has undertaken fund raising campaign
7. Organization engages in or will engage in educational or cultural event or program
8. Support of Truman Fair Deal (not specified elsewhere)
9. Opposition to Truman Fair Deal (not specified elsewhere)
10. Organization engages in "Americanization" program
11. Oppose public housing activities in Chicago
12. Support public housing activities in Chicago
13. Local activity in support of minority group civil rights
14. Local activity in opposition to minority group civil rights
15. Support of legislative action in behalf of minority group civil rights
16. Oppose legislative action in behalf of minority group civil rights
17. Other

MAIN ACTOR OR AGENCY

1. Alderman
2. City administration
3. City council
4. State or national legislature or agency
5. Community council

MAIN ACTOR OR AGENCY—contd.

6. Business man or men (unorganized)
7. Business firm
8. Businessmen's association
9. Property owners' association
10. National business and real estate association
11. A.F. of L.
12. C.I.O.
13. American Veterans Committee
14. Veterans Organization
15. Clergyman
16. Church and church affiliated groups
17. Local social organization
18. Fraternal organization
19. School groups (PTA)
20. Youth groups
21. "Local residents"
22. Not applicable
23. Other
24. Political party or organization

IDENTIFICATIONS

Religion
1. Protestant denomination
2. Catholic, Holy Name
3. Jewish

Political
7. Democratic
8. Republican
9. Independent

Ethnic
4. Polish
5. Italian
6. Other ethnic

II. Readership Survey

A. Sample of Respondents

The sampling procedure for selecting respondents in the readership survey involved three steps: 1) the selection of three community areas from among the seventy-five Chicago community areas (this procedure is described on pages 114-7; 2) the selection of sample points or city blocks within the three communities; 3) and, the selection of respondents within these sample blocks. The sampling procedure had to adapt itself to the varying sizes of the community areas as well as varying degrees of homogeneity within the three sample communities. In all, the sample design required the selection of six hundred respondents, or two hundred from each community of which half would be male heads of households and half female.

Selection of the city blocks. Within each community area ten sample points consisting of a single city block were selected at random. Since Carleton Manor and Bethel Park were relatively homogeneous communities, this was accomplished by listing the blocks in the community area and selecting at random blocks weighted by number of dwelling units. In Atwater, the randomized selection of blocks weighted by dwelling units was accomplished after the community had been divided into relatively homogeneous sectors.

In order to adjust for the relative concentration of population in the three community areas, it was necessary to add additional blocks contiguous to the sample block. In each community, the number of additional blocks varied depending on the population concentration. In Atwater, because of a high concentration of households only one additional block was required; in Bethel Park, two additional blocks were required while in Carleton Manor three neighboring blocks were added. In each case the additional blocks contiguous to the sample point were added on a random basis by randomizing the north, south, east, and west directions from the original sample block.

Selection of the households. Within each sample point, an average of twenty interviews were desired. In order to achieve this objective and to adjust for varying concentrations of population between the three communities the number of households per block in each community sampled were varied. In Atwater every eighth household was sampled; in Bethel Park every tenth, and in Carleton Manor every fifth household was taken. The number of blocks at each sample point and the ratio of households sampled in each block provided in excess of two hundred interviews from each community area in order to compensate for refusals or no responses.

Interviewer assignments began with the original sample block and designated the order by which the neighboring blocks were to be covered. The corner of the block on which the interviewer was to begin, the direction he was to enumerate, and the number of households from the corner of the block to be skipped before the first household was selected, were all designated to the interviewer on the basis of randomization.

From the first assigned household the interviewer counted off to the fifth, eighth, or tenth household, depending on his community, for each succeeding household. Detailed rules for enumerating households were given each interviewer.

Every dwelling unit in which one person or a group of persons resides was considered a household. Households were counted by examination of door bells and mail boxes; the interviewers were instructed to include households living in basements, in houses set back of other houses, or in back of stores. Where there was doubt the interviewers were instructed to ask how many families were living in a particular dwelling structure. Unless the area had many roomers, different names under the same bell were counted as one household. However, where more than one name was listed and different rings assigned to each name, each name in the rooming house was counted as a household. Transient hotels were skipped.

Court buildings were enumerated consecutively. Households in each entrance, of a multiple dwelling unit, were enumerated in the following order: first floor, front; first floor, rear; similarly with the second and third floors. In two-story houses the first floor was counted first. Where basements, garages or back-of-store residences had separate street numbers, that number determined the order of enumeration. Where the street number was the same as the attached house, the basement was counted first. Garage apartments were counted following the attached house.

Selection of the respondent. The sample within each household was drawn from the adult heads (male or female) of the household over twenty-one years of age. Adult heads of households were defined as heads of complete families as well as heads of incomplete families (families where either the father or mother is dead or divorced). If one of the sons or daughters is an adult but continues to live with his parents, his parents were considered as heads of the household. However, where the parents, man and/or wife, were living with one of their married children, the head of the household was selected from the younger generation. An incomplete household was any household that did not have a married couple.

The sampling instructions permitted the substitution of the immediately next household in the event that the sampled household was not at home.

For the first block in each sample point, the interviewer was informed whether his first respondent was to be male or female. Assuming it was a male, the interviewer proceeded to the first household assigned in the block and asked to interview the male head of the household. If the male is not at home, a call back was projected and the interviewer proceeded to the household immediately next door (n plus one). If the male was at home at this household, the interview was completed with this respondent. However, if this respondent was not at home, a call back had to be made. The call back was always made first on the original respondent and then on the immediate next-door respondent.

For the second household falling in the sample, the interviewer selected the female head of the household. He alternated back to a male on the third and so forth until the block was exhausted. For each household, the substitution of immediately-next-door (n plus one) households was possible according to the rules stated above. In no case was the search for a head of the household of the proper sex extended beyond the next-door household.

In the event that the second household falling in the sample was an incomplete household, with no female head of the household, the male head of the household was interviewed. The interviewer then instituted the procedure of alternation and took the female head of the household in the third household in the sample.

The interviewers were required to make at least three call backs at both the n and the n plus one household. However, since the interviewers made numerous trips to the same sample point they had the opportunity to make extensive call backs in certain cases. As a result, the combined refusal and not at home rate did not generally exceed six percent.

B. *Interview Schedule*

1. About how long have you been living in this house?
2. Where was the last place you lived before you moved here? How long did you live there?
   Where have you lived most of your life?
3. Generally speaking, how do you feel about living in this community?
   Like it _____ Dislike it _____ Other _____
   What do you like about it?
   Is there anything else?
   What don't you like about it?
   Is there anything else?
4. Do you have much to do with the people in this neighborhood?
   If yes, in what way?
   Do you visit with them? Yes _____ No _____
5. Incidentally, what is this community called?
   _____Correct _____ambiguous _____incorrect _____don't know
   (specify _____)
6. Would you say that _____ is:
   A pleasant _____ or unpleasant _____ community
   A clean _____ or dirty _____ community
   Do many of your friends live in this community?
   Or do they live elsewhere?
7. Do you think of this community as your real home—where you really belong?
   If "no" or "don't know": What place do you think of as your real home?
8. Do you buy your clothes or house furnishings in the Loop?
9. Which newspapers do you read more or less regularly?
   _____Tribune _____Sun Times _____News _____Herald American
   _____other (specify)
10. Have you ever seen the (name of local community newspaper)?
11. How do you get the _____?
    By mail subscription _____ Delivered to the house _____
    Pick up in store _____ Other _____
    Do you pay for it or do you get it free? Pay _____ Free _____
12. About how often have you read the _____ in the last month?
    Regularly _____(each week) Occasionally _____(about once a month) Rarely _____(less than once a month) Never _____

13. Would you say that you read most (or all) or it; part (or some) of it; or that you just glance through it?

_____Read most _____Read partially _____glance

14.   (For non-readers skip to Question 23)

For Readers:

What do you look for in the _____?

If local news, query: What sort of local news?

15. Do you ordinarily read:

(1) _____store advertisements

Do you get information on where to shop from them?
Yes _____ No _____

(2) _____classified advertisements

Do you ever make use of them? Yes _____ No _____

(3) _____news about (name of community)

What news about the community do you remember reading about in a recent issue?

(4) _____sports (men only)

(5) _____social items (marriages, births and deaths)

What do you think about the social items?

(6) _____club news

(7) _____church news

Do you ever see the names of any of your friends in the _____? _____ Yes _____ No. If yes: For example, when (or similar probe)

(8) _____political news

What do you think the paper stands for in politics?

16. Do you miss the paper when it doesn't come? Why?

17. What do you do to get it when it doesn't come?

18. In general, what do you think about the _____?

Probe: What do you like about it? What don't you like about it?

19. Do you think it pays too little or too much attention to community problems?

Too little _____ About right _____ Too much _____

20. Why would you say you read the _____?

21. Do you think there are too many advertisements in the _____?

Too many _____ About right _____ Too few _____

22. Incidentally, how long have you been reading community newspapers like _____?

(Skip to question 25)

FOR NON-READERS

23. Why don't you read the _____?
24. In general, what do you think about it?

FOR ALL RESPONDENTS

25. Does anyone else in your house read the _____? Who?
26. About how often has _____ read it in the last month?
_____Regularly (each week) _____Occasionally (about once a month) _____Rarely (less than once a month) _____Never
27. As far as you know, would you say he (she) reads most of it; part (or some) of it; or that he (she) just glances through it?
_____Reads most _____Reads partially _____Glance
28. Does he (she) read it more or less carefully than he (she) reads the daily newspaper?
_____more
_____same
_____less
29. Do you think the _____ ought to be published since there are big daily papers in Chicago? _____Yes _____No _____Other
Why do you say that?
30. Do you think the _____ is published:
a. _____To develop community spirit
b. _____To make profit for the owners
c. _____To get better facilities for the community, like playgrounds and new traffic lights
d. _____To help get good people elected to government
31. What clubs or organizations do you belong to?
32. Which of them meet here in the community?
33. About how often do you attend church?
_____Regularly _____Occasionally _____Rarely _____Never
34. To which church do you go?
35. How many movies have you seen in the last month?
_____None _____One _____Two _____Three _____Four
_____Five or more
36. How many hours do you listen to the radio on an average weekday night?
_____Less than one hour _____One to two hours
_____Two to three hours _____Three or more hours
37. Do you have a television set? _____Yes _____No

38. How many hours do you view television on an average week-day night?

_____Less than one hour   _____One to two hours
_____Two to three hours   _____Three or more hours

39. Do you read any magazines more or less regularly?
Which?

40. Would you say that you read most (or all) of the _____; part (or some) of it; or that you just glance through it?

_____Read most _____Read partially _____Glance

41. About how many books do you read in an average month?

_____None _____One _____Two _____Three _____Four
_____Five or more

42. About how often do you use the public library branch in this neighborhood?

_____Once a week or oftener _____Up to once a month _____Up to once a year _____Less or never

43. Where were you born?

44. Where do you work?

45. What do you do for a living?

46. What does your (husband) (wife) do for a living?

47. Where?

48. What was the last grade you finished in school?

_____Some grade school _____Eight _____Ten _____Twelve
_____Some college _____Completed college

49. How old are you?

50. Do you have any children?

51. How old are they?

52. Do they live with you?

53. To which school do they go?

54. Do you own or rent your house?

55. Would you tell me in which of these general groups your family's total weekly income falls before taxes? (Hand respondent card)

_____A (under $25) _____B ($25-$35) _____C ($35-50)
_____D ($50-$75) _____E ($75-$100) _____F ($100-$125)
_____G ($125 and over)
_____Refused

We need this information simply to make sure we are getting a good sample.

56. What do you feel needs to be done in this community?
What else?

(If a specific answer is given)
57. Of what help are the precinct captain or the alderman in getting this (or these) things done?
58. Do you think the political parties can do anything to improve the community?
(If the respondent's reply is "nothing" to question 56):
59. Do you think it will stay the way it is?
60. Do you think the political parties can do anything else to help?

_____MALE _____SINGLE
_____FEMALE _____MARRIED   HOUSE TYPE
            _____WIDOWED OR   _____Single family house
            DIVORCED   _____Two-family house
                                _____Multiple unit house (4 and
                                6 units)
                                _____Apartment house
                                HOUSE CONDITION
                                _____Above average
                                _____Average
                                _____Below average
Date of interview _____   Time of interview _____
Address of respondent _____   Name of interviewer _____
Call _____

III. Basic Data on the Three Sample Communities

A. Historical Sketches

ATWATER

Atwater has had a very long and colorful past. Traders and explorers in the last half of the seventeenth century made portage across this district from Lake Michigan to the Des Plaines River, and the local historian claims that Father Marquette passed the winter of 1674–75 in the vicinity. Around 1810 the first permanent settlement was made, only to be temporarily wiped out at the time of the Fort Dearborn massacre.

By 1831, the Chicago Council ordered a road laid from the Chicago river to Joliet. Following an Indian trail diagonally southwestward, this was the first good farmer's road to Chicago and since it passed through Atwater, it is today the community's main thoroughfare. When Irish immigrants arrived in 1836 to work on the Illinois-Michigan Canal they settled in this district and gave it its early predominantly Irish flavor. These early immigrants founded a glue factory, as well as a slaughter and packing house on the outskirts of the district, making the area particularly malodorous. Today, over one hundred years later, the residents of part of the community are still afflicted with a like odor, for these slaughter houses have developed into the Chicago packing house area in a nearby community.

Atwater, with its predominantly early Irish settlement, became the home of many prominent politicians and developed a strong community spirit. In fact, "true" residents had to reside in a small section in the west sector of the district and be of early residence. During the Civil War the community was pro-southern, and rebel victories were celebrated in the village. In 1863, Atwater was annexed to Chicago.

In the 1880's and 1890's many famous Chicago politicians continued to come from the district. Industry grew up in a solid wall around the residential section, breweries, foundries, brick yards and steel mills. The isolation of the community was insured by its physical boundaries; on two sides the branch of a river flows, and on the third side there is an elevated railroad embankment.

Through the years its predominantly Irish population gave way slowly to the immigration of Poles, Lithuanians, and Italians. In 1940, the Lithuanians constituted the largest foreign born group in the community whose total foreign born was then 17.5 percent. First and second generation Lithuanians, Poles and Italians have been joined by a slight admixture of Southern whites.

The ethnic groups are mainly employed as semi-skilled workers in the industrial establishments and packing houses which encircle the community. While semi-skilled occupations predominate (32.5 percent of the heads of households in our sample), the proportion of skilled workers and foremen is less but not markedly less than the other two communities studied. In Atwater, 16.0 percent were classed as skilled workers and foremen representing the mobility which resulted from accumulation of skill and low managerial positions over even lower status groups, especially Negroes. The concentration in the clerk, sales and kindred group (20.5 percent) is in part due to a large nearby mail order house which employs local residents, many of whose jobs though nominally clerical have aspects of semi-skilled work.

Economically, Atwater is of course at the bottom of the three communities. This is not because the proportion of its families with lowest incomes is so much greater than the other communities; it is because it has so very few in the upper ranges of the salary scale. Atwater's "low" position is more clearly a matter of status, if status is viewed in terms of occupational prestige.

As in other parts of working class Chicago, home ownership is a desired goal and quite prevalent (37.5 percent of the dwelling units are owner occupied.) The extreme age of the physical structure of the community can be seen from the data on the years in which construction took place. Over 65 percent of the houses were built before the turn of the century; 28 percent between 1900 and 1919; and only 4 percent since then, with almost none since the Great Depression. Through the ethnic successions, Atwater has maintained a high birth rate but its population has not grown rapidly. Housing shortages and no building for over three decades has forced outmigration.

The main intersection which dominates the commercial life of Atwater lies in the southeastern sector of the area and is two and one-half miles, or 15-20 minutes by street car, from the edge of the Loop. There are no branches of downtown department stores, but the shopping center is equipped with all sorts of outlets that offer credit to the working class. The nationality character (e.g. Polish and Lithuanian) of many of the stores is apparent. Closeness of the Loop is a powerful attraction, nevertheless 42.5 percent of the sample shop predominate in Atwater.

BETHEL PARK

The Bethel Park community [1] grew out of three old towns, Riverview, Washington and Robinswood. As early as 1835 real

_____
1. The name by which the local residents refer to this community area is not the same as designated by the *Local Community Fact Book, op. cit.*

estate was purchased and the first settler was a farmer from New York State, who came to the area in 1837. In 1852 the Chicago and Milwaukee Railroad built its line through the eastern edge of the present community, and soon the streets were laid out.

In the middle of the 1880's the first ethnic immigration began when German laborers and businessmen moved into real estate subdivisions. Most of the settlers worked in the brick yards or in the farm implements works just north of the area. There was a large adjoining wooded tract in which local German societies held marksmanship contests and festivals. Originally called Sharpshooters' Park, this land later became the site of a commercialized amusement park which serves the area and many adjoining communities. In 1900, the surface lines were extended from the Loop, and in 1907, the extension of the elevated established a firm link between the community and the city.

Today, the community is mainly a residential community with physical barrier of a belt of industry on one side.

Bethel Park's social structure differs from that of Atwater mainly because of its much larger lower-middle class which is accompanied by a relative absence of lower-lower class groups. Occupationally, its lower-middle class is composed in good measure of the clerical, sales and kindred category which is the largest occupational grouping in the district (30.0 percent). In addition to the privately employed clericals, Bethel Park has numerous governmental and institutional white collar workers. The skilled workers (23.0 percent) are employed in the factories in the adjoining belt of industry and in the building trades throughout the city. Higher income level is due to its proprietor, managerial group (8.5 percent), salesmen in the white collar group, and certain of the skilled labor workers.

Bethel Park has a high population with a very heavy population density of 30,788 per square mile. Its average birth rate does not result in more than nominal increases in population because of the lack of housing, and because the sons and daughters of the community tend to migrate out. The population is subject to pronounced aging therefore; the new residents are South and East Europeans who move into the homes of old residents who have died. Building in the community has been gradual over many years with almost one third of its buildings erected before the turn of the century. Since 1920, then, there has been no building. The older homes were predominantly single and two family homes while new construction took the form of middle-size apartment units which made for the high concentration of population.

Bethel Park's main shopping center boasts of many branches of the largest downtown department stores and an extremely high volume of business. This shopping intersection, which lies about 4½ miles from the Loop, requires a 25 minute ride by street car and a slightly faster ride by elevated. Over 73.5 percent of our sample list themselves as predominately local shoppers, which is an indicator of markedly high local orientation.

CARLETON MANOR

Carleton Manor is the most recent of the three communities. Historical details can be traced back to 1858 when the U.S. Government deeded 160 acres of land within the district's boundaries to a private citizen. One of the earliest pioneers in this neighborhood was a retired street car conductor who with his wife "moved out into the country" bringing their possessions in a wagon. Soon the district was called "Penny's Town" because of the strong personality of the owner of the Penny General Store. Since most of the residents resented this nickname, they decided formally to choose a new name, and in 1910 Carleton Manor was decided upon.

Most of the sub-divisions's first citizens arrived during the World's Fair in 1893 and immediately afterward. Many were skilled mechanics employed in the railroad shops on the Southside. They were principally of German extraction, eager to own and establish their own homes, and they established the quiet middle-class character of the community which still persists. The character of the community was also affected by the fact that private investors owned large tracts of land in this region which were not built up until a much later period.

In fact, Carleton Manor remained relatively undeveloped until after World War I. Within the area a city park with a lake was a popular place for fishing, duck hunting, rabbit shooting, and picknickers on summer days. When a modern sewerage system was installed, Carleton Manor took its place in the list of Chicago's expanding communities.

Throughout its population increases, the foreign born element has remained low. Until recently, second and third generation Germans and Scandinavians were in the majority, while the foreign born element was of the same stock. Recently older Irish and some second generation East Europeans have started to come into the area.

Before 1919, less than 20 percent of its dwelling units had been constructed. During the 1920 decade the bulk of its houses went up. Again, in the years after the second World War, a building boom took place. The recent building expansion accounts for the difference in types of dwelling units in the 1940 Census and in our sample survey. The single family homes are predominantly owner-occupied with a median rental which is very high for a district within the city limits.

Carleton Manor is small in acreage comprising about ¾ of a square mile, with a very low population density of 13,180 per sq. mile in 1940, but which as indicated has increased since then. Its triangular shape is bounded by a park on one side, a main thoroughfare on the second, and a lesser thoroughfare on the third.

The district approximates suburbia in elements other than its housing. Although located about 9½ miles from the Loop, an interurban rapid transit system links it with the Loop in less than 25 minutes. Within the area there is no satellite shopping district; even the tertiary shopping centers are relatively undeveloped. Two shopping centers at a short distance serve the community, but the pull to the Loop is great. The rapid transit system and social character of the residents result in the low number of community satellite shoppers (36.5 percent of our sample reported themselves as predominantly non-Loop shoppers.)

Occupationally, the professionals together with proprietors, managers, and officials constitute the largest group (29.0 percent), while the clerical, sales, and kindred workers are of almost equal number. Heads of households who are skilled workers are almost invariably building trades workers, and are seldom employed in industrial factories. This occupational structure produces not only relatively high income but also relatively high social status, especially since the clerical, sales and kindred workers are heavily represented by moderately prosperous and prestigeful occupations.

B. Socio-Economic Data on the Three Sample Communities

1940 data based on U. S. Census. 1950 data based on Sample Survey.

	ATWATER	BETHEL PARK	CARLETON MANOR
Miles from Loop	2.5	4.5	9.0
Travel Time to Loop (minutes)			
Street car	15-20	25-30	45-50
Suburban train	—	20-25	20-25
Square Miles	2.54	1.58	.79
Density per square mile	19,277	30,788	13,180
Foreign Born			
1930	28.6	27.2	13.6
1940	22.1	22.7	12.6
1950	17.5	26.5	12.0
% Owner-Occupied Dwelling Units			
1930	33.7	36.6	58.3
1940	29.8	30.5	55.2
1950	37.5	36.4	77.5
House Types			
1940—single	19.7	17.4	61.6
—two	36.2	41.4	9.9
—multiple	44.1	41.2	28.5
1950—single	18.5	19.5	72.5
—two	36.0	44.5	8.0
—multiple	45.5	36.0	19.5
Median Value of Owner-occupied unit, 1940	$1,859	$3,116	$6,391
Monthly Rental, 1940	$16.38	$29.27	$44.69

	ATWATER	BETHEL PARK	CARLETON MANOR
Dwelling Units by Years Built			
1930–1940	.5	1.4	8.1
1920–1929	3.8	28.0	71.7
1900–1919	28.5	42.4	14.4
1899 or earlier	67.2	28.2	5.8
Size of Private Households, 1940	3.76	3.35	3.61
Percent Normal Households, 1940	71.4	79.6	87.5
Age, 1950			
Under 29	20.5	15.5	6.0
30-39	30.0	23.5	31.5
40-49	20.5	21.5	26.5
50-59	17.0	20.5	20.5
60 and over	12.0	19.5	15.5
Education, 1950			
Grade School	57.0	41.5	21.0
10 years	16.0	21.0	11.0
12 years	20.5	25.5	42.5
Some college	6.0	11.5	30.0
No school, no data	.5	.5	.5
Place of Education, 1950			
Educated abroad	9.0	21.0	5.0
Income, 1950			
Under $50	21.5	15.5	5.5
$50-$75	43.0	37.5	22.0
$75-$100	22.0	28.0	28.0
$100-$125	10.5	14.0	24.0
Over $125	2.0	4.0	19.0
No data	1.0	1.0	1.5
	100.0	100.0	100.0
Occupation, 1950 *			
Professional	2.0	3.0	12.0
Propr., manager, off	4.5	8.5	17.0
Clerks, sales, kindred	20.5	30.0	28.5
Skilled workers & foremen	16.0	23.0	23.0
Semi-skilled workers	32.5	22.0	11.0

* Head of household.

	ATWATER	BETHEL PARK	CARLETON MANOR
Service workers	12.5	2.0	0.0
Unskilled workers	5.5	4.0	2.0
Students	.5	1.5	.5
No data	6.0	6.0	6.0
Status, 1950			
Upper-Middle	2.0	3.5	17.5
Lower-Middle	34.5	45.0	54.0
Upper-Lower	33.0	33.5	16.0
Lower-Lower	23.5	8.5	5.0
Not classifiable	7.0	9.5	7.5
Length of residence (Present House), 1950			
Up to 4 years	30.0	34.5	27.0
5-14 years	32.5	34.0	46.0
15 or over	37.5	31.5	27.0
Local Shopper (pred.), 1950	42.5	73.5	36.5
Church attendance, 1950			
Regular	77.0	36.5	53.5
Occasional	12.5	32.0	26.5
Rare	5.5	17.0	14.0
Never	5.0	14.5	6.0
Church Attend. in community, 1950	96.8	71.5	83.0
No. of Children, 1950			
No children	25.0	27.0	16.5
One	18.5	32.0	21.5
Two	23.5	23.0	40.0
Three or more	33.0	18.0	22.0

IV. List of Chicago Community Newspapers, June, 1951

Publication	Publisher	Address
Albany Park Times	Leo Lerner	5332 W. Ainslie Ave.
Auburn Parker	M. L. Novitt	8038 S. Racine Ave.
Austinite	Telfer MacArthur	5625 W. Lake St.
Austin News	Walter H. Buescher	5241 W. Chicago Ave.

Publication	Publisher	Address
Belmont-Central News	R. J. Peacock	2319 N. Milwaukee Ave.
Beverly Review	Weekly Review Publishing Co.	1829 W. 103rd St.
Booster	Leo Lerner	5332 W. Ainslie Ave.
Bridgeport News	Maurice Feldman	751 W. 25th St.
Brighton Park-McKinley Park Life	Brighton Publishing Co.	2949 W. 43rd St.
Calumet Index	Floyd Haas	11242 S. Michigan Ave.
Central Northwest Topics	Harry S. Weimer	4302 W. Wrightwood Ave.
Community News	R. J. Peacock	1117 N. Ashland Ave.
Community Register	A. J. Monaco	2549 S. Pulaski Ave.
Daily Calumet	Calumet Publishing Co.	9120 S. Baltimore Ave.
Edgebrook Events	———	6519 N. Algonquin Ave.
Edgebrook News	Leo Lerner	5332 W. Ainslie Ave.
Edgewater News	Leo Lerner	7519 N. Ashland Ave.
Edison-Norwood Review	Fred A. Fulle	6995 North-West Highway
Edison Parker	J. W. Carroll	6118 North-West Highway
Edison Park Times	Leo Lerner	5332 W. Ainslie Ave.
Garfieldian and Garfield News	Walter H. Buescher	3935 Washington Blvd.
Garfield Ridge News	Thomas J. Cody	5542 S. Natona Ave.
Gold Coast Independent	Charles Weber	3126 N. Ashland Ave.
Higgins-Harlem Press	Morton Steinman	5353 W. Lawrence Ave.
Higgins-Oriole Times	Leo Lerner	3434 W. Lawrence Ave.
Hyde Parker-Southeast News	A. C. Zeller	1201 East 55th St.
Hegewisch News	———	3142 East 133rd St.
Hyde Park Herald	Great Lakes Publ.	1223 East 55th St.
Irving Park News	R. J. Peacock	2319 N. Milwaukee Ave.
Jefferson-Norwood News	R. J. Peacock	2319 N. Milwaukee Ave.

Publication	Publisher	Address
Jefferson-Park Press	Morton Steinman	5353 W. Lawrence Ave.
Jefferson Park Times	Leo Lerner	5332 W. Ainslie Ave.
Journal, Back of the Yards	A. Hurwitz and J. Haffner	4601 S. Ashland Ave.
Lakeview Booster	Leo Lerner	3114 N. Greenview Ave.
Lakeview Economist	Saul R. Fellars	1606 N. Larabe Ave.
Lakeview Independent	Charles Weber	3126 N. Ashland Ave.
Lawndale News	Arthur J. Weiss	2530 S. Kedzie Ave.
Lincoln-Belmont Booster	Leo Lerner	3114 N. Greenview Ave.
Lindblom Weekly	———	6130 S. Wolcot Ave.
Logan Square Herald	Harry G. Weimer	4302 W. Wrightwood Ave.
Logan Square News	R. J. Peacock	2319 N. Milwaukee Ave.
Mayfair Times	Leo Lerner	5332 W. Ainslie Ave.
Mid-Week News	Edward Fahner	2728 W. Ainslie Ave.
Mid-West Herald	Arthur H. Weiss	2530 S. Kedzie Ave.
Mid-West Times	Robert R. Petrone	3437 W. Chicago Ave.
Montclare News	R. J. Peacock	2319 N. Milwaukee Ave.
Montrose Times	Leo Lerner	5332 W. Ainslie Ave.
Mount Greenwood Express	Roy G. Andrews	3058 West 111th St.
Northcenter News	C. W. Wermick	2050 W. Irving Park Ave.
North Loop News	B. R. Albanese	800 N. Clark St.
North Park Times	Leo Lerner	5332 W. Ainslie Ave.
North Side Star	Leo Lerner	7519 N. Ashland Ave.
North Town Economist	Saul R. Fellars	1606 N. Larabe Ave.
North Town Independent	Charles Weber	3126 N. Ashland Ave.
North Town News	Leo Lerner	7519 N. Ashland Ave.
North West News	R. J. Peacock	2319 N. Milwaukee Ave.
North West Side News	Morton Steinman	5353 W. Lawrence Ave.
North West Sunday Times	Leo Lerner	5332 W. Ainslie Ave.

Publication	Publisher	Address
North West Times	Leo Lerner	5332 W. Ainslie Ave.
North Westtown Booster	Aladdin Publ. Co.	3749 W. North Ave.
Norwood Park Citizen	William Carroll	6132 N. Northwest Highway
Norwood Park Times	Leo Lerner	3424 W. Lawrence Ave.
Portage Park News	R. J. Peacock	2319 N. Milwaukee Ave.
Portage Park Times	Leo Lerner	5332 W. Ainslie Ave.
Ravenswood-Lincolnite	Leo Lerner	7519 N. Ashland Ave.
Rogers Park News	Leo Lerner	7519 N. Ashland Ave.
Sauganash Star	Leo Lerner	7519 N. Ashland Ave.
Sheridan Center Booster	Leo Lerner	3114 N. Greenview Ave.
Southeast Economist	W. F. McDonnell	728 W. 65th St.
Southend Reporter	J. W. Crane	105 E. 115th St.
South Side Courier	———	7646 S. Cottage Grove Ave.
South Side News	Walter M. Convey	9257 S. Cottage Grove Ave.
Southtown Economist	W. H. McDonnell	728 W. 65th St.
Southwest News Herald	Edward Vondrak	5855 S. Kedzie Ave.
Spectator of Edge-brook Lincoln	William Carroll	6132 N. Northwest Highway
Sunday Booster	Leo Lerner	3114 N. Greenview Ave.
Sunday Northwest	R. J. Peacock	2319 N. Milwaukee Ave.
The Tattler	T. D. Costello	7031 N. Ridge Ave.
Uptown News	Leo Lerner	7519 N. Ashland Ave.
West Side Times	Arthur J. Weiss	2530 S. Kedzie Ave.
West Suburban Times	R. J. Peacock	2319 N. Milwaukee Ave.
West Town Herald	Arthur J. Weiss	2530 S. Kedzie Ave.
Woodlawn Booster	Allen Osherman	1153 E. 63rd St.

Postscript:
Communication
and Community

by Scott Greer

Why should the study of the neighborhood press in Chicago have major importance for the study of urban society? The neighborhood throw-away or the neighborhood shopper had usually been dismissed, even by social scientists, as trivial. Yet for me *The Community Press in an Urban Setting* was a breakthrough. I think it was important for one reason: it presented a dramatic new image of the great city as a human environment. It was an image which contributed to challenging our theory about urbanism and massive social change yet one conducive to the precise investigation of people's behavior where they live. It demonstrated the power of newer tools (the sample survey, content analysis) to criticize and clarify the grand speculations which had guided our treatment of urbanization.

Janowitz rediscovered community within the metropolis, and did so through the study of communications. Emphasizing the requirement for integration in the complex and delicately calibrated social system of the contemporary city, he demonstrated the emergence of social mechanisms which facilitate such integration. His emphasis was upon the community press, but he showed in detail the groups which supported it: household, neighborhood, voluntary associations, and the decentralized commercial center. Together these mechanisms allowed individuals to participate meaningfully in a small unit of larger structure—the fabric of the metropolis. This, he hypothesized, resulted in participation for the social structure, identification for the individual. In other words, the person gained significant relations while the society gained patterned behavior.

This approach avoids the easy generalities that have plagued urban sociology. Those crude dichotomies known as ideal types, which led us to try characterizing societies as *either* gemeinschaft or gesellschaft, mechanic or organic, folk or urban, are brought into serious question. The result is more complex, more interesting, and more relevant to the world we must describe.

Janowitz shifted the discussion to a question of the existence —and relative importance—of components in a totality. He showed the strength of informal relations rooted in family and friendship. He also showed their importance as limits and directives for the larger systems of organization: the market, polity, and press. Thus the metropolis need not destroy the roots of localized community; the urbanite can be neighbor and gossip; the denizen of Chicago's streets (described by Sherwood Anderson as "going on and on forever, out of nowhere into nothing") can also be a citizen of his local community in that enormous grid of urban sites and scenes. To be sure, he will not be *solely* committed to the locality; it is a "community of limited liability," for he has commitments otherwhere, to other groups. But is this not an accurate reflection of a segmentalized, nationalized society? In short, dropping either/or as a logical framework, we ask once more: how much and under what circumstances, what produces it and what comes of it?

The value of an approach can be gauged only in pragmatic terms. Thus, in commenting on *The Community Press in an Urban Setting* I will try to indicate the value and the limits of the framework through reporting studies in a number of cities which bear upon important hypotheses. Some hypotheses deal specifically with the press; more deal with what seems to me the major value of Janowitz's work: the use of the local press as a "tracer" to illuminate the structure of the local community within the metropolis.

The Community Press and Styles of Life

In the central city areas studied by Janowitz some 84 per cent of the adults interviewed were readers of their local press. In a Los Angeles sample, distributed among four census tracts, 70 per cent of the adult women interviewed were regular readers.[1] These census tracts were scattered in the central city of Los Angeles; one was only 15 minutes by automobile from the center, while one was on the outer edge of the city with characteristics similar to those of the stereotypical suburb. In the close-in neighborhood 60 per cent of the sample were readers, while in the other the percentage was 78. Thus the press was consistently important in these various neighborhoods, but its importance varied substantially.

---

1. "Urban Worlds: A Comparative Study of Four Los Angeles Areas," by Scott Greer and Ella Kube (Los Angeles: The Laboratory in Urban Culture of Occidental College, 1955) (processed). The study is reported in more detail in "Urbanism and Social Structure: A Los Angeles Study," by Scott Greer and Ella Kube, in *Community Structure and Analysis*, edited by Marvin B. Sussman (New York: Thomas Y. Crowell Company, 1959).

The Los Angeles neighborhoods studied varied among themselves, not only in distance from the center, but also in important social characteristics. Indeed, they were chosen to do so. According to Shevky's technique of Social Area Analysis, these four areas were similar in Social Rank, were almost entirely non-ethnic, but varied widely in their average style of life.[2]

The latter ranged from neighborhoods where urbanism was a way of life to others where familism was the norm. In the first, we found areas with few children, with many working women, and with most households living in apartments. In the second, these aspects were reversed; there were many children, fertility was high, few women worked outside the home, and most households lived in single-family dwellings. These neighborhoods approached the stereotype of suburbia—child-centered, neighborhood-centered, home-centered families were the norm. The four census tracts ranged from the extremely urban to the extremely familistic neighborhoods to be found at middle social rank in Los Angeles in the 1950's.

There were consistent differences in social structure as we went from the highly urban to the familistic neighborhood. Participation in locally based organizations increased, including most types of voluntary organizations. Neighboring increased and with it the play of children in the neighborhood. (In the highly urban neighborhoods, there were so few other children around that opportunities were scant). Most importantly for Janowitz's hypotheses, commitment to the neighborhood (as determined by lack of willingness to move) also increased and with it readership in the local community press

---

2. For an explication of the Shevky framework and the technique of Social Area Analysis, see *Social Area Analysis*, by Eshref Shevky and Wendell Bell (Stanford: Stanford University Press, 1955).

and ability to name local leaders. Thus an entire complex of localism seemed to vary positively with the increasing familism of the local area. And with this increasing localism went increasing importance for the local community press.

There were serious limitations in the Los Angeles study design. Representing only four tracts out of hundreds, and tracts designated as "named places," it could—like the Janowitz study —be questioned as a possibly biased sample.[3] Still, as a pilot study it demonstrated the strength of the local area as social fact (and the accompanying importance of the press) in some parts of a city as well as considerable variation in that strength among local areas.

It was possible to complement these studies with data collected in connection with the Metropolitan St. Louis Survey.[4] The new study design allowed for more rigorous testing and more elaborate analysis. Eighteen hundred urban residents of metropolitan St. Louis, Missouri, were interviewed—1,285 in the suburbs and 515 in the central city. Although we could not, as in Los Angeles, speak with confidence about any specific local area (for the sample yielded only a few interviews in any census tract), this sample had two major advantages. First, by assigning each interviewee to his census tract and then aggregating respondents in given types of tracts, we could estimate for types of populations without respect to where they lived— thus avoiding the danger of bias always present in a sample of a few communities. Second, since all tracts in the metropolis

---

3. The comparability of the community press in the four areas was marred by the publication in Hollywood (most highly urban of the tracts), of an old established local daily which many considered their community paper.

4. The study was financed by the Ford Foundation and the McDonnel Aircraft Charitable Trust. It is reported in many places; the summary volume is *Exploring the Metropolitan Community*, under the general editorship of John C. Bollens (Berkeley and Los Angeles: University of California Press, 1961).

were represented, we could vary all three indexes at once: Social Rank, Ethnicity, and Life Style.[5]

Center City and Suburbia

In popular discourse today there is a widespread assumption that suburbanization is something different in kind from urbanization. And it will be remembered that the Los Angeles census tract near the center differed considerably from that on the outer edge of the city, the one which was in many ways similar to suburbia as it is generally conceived. For this reason it is useful to examine city-suburb differences. Janowitz's study areas, it will be remembered, were all in center city Chicago.

There are, indeed, differences in localism and the use of the local press between city and suburbs. Two-thirds of the St. Louis sample received a community paper, compared with 94 per cent in the suburbs; those reading it regularly were 58 per cent in the city but 81 per cent in the suburbs. Furthermore, when those who read it regularly were asked what they liked best about the paper, six out of ten in the suburbs emphasized local news about local people and events; in the city only four out of ten did so. As many city dwellers preferred advertisements as preferred local news, but twice as many suburbanites preferred news.

These gross differences were accompanied by others, and all were in the same direction. The suburbs are more localistic. Thus all but 2 per cent of the suburbanites gave specific names for their local area; in the city this was true for only 28 per cent (another 16 per cent gave local street names, and the remainder spoke vaguely of "South St. Louis," "North St. Louis," or simply confessed their ignorance). More suburbanites participated in their local area's social group. They neighbored more (57 per

---

5. The analysis reported here focusses upon two: Social Rank, and Life Style.

cent visited neighbors at least once a month, compared with 44 per cent in the city); they were more likely to belong to voluntary organizations (74 per cent and 61 per cent). Finally, suburbanites were much more likely to be committed to remaining in their locale. Asked if there was any neighborhood or community in the metropolis where they would rather live than their present home, only one-fifth of the suburbanites said there was, compared with 45 per cent of the city respondents.

Thus the stereotype of suburbia seemed confirmed: they were dependent villagers within the urban ambit. Suburbs are, however, different from the city in several ways. They are not only farther from the old center; they are also outside the municipal boundaries of the center city, and there are broad differences in population characteristics between the two halves of metropolis. Of these differences, the first seems least important; in the day of automobiles and freeways, radio and television, the number of miles from the center has little independent theoretical significance. It does have a dependent significance, however, as an indicator of newer residential developments. As such it points toward newer families who are able to choose (and do choose) familism as a style of life. If this is true, the key variable is population type.

Population Type and the Press

Attribute space, defined by Shevky's dimensions, is more important than physical space, for the indicator is more accurately related to what is meant. With this in mind we "poststratified" the St. Louis sample by City and Suburb, then for the characteristics of the neighborhoods in which they lived. In Table 1, for each social area type, is the rate of use of the local community press. The horizontal dimension indicates the social rank of the area of residence, with the range broken into quartiles. The vertical dimension indicates the urbanism (high pole) and familism (low pole) of the areas, also in quartiles.

TABLE NO. 1—*Per Cent Readers and Readers of Local News in the Social Areas of St. Louis City and the St. Louis Suburbs**

City
Urban

	Low		SOCIAL RANK	High	
High					
All Readers	..	..	16	11	D
Local News	..	..	8	6	
All Readers	70	75	53	16	C
Local News	24	26	31	0	
All Readers	46	79	15	..	B
Local News	15	35	34	6	
All Readers	..	..	..	..	A
Local News	..	..	..	..	
Low	1	2	3	4	

Suburbs
Urban

	Low		SOCIAL RANK	High	
High					
All Readers	..	..	..	..	D
Local News	..	..	..	..	
All Readers	..	..	86	73	C
Local News	..	..	41	45	
All Readers	92	85	82	75	B
Local News	46	47	43	37	
All Readers	100	84	84	87	A
Local News	55	55	56	55	
Low	1	2	3	4	

* The blank cells are those in which there is no census tract in the area whose population has the appropriate characteristics. The social differences between city and suburb are clear from this table.

Janowitz suggested a decline in readership with increasing social rank of the sub-community. Such a decline is evident in Table 1, but even more impressive is the decline in readership with the increasing urbanism of the tract population. Non-readers are rare indeed in the most familistic neighborhoods, but in the areas of high urbanism they are an overwhelming majority. The relative importance of life style (urbanism) as compared to social rank is even greater when we consider the content of the press which the readers find most interesting. Readership for local news declines from a majority of those in the most familistic areas to a tiny minority of the most urbane. The latter read chiefly for advertisements.

The most striking aspect of these data is the quite different, almost mutually exclusive, nature of the sub-communities in the two halves of the metropolis. The city sample has no population in the lower quartiles: the most familistic tracts. The suburban sample has very few persons from neighborhoods above the median in urbanism. Similarly, the city sample is concentrated in the lower half of the social rank range, while the suburban sample is about equally divided between upper and lower.

There is a rough pattern of declining interest in local news with increasing urbanism in each half of the metropolis and a tendency for readership to decrease with higher social rank. More interesting, however, are the differences between suburbs and central city. In every comparable population type (B1, B2, B3; and C3, C4) a higher proportion of the suburban sample read the community press for local news. Further, there is very little difference in such readership by social rank in the suburban areas, and only a small difference by urbanism (around 10 per cent for each level of social rank). In the city, however, there are sharp differences in readership and in content preferred (even allowing for the size of some of the sub-samples).

It seems clear that the strength of the community press is much greater in suburban St. Louis than in the central city when population type is controlled.

One obvious reason is the lack of circulation in the central city—the smaller number and weaker spread of community papers. This may be related to the strength of the two dailies, the *Post-Dispatch* and the *Globe-Democrat*, for they constitute something of a community press themselves for the city of St. Louis. This explanation, however, only produces further questions—as Janowitz notes, the community press has been very vigorous in its search for new markets. It seems likely then that the markets are simply not as good in central city; but why should this be so? Perhaps there are important differences in the organizational structure of local community in the two parts of the metropolitan area.

Local Community Organization

The spatially defined organization of the urban populations may be conceived in a series of concentric circles. These increase in scale as we go outward from household to neighborhood, from neighborhood to the named place or local community, and from the latter to the municipality or municipal subdivision. We have already noted one difference between city and suburb: the much larger proportion of suburban respondents who gave a distinctive name to their area. Sunset Hills, Bellefontaine Gardens, Country Club Hills—such names, often originating in the fancy of the developer who launched the residential enclave, have a way of taking hold. They help identify where one lives in the vast fabric of the metropolis.

These identifications are greatly reinforced, moreover, by another structure. The named place in suburbia is usually incorporated, separately or with others, in an independent municipality. Some of these are the site and market for community papers, and even if they alone are not large enough to support a paper their identity is broadcast through the community press in much the same way that the open-country neighborhoods are identified in the small-town weeklies. And their incorporation provides a governmental "game" which produces news; there are mayors, councilmen, constables, and fire companies on the stage; there are issues resulting from the fiscal problems, service provision, and electoral contests of the municipality.

When we asked people to name a leader in their local community, we found a sharp difference between central city and suburbs. In the former, one-third could do so; in the latter, one-half named at least one local leader. The separate importance of incorporation is made clear when we separate the local political-governmental leaders from all others. In the unincorporated suburban areas the proportion naming local leaders falls to 42 per cent, but it is 60 per cent in the municipalities. When, however, political leaders were omitted, the proportions naming leaders are 31 per cent in the unincorporated areas and 24 per cent in the municipalities. (The reversal may indicate that where there are elected officials they shoulder aside the non-officials, in fact or in the awareness of the respondents.)

It will be remembered that Janowitz found the most prominent news in the Chicago community press dealt with municipal affairs, public programs, and public space. In the hundred-odd suburban municipalities of St. Louis these affairs are localized and personalized, an obvious supply of grist for the community papers' mills. At the same time these municipalities are significant at just the points where a familistic population is most sensitive: they control the streets and land use of the neighborhoods; they affect local commercial facilities; they levy taxes and often (when they are coterminous with school districts) control the public schools. In short, they affect the well-being of the family, its home and children, in dozens of ways.

Since the local community is of greater significance when it is also a village or city, the press, as a major medium of communication about the community, is correspondingly more important.

Significance of the Press: Social Types

Janowitz found readership of the local press to be related to political competence and involvement. However, he found it correlated with many other attributes, including family integration, residential stability, and voluntary organization membership. Thus we must question the independent importance of the press; is it a facilitator as he suggests, a reinforcer of localistic tendencies and public interest, or in some way a causal agent? Does it help to create community and, if so, how?

In the analysis of local community ties among the metropolitan St. Louis sample, the concentric circle metaphor was employed. That is, persons were classified as neighbors by their frequency of face-to-face contact; they were classified as community participators by membership in voluntary organizations which met locally; they were classified as community communicators by their readership of the local press for local news. A subsample of 196 was drawn from the suburban residents to use for analysis and the construction of types.[6]

In this sample, 44 per cent were neighborhood actors, 49 per cent belonged to local organizations, and 49 per cent read the

---

6. The logic of the subsample is as follows: "It was crucial that the indicators be developed independently of their use as a test of the theory, for the analysis aims at verification. . . . For this reason the sample [after the elimination of 89 people who were ineligible to vote] was divided into a 'laboratory sample' of 196 cases and a 'test sample' of 1,000 cases. The laboratory sample was analyzed by various possible indicators, and three were finally selected. Both the items selected and the discriminating categories of answers were determined with the small sample: they were not changed in the analysis of the testing sample." "The Social Structure and Political Process of Suburbia: An Empirical Test," by Scott Greer, *Rural Sociology* 27 (Dec., 1962): 44.

local paper for local news. It seemed likely that these were approximately the same persons: a trivariate analysis demonstrated they were not. There are associations here, but weak

TABLE NO. 2—*Percentage of the Laboratory Sample by Indicators of Social Participation (N = 188)**

	Neighbors			Does Not Neighbor		
		44				
	Reads local paper	Does not read local paper	Total	Reads local paper	Does not read local paper	Total
Belongs to local organizations	20	8	28	10	11	21
Does not belong to local organizations	6	10	16	13	22	35

Reproduced from "The Social Structure and Political Process of Suburbia: An Empirical Test," *Rural Sociology* 27 (Dec., 1962): 44.

* Omitted are eight cases which do not receive local paper.

ones. Of those who neighbor, 36 per cent do not belong to organizations and 40 per cent do not read the local paper for local news. Of those who belong to local organizations, 40 per cent do not read the paper and more than 40 per cent do not neighbor. Of those who read the local community press for local news, 45 per cent do not neighbor and 38 per cent belong to no local voluntary organization.

The relative independence of the three aspects of behavior made the construction of organizational types possible. This was done through logical permutation; the eight types in Table 4 resulted.

These types were expected to vary in their political involvement by their role in community organization; they were ex-

TABLE NO. 3—*"Organizational Types" in Suburbia*

	Neigh-borhood Inter-action	Local Com-munity Role	Access to Com-munication Flow	Type
I.	Yes	Yes	Yes	Multilevel Participator
II.	Yes	Yes	No	Community Actor (A)
III.	No	Yes	Yes	Community Actor (B)
IV.	Yes	No	Yes	Neighborhood Actor (A)
V.	Yes	No	No	Neighborhood Actor (B)
VI.	No	No	Yes	Voyeur
VII.	No	No	No	Isolate
VIII.	No	Yes	No	Error

Reproduced from "The Social Structure and Political Process of Suburbia: An Empirical Test," *Rural Sociology, op. cit.*

pected to vary in political competence by their access to the local communication flow through readership of the local press. According to Janowitz's findings, type VI (the Voyeur, who reads the paper but is otherwise isolated) was expected to include only a small minority of the sample. Table 5 shows the variation in political involvement (as measured by voting in local elections) and competence (indicated by ability to name local leaders) for each of the eight types.

It is clear from these findings that the *only* important variable associated with voting in local elections is membership in local voluntary organizations. Press readership and neighboring are unimportant when not accompanied by such membership, and in fact those who are totally isolated from the locale are about as likely to vote as any who are not organization members. When, however, we inspect the column presenting percentages who named local leaders, we find a different story. In the first place, political competence varies directly with access to communication. In the second place, it does not matter whether one communicates by reading the local press

TABLE NO. 4—*Percentage of Participational Types Who Had Voted in Municipal Elections and Could Name Local Leaders for the Laboratory Sample*

Types	% who had voted	No. of type	% who named leader	No. of type
I. Multilevel Actor	77	31	71	38
II. Community Actor (A)	85	13	78	14
III. Community Actor (B)	86	14	72	18
IV. Neighborhood Actor (A)	42	12	46	13
V. Neighborhood Actor (B)	36	14	47	19
VI. Voyeur	45	20	37	24
VII. Isolate	45	31	22	40
VIII. Error	78	18	23	22
Total number		153*		188**

Reproduced from "The Social Structure and Political Process of Suburbia: An Empirical Test," *Rural Sociology, op. cit.*

* Omitted are eight persons who do not receive local paper and thirty-five persons who live in unincorporated areas and cannot vote in municipal election.

** Omitted are eight persons who do not receive a local paper.

or by neighboring—they are interchangeable. There is little difference in competence among the three types of Community Actor, the two types of Neighborhood Actor, and the two types of non-communicator (Isolate and Error). The Voyeur was slightly more competent than the last, but no more likely to vote than was the Isolate; the Error type was as ignorant as the Isolate, but as likely to vote as the Community Actors.

From this analysis it would appear that the local community press is chiefly a facilitator, not a creator, of community political activity. Neighboring can do about the same thing as a political communications channel, while membership in voluntary organizations is most important for the development of political involvement.

These findings from the analysis of the laboratory sample indicated that the eight social types could be collapsed with little loss in accuracy and a resulting parsimony. The result was three categories: Community Actors who either neighbored, read the community press, or both, and who in any event belonged to voluntary organizations in the local area. Neighbors were those who saw their neighbors regularly but did not belong to organizations and might or might not read the paper. Isolates neither neighbored nor participated in organizations, though they might read the paper. A fourth category (the Error types) belonged to organizations but neither neighbored nor read the local press. These types were used to predict competence and involvement for the sample of a thousand suburbanites.

There is of course some variation by social background characteristics among the four types. Community Actors are less likely to be under thirty and less likely to have only an eighth-grade education (women, however, are represented proportionally among them, in contrast to the Isolates and the Deviants). These background differences are far from accounting for the differences in political competence and involvement: the latter are products of organizational role in the local community. Thus: "Young Community Actors are more competent than older people in all other categories; female Community Actors are more competent than males in all other categories; Community Actors with grade-school educations are more competent than the college-educated in all other categories." The same regularities hold for voting.[7]

Since organizational role varies widely among the urban population, major questions emerge. How does the distribu-

---

7. "The Social Structure and Political Process of Suburbia." Other control variables were used with similar results, and other dependent variables were predicted in a consistent fashion.

tion of these social types vary among the different sub-areas of the metropolis? Where are the Community Actors, the Neighbors, the Isolates? And how do political competence and involvement vary between those living in the suburbs and those in the central city? With Social Area Analysis as a differentiator, the distribution of each type (for the nine cells in the grid for which adequate samples were at hand) is presented in Table 6.

TABLE NO. 5—*Percentage Distribution of Four Types of Social Participation by Social Area for the Metropolitan St. Louis Combined Sample (N = 629)**

high								
Urbanism	1D	2D	3D	4D		74	107	54
	1C	2C	3C	4C			116	56	30
	1B	2B	3B	4B			99	63	30
	1A	2A	3A	4A			*Number of*	
	low			*high*		*Respondents*	
		Social Rank					

39	50	40			22	12	14
	34	28	36			26	20	16
	36	31	14			20	23	13
	Isolates					*Neighbors*	

23	26	28		16	12	18
	30	37	39		10	15	9
	38	40	61		6	6	12
	Community Actors				*Deviants*	

Reproduced from "The Mass Society and the Parapolitical Structure," *American Sociological Review* 27 (October, 1962): 643-46.

* City and suburban respondents residing in segregated areas (as defined according to the Shevky-Bell Social Area Index) have been deleted from the sample. In addition, forty-seven city respondents and sixteen (weighted) suburban respondents in social areas 1A, 1B, 3D, 4C, and 4D have been deleted as the total n's for these social areas were too small to allow for computation of meaningful percentages. Of the sample arrayed above, all residents of the highest quartile on urbanism are in the city; all in the lowest quartile are in the suburbs.

TABLE NO. 6—*Percentage Distribution of Political Involvement Scale Scores for Three Types of Social Participation in City and Suburban Samples in the Non-Segregated Social Areas of Metropolitan St. Louis*

City Sample		TYPE	OF	SOCIAL	PARTICIPATOR	
Political						Community
Involvement		*Isolates*		*Neighbors*		*Actors*
	N	%	N	%	N	%
None (0)	40	25	17	25	11	11
Low (1-2)	96	61	42	61	62	65
High (3-4)	22	14	20	14	23	24
Total	158	100	69	100	96	100

$x^2 = 11.2 \ p < .05$

Surburban Sample		TYPE	OF	SOCIAL	PARTICIPATOR	
Political						Community
Involvement		*Isolates*		*Neighbors*		*Actors*
	N	%	N	%	N	%
None (0)	29	29	14	23	11	10
Low (1-2)	57	57	36	58	59	49
High (3-4)	14	14	12	20	49	41
Total	100	100	62	101	119	100

$x^2 = 27.8 \ p < .001$

Reproduced from "The Mass Society and the Parapolitical Structure," *American Sociological Review, op. cit.*

The proportion of Community Actors increases consistently with social rank and with declining urbanism (or increasing familism). Though not as regular, the pattern for Isolates is roughly complementary. Neighbors are somewhat more common at levels of lower social rank and lower urbanism.

In view of the comparative distribution of central city and suburban tracts in the social area attribute space, a difference in the incidence of these social types would be expected. Community Actors are much more common in the suburban municipalities (43 per cent compared to 30 per cent); Isolates, in the central city (50 per cent compared to 35 per cent). Since we have spoken of the difference in the scale of the polity in these halves of the metropolis, it is useful to consider organizational type and governmental structure simultaneously, observing variations in competence and involvement.

Political involvement is measured by a Guttman type scale on which zero indicates no involvement in local issues; 1, voting only; 2, the respondent also usually takes sides on local issues; 3, also tries to persuade others; and 4, has attended meetings dealing with local governmental issues. By these measures, Community Actors are much more involved in both city and suburb. Neighbors are between them and the Isolates in the suburbs; but in the city, Neighbors are equally uninvolved. As between the halves of the metropolis, the major difference is the higher proportion of suburban Community Actors in the suburbs who fall in the highest categories of involvement, perhaps indicating the easier access to local politics in small municipalities. Otherwise the types behave in a very similar fashion regardless of residence.

While suburbanites are more likely to read a local paper for local news, they rely heavily on word of mouth. When asked "Which helps you most in making up your mind about local elections—talking with people, or things like radio, television, and the newspapers?" 56 per cent of Isolates and 69 per cent of Community Actors in the suburban sample chose people. In the city, however, 54 per cent of the Isolates and 60 per cent of the Community Actors opted for the mass media. The results of such communications, as measured by ability to name local leaders, are in favor of the suburbanites for Neighbors (65 per cent could, compared with 36 per cent) and Community Actors (59 per cent and 43 per cent). There was no difference for Isolates (28 per cent and 27 per cent). This would support Janowitz's contention that the local community press functions in a complex of personal and organizational relations at the local level and is not a substitute for such relations.

The Community Press and Metropolitan Reform

The community press profits from, and encourages, that localization of activities and bonds within urban sub-areas which we have termed local community. In doing so, it develops a vested interest in the persistence and socioeconomic strength of the named places within the urban area, and speaks in the rhetoric of our town—not our metropolitan community. The rapid development of small suburban enclaves—and even more, their incorporation as municipalities—is both an opportunity for the press and a challenge, for the editor may see himself as a community-building agent.

Jerrold Werthimer, a journalist and social scientist, has carried out a study in depth of one community press chain. The Paddock newspapers, in the northwest suburbs of Cook County, were his subjects. These papers, begun with a small town weekly, are now among the most successful and influential in the Chicago metropolitan complex. Far from defining themselves as primarily sales sheets and secondarily bulletin boards, they have developed a distinct sense of mission. As public conscience, commentator, and innovator, they attempt to do for the affairs of the local communities what they believe the dailies should do for the metropolis.

Janowitz has spoken of the community press editor as surrogate for local leadership when the area suffers social absenteeism. The case of the Paddock papers is relevant and fascinating. Setting up shop at the beginning of new enclaves, they have preceded the development of leadership, fostered it, and tried to focus it upon what they consider pressing problems: education, ethnic relations, land use commitments, public capital development. They have been—in some cases literally —among the first citizens of their various local areas.[8]

Such strengthening of the sub-areas in a metropolis may, however, integrate the small area at the cost of anarchy and anomie for the entire city. This is evident in the typical governmental pattern of American urban places. In St. Louis, for example, there were 98 municipalities and a total of 149 units of local government, yet there was no governmental body for the metropolitan area as a political community. (The closest equivalent was a single-purpose sewer district.) In the circumstances the unity of the metropolis as a transportation grid, a labor market, a housing market, and a geographical area could not be the grounds for any unified policy.

For these reasons a movement developed to create a metropolitan district government, one with limited powers over the area as a whole. The new government would not have resulted in abolishing any local government within the district; its powers were strictly limited. It appeared a reasonable compromise between localism and metropolitanism. Such a change was possible in Missouri only if approved in referendum by both the central city and the suburban areas. Thus we have here a test case for gauging: (1) the policy of the local community press, and (2) its effectiveness.

Most of the local community press opposed the district plan, those who did not remained neutral. Their reasons emphasized the moral value of "keeping government close to the people," of small-scale government, and of local leadership. They also emphasized fear of increase in property taxes, bureaucracy, and

8. "The Community Press of Suburbia: A Case Study of Paddock Newspapers," by Jerrold Werthimer, unpublished Ph. D. dissertation, Northwestern University.

the loss of responsiveness to the local electorate. (The more rabid papers printed articles in which the Public Administration Service and the International City Managers' Association were dubbed Communist fronts.) So much for ideology.

Janowitz has noted the basically integrative nature of the community press. It avoids highly divisive issues, and takes a stand only when it can speak for the community as a whole in opposition to some outside force. Identifying the community with the existing tissue of municipal governments in St. Louis County, the suburban community press had a superb opportunity to take a stand for this community against the big city and big government. The editors may also have sensed a threat to their local business districts and neighborhoods in the powers of general planning conferred on the proposed St. Louis Metropolitan District. They certainly had an opportunity to attack the metropolitan dailies (both of whom favored the plan), thus identifying their special and parochial interests with the general interest of the local communities. They used this opportunity, going to the extremes of publishing special issues devoted to attacks on the plan just before election day.

Of the voters, 40 per cent in the suburbs and 20 per cent in the city registered their opinion of the plan. It was defeated by two to one in the city, three to one in the suburbs. Whether the community press had much to do with this or not, it had certainly gauged accurately the direction of opinion. Let us look briefly at some measures of their effectiveness.[9]

One-half of the suburban residents and one-quarter of the city residents had heard of the district plan through the community press. (This compares with 74 per cent and 57 per cent

---

9. These data are derived from a survey, carried out after the Plan, of 300 adults; they are reported in *Metropolitics: A Study of Political Culture*, by Scott Greer, especially Chapter 5, "Who Was Listening?" (New York: John Wiley and Sons, 1963).

who heard through the *Post-Dispatch*.) Of these, 56 per cent in the city and 68 per cent in the suburbs had an accurate knowledge of the community press's position on the issue.

In the suburbs, where the readership is most widespread and the press most opposed, one-fifth of those with opinions thought the community press the most trustworthy source of information on the plan—but 36 per cent thought it least trustworthy.

The 42 per cent of suburban residents who stated the community press's position accurately were asked why they thought it took that position. Thirty-two per cent thought it was because it was in the interest of the suburban county to defeat it; 21 per cent cited belief in progress; 14 per cent thought it was self-serving. Thus the community press was not seen by many respondents as simply preserving its self-interest. (In the smaller city sample, few persons had any idea why the press said what it did.)

When asked where they had heard or read the best and worst arguments, pro and con the plan, only a trivial number mentioned the community press. But—more important—of those suburban respondents who remembered where they had heard the strongest argument *against* the Plan (31 per cent), more than half said it was from a specific relative, friend, or neighbor. The people orientation of suburbia seems evident here.

Of the two dozen suburbanites in the sample who favored the press over talking with people as a source of political information, those who preferred the community press tended to oppose; those who favored the metropolitan dailies tended to favor. More important, however, the general findings pointed to agreement between one's personal opinion on one hand and the tone of conversations about the plan among one's relatives and friends.

Using the social types constructed with the 1957 survey data, we analyzed the respective knowledge and opinions of Isolates, Neighbors, and Community Actors. Community Actors were somewhat more likely to have a definite opinion on the issue. More important, if they did have an opinion, they were much more likely to vote; thus 50 per cent of Isolates, 60 per cent of Neighbors, but 79 per cent of Community Actors who had opinions voted. Not opinion formation but activation is strongly associated with social type. This activity was not accompanied by an equal difference in competence. Community Actors and Neighbors were both less likely to be completely ignorant of the plan than were Isolates (25 per cent compared to 42 per cent), but otherwise the differences are meaningless. However, personal knowledge of the intricate proposal was not widespread, and interpersonal communication was as likely to be false as true. This leads to another finding: there was no difference in direction of the vote among the three types. Each voted overwhelmingly against the plan.

In summary then, the community press in St. Louis took a strong position against governmental integration of the metropolis. Identifying the existing political units with the totality of the local communities they served and earned a living from, they heatedly disputed the need or desirability of any larger framework for facing the problems of the complex metropolis. While they accurately reflected public opinion on the issue, it is doubtful that they had a major impact on the formation of that opinion. They did have an exciting issue to exploit, one on which they could take sides; they communicated their position to a large minority of the suburban residents. They probably helped activate some of the conservative social norms and belief systems which were evidenced by the voters in the post-election surveys. On the one hand, their authority to speak on the issue was seriously doubted by a sizable proportion of their readership; on the other hand, few people accused them of self-interest in the affair. They were seen, not as commercial enterprises searching for profits, but as organs of the local communities and of suburbia as a whole.

Some Notes on Futures

As our society increases in scale, locational freedom increases. The technology of equal cost, manifest in truck and automobile, electronic communications and electricity, increases the spread of areas in which human behavior can be adequately integrated. Thus the peripheries of the cities become usable for many activities once demanding location near the center, and centripetal forces decline. The result is dispersion, scatteration, sprawl. Comparative studies of American cities at mid-twentieth century indicate that the newer, the richer, the more rapidly expanding is the city, the larger the proportion of it which resembles the horizontal neighborhoods of suburbia. And in the older cities it is the same story: the growing edge is in the suburbs, while urban renewal is chiefly a holding action at the center. Nor is this surprising, given the shifts in use values accompanying the equal-cost technology.

The pattern that seems to be emerging is one in which giant sub-nuclei form within the continuous, low-density city. The places of work and residence, commerce and public facilities, religious institutions, the networks of friend and kin, may all be included within one of the large fractions of the metropolis. In such a pattern, the older center is one among equals. In such a city the typical local community is likely to be oriented increasingly toward the sub-center.

As this occurs, we can adopt one of two strategies. We can remain fixated on the older center and attempt, with such weak tools as urban renewal and metropolitan government, to re-create boundaries forcing centrality. Or we can look to the sub-centers, where the massive growth is taking place, and consider the feasibility of making each such area a complete urban world, a set of opportunities for experience and growth such as was once found only in the central city. (After all, such sub-areas as the San Fernando Valley are now larger than the entire Los Angeles complex was a few decades ago.)

In building a new kind of a city, the city of many centers, one of the critical tasks will be the development of a much more competent and more highly differentiated communication system. In this enterprise it seems likely that the local community press will have a major role. Whether it develops into a major organ for a great sector of the metropolis (as with *Newsday* on Long Island) or whether it remains focused on the smaller shopping center, its utility as a social integrator will increase only with its ability to integrate the sub-unit within the relevant whole. Integrating people in extended neighborhoods is not enough when these neighborhoods themselves are creatures and victims of a larger and largely uncontrolled system: the contemporary metropolitan fabric.

Index